STYLISTICS

Routledge English Language Introductions cover core areas of language study and are one-stop resources for students.

Assuming no prior knowledge, books in the series offer an accessible overview of the subject, with activities, study questions, sample analyses, commentaries and key readings – all in the same volume. The innovative and flexible 'two-dimensional' structure is built around four sections – introduction, development, exploration and extension – which offer self-contained stages for study. Each topic can be read across these sections, enabling the reader to build gradually on the knowledge gained.

Stylistics:

- ❑ provides a comprehensive overview of the methods and theories of stylistics: from metre to metaphor, dialogue to discourse
- ❑ enables students to uncover the layers, patterns and levels that constitute stylistic description
- ❑ helps the reader to develop a set of stylistic tools of their own, which can be applied to any text
- ❑ is written in a clear and entertaining style with lively examples from authors as diverse as Shakespeare and Irvine Welsh
- ❑ provides classic readings by key names in the field, such as Roger Fowler, Mick Short, Walter Nash and Mary Louise Pratt.

Written by an experienced teacher and researcher, this accessible textbook is an essential resource for all students of English language, linguistics and literature.

Paul Simpson is a Professor of English Language at Queen's University, Belfast. He edits the journal *Language and Literature* and is the author of *On the Discourse of Satire* (2003). His other books for Routledge include *Language, Ideology and Point of View* (1993) and *Language through Literature* (1997).

Series Editor: Peter Stockwell
Series Consultant: Ronald Carter

ROUTLEDGE ENGLISH LANGUAGE INTRODUCTIONS

SERIES EDITOR: PETER STOCKWELL

Peter Stockwell is Senior Lecturer in the School of English Studies at the University of Nottingham, UK, where his interests include sociolinguistics, stylistics and cognitive poetics. His recent publications include *Cognitive Poetics: An Introduction* (Routledge 2002), *The Poetics of Science Fiction, Investigating English Language* (with Howard Jackson), and *Contextualized Stylistics* (edited with Tony Bex and Michael Burke)

SERIES CONSULTANT: RONALD CARTER

Ronald Carter is Professor of Modern English Language in the School of English Studies at the University of Nottingham, UK. He is the co-series editor of the forthcoming *Routledge Applied Linguistics* series, series editor of *Interface*, and was co-founder of the Routledge *Intertext* series.

OTHER TITLES IN THE SERIES:

Sociolinguistics
Peter Stockwell

Pragmatics and Discourse
Joan Cutting

Grammar and Vocabulary
Howard Jackson

Psycholinguistics
John Field

World Englishes
Jennifer Jenkins

Practical Phonetics and Phonology
Beverley Collins & Inger Mees

FORTHCOMING:

Child Language
Jean Stilwell Peccei

Language in Theory
Mark Robson & Peter Stockwell

STYLISTICS

A resource book for students

A

B

C

D

PAUL SIMPSON

Routledge
Taylor & Francis Group
LONDON AND NEW YORK

First published 2004
by Routledge
2 Park Square, Milton Park, Abingdon, OX14 4RN

Simultaneously published in the USA and Canada
by Routledge
270 Madison Ave, New York, NY 10016

Reprinted 2006 (twice), 2007

Routledge is an imprint of the Taylor & Francis Group, an informa business

Typeset in Minion and Univers by Florence Production Ltd, Stoodleigh, Devon
Printed and bound in Great Britain by TJ International Ltd, Padstow, Cornwall

British Library Cataloguing in Publication Data
A catalogue record for this book is available from the British Library

Library of Congress Cataloging in Publication Data
A catalog record for this book has been requested

ISBN10: 0–415–28104–0 (hbk)
ISBN10: 0–415–28105–9 (pbk)

ISBN13: 978–0–415–28104–1 (hbk)
ISBN13: 978–0–415–28105–8 (pbk)

HOW TO USE THIS BOOK

The Routledge English Language Introductions are 'flexi-texts' that you can use to suit your own style of study. The books are divided into four sections:

A Introduction – sets out the key concepts for the area of study. The units of this section take you step-by-step through the foundational terms and ideas, carefully providing you with an initial toolkit for your own study. By the end of the section, you will have a good overview of the whole field.

B Development – adds to your knowledge and builds on the key ideas already introduced. Units in this section might also draw together several areas of interest. By the end of this section, you will already have a good and fairly detailed grasp of the field, and will be ready to undertake your own exploration and thinking.

C Exploration – provides examples of language data and guides you through your own investigation of the field. The units in this section will be more open-ended and exploratory, and you will be encouraged to try out your ideas and think for yourself, using your newly acquired knowledge.

D Extension – offers you the chance to compare your expertise with key readings in the area. These are taken from the work of important writers, and are provided with guidance and questions for your further thought.

You can read this book like a traditional text-book, 'vertically' straight through from beginning to end. This will take you comprehensively through the broad field of study. However, the Routledge English Language Introductions have been carefully designed so that you can read them in another dimension, 'horizontally' across the numbered units. For example, Units A1, A2, A3 and so on correspond with Units B1, B2, B3, and with Units C1, C2, C3 and D1, D2, D3, and so on. Reading A5, B5, C5, D5 will take you rapidly from the key concepts of a specific area to a level of expertise in that precise area, all with a very close focus. You can match your way of reading with the best way that you work.

The index at the end, together with the suggestions for further reading, will help to keep you orientated. Each textbook has a supporting website with extra commentary, suggestions, additional material and support for teachers and students.

STYLISTICS

In this book, the twelve numbered units in section A introduce you to key concepts in stylistics. These introductions are compact and are ordered in a linear way, so if you read progressively through this section you can assemble a composite picture of the core issues in both stylistic theory and practice. Then, or alternatively, you can use the numbered units of section A to follow a particular strand through the book. The units which comprise section B develop the topic introduced in the equivalent numbered unit in section A. In this book in the Routledge English Language Introductions (RELI) series, B units are either illustrative expansions of the model introduced in A or surveys of important research developments in the relevant area of stylistics. For example, unit A3 sets out a compact model for the study of grammar and style. In B3 you will find some applications of this grammatical model to a variety of texts. In unit A6, the concept of transitivity is developed but the corresponding unit in Section B is in this case a survey of the uses stylisticians have made of this model over the years.

Of course, the most productive way of learning about stylistics is simply to do it. The units that make up section C provide the opportunity to try out and apply what you have learned from A and B. For example, following from A3 and B3, unit C3 offers a practical activity involving the exploration of patterns of grammar in a short poem. Similarly, following from A6 and B6, unit C6 offers a chance to investigate the concept of transitivity in different kinds of texts. Finally, section D allows you to read what other scholars have written on the relevant subject over the years and to this effect, it offers a wide-ranging selection of readings by some of the best known stylisticians in the world.

This then is the basic blueprint for the better part of the book. There are some minor exceptions: for example, the reading in unit D5, because of its broad subject matter, covers strand 7 also. As strand 8 includes a detailed workshop programme which goes right down to the micro-analytic features of textual patterning, the space for the reading has been vacated to carry extra practical material. Whatever its narrower variations in structure, the core organising principle of this book is that in every strand a key topic in stylistics is introduced, defined and then elaborated progressively over the remainder of the strand.

CONTENTS

ILLUSTRATIONS

Figures

Tables

ACKNOWLEDGEMENTS

I would like to thank Sonia Zyngier and Greg Watson for their helpful comments on an earlier proposal for this book, and Fran Brearton and Michael Longley for their help during the book's later stages. As ever, special thanks go to Janice Hoadley for her patience and perseverance, on both the family and academic fronts. I am also grateful to my friends and colleagues in the Poetics and Linguistics Association for their support over the years, and to my students, well, everywhere I suppose, for their participation in the various seminars and tutorials that helped shape parts of section C of the book. I am especially indebted to Derek Attridge, Mary Louise Pratt, Katie Wales, Mick Short, Margaret Freeman and Bill Nash for kindly allowing me to reproduce some of their work in section D.

My thanks are due to Routledge's steadfast team of Louisa Semlyen, Christy Kirkpatrick and Kate Parker, and to series consultant Ron Carter for his friendship and support for the best part of a quarter of a century. Finally, a huge debt of gratitude goes to series editor Peter Stockwell, not least for his uncanny knack of weeding out superfluous blarney which helped keep the length of the book within the bounds of decency. Any waffle, nonsense or unnecessary digression that may remain is of course entirely the fault of the author.

Derek Attridge, 'Fff! Oo!; Nonlexical Onomatopoeia' from *Peculiar Language: Literature as Difference from the Renaissance to James Joyce* Methuen, 1988. Reproduced by permission of Taylor and Francis Books Ltd (Methuen).

D. Burton, extract from 'Through Glass Darkly, Through Dark Glasses' from *Language and Literature* by Ronald Carter, published by Unwin Hyman/Routledge 1982. Reproduced by permission of Taylor & Francis Ltd.

Ronald Carter, 'What is Stylistics and Why Can We Teach it in Different Ways?' from *Reading, Analysing and Teaching Literature* edited by Mike Short, Longman 1989. Reproduced by permission of Ronald Carter.

e e cummings, 'love is more thicker than forget' is reprinted from *Complete Poems 1904–1962*, edited by George J. Firmage, by permission of W. W. Norton & Company. Copyright © 1991 by the Trustees for the e e cummings Trust and George James Firmage.

Roger Fowler, extracts from *The Languages of Literature* published by Routledge & Kegan Paul Ltd, 1971. Reproduced by permission of Taylor & Francis Ltd.

Ralph W. Franklin, ed., text reprinted from *The Poems of Emily Dickinson*, by permission of the publishers and the Trustees of Amherst College, Cambridge, Mass.:

The Belknap Press of Harvard University Press, Copyright © 1998 by the President and Fellows of Harvard College. Copyright © 1951, 1955, 1979 by the President and Fellows of Harvard College.

Ralph W. Franklin, ed., poetry text reprinted from *The Manuscript Books of Emily Dickinson: A Facsimile Edition*, by permission of the publishers and the Trustees of Amherst College, Cambridge, Mass.: The Belknap Press of Harvard University Press, Copyright © 1981 by the President and Fellows of Harvard College.

Margaret Freeman, reprinted by permission of Sage Publications Ltd from 'Grounded spaces: deictic *-self* anaphors in the poetry of Emily Dickinson', Copyright (© Sage Publications Ltd, 1997).

Ernest Hemingway, extract from *The Old Man and the Sea* published by Jonathan Cape. Used by permission of The Random House Group Limited (UK). Reprinted with permission of Scribner, an imprint of Simon & Schuster Adult Publishing Group (US). Copyright 1952 by Ernest Hemingway. Copyright renewed © 1980 by Mary Hemingway.

Michael Longley, 'The Comber' from *The Weather in Japan* published by Jonathan Cape. Used by permission of the Random House Group Limited

Roger McGough, '40 – Love' from *After the Mersey Sound* by Roger McGough. Reprinted by permission of PFD on behalf of Roger McGough © Roger McGough.

Edwin Morgan, 'Off Course' from *Collected Poems* by Edwin Morgan. Reproduced by permission of Carcanet Press Limited.

Walter Nash, extracts from *The Language of Humour* by Longman, 1985. Reproduced by permission of Pearson Education Limited.

Dorothy Parker, 'One Perfect Rose' from *The Portable Dorothy Parker* edited by Brendan Gill. Used by permission of Duckworth Publishers (UK) and Viking Penguin, a division of Penguin Putnam Inc. (US). Copyright 1926, renewed © 1954 by Dorothy Parker.

Ezra Pound, 'In a Station of the Metro' from *Collected Shorter Poems*, reproduced by permission of Faber and Faber (UK). From *Personae*, copyright © 1926 by Ezra Pound, reprinted by permission of New Directions Publishing Corp (US).

Mary Louise Pratt, extracts from *Toward a Speech Theory of Literary Discourse*, Indiana University Press, 1977. Reproduced by permission of Indiana University Press.

Mick Short, 'Graphological Deviation, Style Variation and Point of View in *Marabou Stork Nightmares* by Irvine Welsh'. Reproduced by permission of Mick Short and Journal of Literary Studies/Tydskrif vir Literatuurwetenskap.

Peter Stockwell, 'The Inflexibility of Invariance', reprinted by permission of Sage Publications Ltd Copyright (© Sage Publications Ltd, 1999).

Kate Wales, 'Zodiac Mindwarp meets the Horseflies' reprinted from *English Today*, 29, January 1992. Reprinted by permission of Cambridge University Press.

Irvine Welsh, extract from *Marabou Stork Nightmares*, published by Jonathan Cape. Used by permission of The Random House Group Limited (UK) and W. W. Norton & Company, Inc. (US). Copyright © 1995 by Irvine Welsh.

Irvine Welsh, extract from *Trainspotting* published by Secker & Warburg. Used by permission of The Random House Group Limited.

SECTION A

INTRODUCTION

KEY CONCEPTS IN STYLISTICS

A1

WHAT IS STYLISTICS?

Some years ago, the well-known linguist Jean-Jacques Lecercle published a short but damning critique of the aims, methods and rationale of contemporary stylistics. His attack on the discipline, and by implication the entire endeavour of the present book, was uncompromising. According to Lecercle, nobody has ever really known what the term 'stylistics' means, and in any case, hardly anyone seems to care (Lecercle 1993: 14). Stylistics is 'ailing'; it is 'on the wane'; and its heyday, alongside that of structuralism, has faded to but a distant memory. More alarming again, few university students are 'eager to declare an intention to do research in stylistics'. By this account, the death knell of stylistics had been sounded and it looked as though the end of the twentieth century would be accompanied by the inevitable passing of that faltering, moribund discipline. And no one, it seemed, would lament its demise.

Modern stylistics

As it happened, things didn't quite turn out in the way Lecercle envisaged. Stylistics in the early twenty-first century is very much alive and well. It is taught and researched in university departments of language, literature and linguistics the world over. The high academic profile stylistics enjoys is mirrored in the number of its dedicated book-length publications, research journals, international conferences and symposia, and scholarly associations. Far from moribund, modern stylistics is positively flourishing, witnessed in a proliferation of sub-disciplines where stylistic methods are enriched and enabled by theories of discourse, culture and society. For example, feminist stylistics, cognitive stylistics and discourse stylistics, to name just three, are established branches of contemporary stylistics which have been sustained by insights from, respectively, feminist theory, cognitive psychology and discourse analysis. Stylistics has also become a much valued method in language teaching and in language learning, and stylistics in this 'pedagogical' guise, with its close attention to the broad resources of the system of language, enjoys particular pride of place in the linguistic armoury of learners of second languages. Moreover, stylistics often forms a core component of many creative writing courses, an application not surprising given the discipline's emphasis on techniques of creativity and invention in language.

So much then for the current 'health' of stylistics and the prominence it enjoys in modern scholarship. It is now time to say a little more about what exactly stylistics is and what it is for. Stylistics is a method of textual interpretation in which primacy of place is assigned to *language*. The reason why language is so important to stylisticians is because the various forms, patterns and levels that constitute linguistic structure are an important index of the function of the text. The text's functional significance as discourse acts in turn as a gateway to its interpretation. While linguistic features do not of themselves constitute a text's 'meaning', an account of linguistic features nonetheless serves to ground a stylistic interpretation and to help explain why, for the analyst, certain types of meaning are possible. The preferred object of study in stylistics is literature, whether that be institutionally sanctioned 'Literature' as high art or more popular 'noncanonical' forms of writing. The traditional connection between stylistics and literature brings with it two important caveats, though.

The first is that creativity and innovation in language use should not be seen as the exclusive preserve of literary writing. Many forms of discourse (advertising, journalism, popular music – even casual conversation) often display a high degree of stylistic dexterity, such that it would be wrong to view dexterity in language use as exclusive to canonical literature. The second caveat is that the techniques of stylistic analysis are as much about deriving insights about linguistic structure and function as they are about understanding literary texts. Thus, the question 'What can stylistics tell us about literature?' is always paralleled by an equally important question 'What can stylistics tell us about language?'.

In spite of its clearly defined remit, methods and object of study, there remain a number of myths about contemporary stylistics. Most of the time, confusion about the compass of stylistics is a result of confusion about the compass of language. For instance, there appears to be a belief in many literary critical circles that a stylistician is simply a dull old grammarian who spends rather too much time on such trivial pursuits as counting the nouns and verbs in literary texts. Once counted, those nouns and verbs form the basis of the stylistician's 'insight', although this stylistic insight ultimately proves no more far-reaching than an insight reached by simply intuiting from the text. This is an erroneous perception of the stylistic method and it is one which stems from a limited understanding of how language analysis works. True, nouns and verbs should not be overlooked, nor indeed should 'counting' when it takes the form of directed and focussed quantification. But the purview of modern language and linguistics is much broader than that and, in response, the methods of stylistics follow suit. It is the full gamut of the system of language that makes all aspects of a writer's craft relevant in stylistic analysis. Moreover, stylistics is interested in language as a function of texts in context, and it acknowledges that utterances (literary or otherwise) are produced in a time, a place, and in a cultural and cognitive context. These 'extra-linguistic' parameters are inextricably tied up with the way a text 'means'. The more complete and context-sensitive the description of language, then the fuller the stylistic analysis that accrues.

The purpose of stylistics

Why should we do stylistics? To do stylistics is to explore language, and, more specifically, to explore creativity in language use. Doing stylistics thereby enriches our ways of thinking about language and, as observed, exploring language offers a substantial purchase on our understanding of (literary) texts. With the full array of language models at our disposal, an inherently illuminating method of analytic inquiry presents itself. This method of inquiry has an important reflexive capacity insofar as it can shed light on the very language system it derives from; it tells us about the 'rules' of language because it often explores texts where those rules are bent, distended or stretched to breaking point. Interest in language is always at the fore in contemporary stylistic analysis which is why you should never undertake to do stylistics unless you are interested in language.

Synthesising more formally some of the observations made above, it might be worth thinking of the practice of stylistics as conforming to the following three basic principles, cast mnemonically as three 'Rs'. The three Rs stipulate that:

- stylistic analysis should be rigorous
- stylistic analysis should be retrievable
- stylistic analysis should be replicable.

To argue that the stylistic method be *rigorous* means that it should be based on an explicit framework of analysis. Stylistic analysis is not the end-product of a disorganised sequence of *ad hoc* and impressionistic comments, but is instead underpinned by structured models of language and discourse that explain how we process and understand various patterns in language. To argue that stylistic method be *retrievable* means that the analysis is organised through explicit terms and criteria, the meanings of which are agreed upon by other students of stylistics. Although precise definitions for some aspects of language have proved difficult to pin down exactly, there is a consensus of agreement about what most terms in stylistics mean (see A2 below). That consensus enables other stylisticians to follow the pathway adopted in an analysis, to test the categories used and to see how the analysis reached its conclusion; to retrieve, in other words, the stylistic method.

To say that a stylistic analysis seeks to be *replicable* does not mean that we should all try to copy each others' work. It simply means that the methods should be sufficiently transparent as to allow other stylisticians to verify them, either by testing them on the same text or by applying them beyond that text. The conclusions reached are principled if the pathway followed by the analysis is accessible and replicable. To this extent, it has become an important axiom of stylistics that it seeks to distance itself from work that proceeds *solely* from untested or untestable intuition.

A seemingly innocuous piece of anecdotal evidence might help underscore this point. I once attended an academic conference where a well-known literary critic referred to the style of Irish writer George Moore as 'invertebrate'. Judging by the delegates' nods of approval around the conference hall, the critic's 'insight' had met with general endorsement. However, novel though this metaphorical interpretation of Moore's style may be, it offers the student of style no retrievable or shared point of reference in language, no *metalanguage*, with which to evaluate what the critic is trying to say. One can only speculate as to what aspect of Moore's style is at issue, because the stimulus for the observation is neither retrievable nor replicable. It is as if the act of criticism itself has become an exercise in style, vying with the stylistic creativity of the primary text discussed. Whatever its principal motivation, that critic's 'stylistic insight' is quite meaningless as a description of style.

Unit A2, below, begins both to sketch some of the broad levels of linguistic organisation that inform stylistics and to arrange and sort the interlocking domains of language study that play a part in stylistic analysis. Along the thread, unit B1 explores further the history and development of stylistics, and examines some of the issues arising. What this opening unit has sought to demonstrate is that, over a decade after Lecercle's broadside, stylistics as an academic discipline continues to flourish. In that broadside, Lecercle also contends that the term *stylistics* has 'modestly retreated from the titles of books' (1993: 14). Lest they should feel afflicted by some temporary loss of their faculties, readers might just like to check the accuracy of this claim against the title on the cover of the present textbook!

STYLISTICS AND LEVELS OF LANGUAGE

In view of the comments made in A1 on the methodological significance of the three Rs, it is worth establishing here some of the more basic categories, levels and units of analysis in language that can help organise and shape a stylistic analysis. Language in its broadest conceptualisation is not a disorganised mass of sounds and symbols, but is instead an intricate web of levels, layers and links. Thus, any utterance or piece of text is organised through several distinct *levels of language*.

Levels of language

To start us off, here is a list of the major levels of language and their related technical terms in language study, along with a brief description of what each level covers:

Level of language	**Branch of language study**
The *sound* of spoken language; the way words are pronounced.	phonology; phonetics
The patterns of *written* language; the shape of language on the page.	graphology
The way words are constructed; words and their constituent structures.	morphology
The way words combine with other words to form phrases and sentences.	syntax; grammar
The words we use; the vocabulary of a language.	lexical analysis; lexicology
The *meaning* of words and sentences.	semantics
The way words and sentences are used in everyday situations; the meaning of language in context.	pragmatics; discourse analysis

These basic levels of language can be identified and teased out in the stylistic analysis of text, which in turn makes the analysis itself more organised and principled, more in keeping so to speak with the principle of the three Rs. However, what is absolutely central to our understanding of language (and style) is that these levels are interconnected: they interpenetrate and depend upon one another, and they represent multiple and simultaneous linguistic operations in the planning and production of an utterance. Consider in this respect an unassuming (hypothetical) sentence like the following:

(1) **That puppy's knocking over those potplants!**

In spite of its seeming simplicity of structure, this thoroughly innocuous sentence requires for its production and delivery the assembly of a complex array of linguistic components. First, there is the palpable physical substance of the utterance which, when written, comprises *graphetic substance* or, when spoken, *phonetic substance*. This 'raw' matter then becomes organised into linguistic structure proper, opening up the level of *graphology*, which accommodates the systematic meanings encoded in the written medium of language, and *phonology*, which encompasses the meaning potential of the sounds of spoken language. In terms of graphology, this particular sentence is written in the Roman alphabet, and in a 10 point emboldened 'palatino' font. However, as if to echo its counterpart in speech, the sentence-final exclamation mark suggests an emphatic style of vocal delivery. In that spoken counterpart, systematic differences in sound sort out the meanings of the words used: thus, the word-initial /n/ sound at the start of 'knocking' will serve to distinguish it from, say, words like 'rocking' or 'mocking'. To that extent, the *phoneme* /n/ expresses a meaningful difference in sound. The word 'knocking' also raises an issue in *lexicology*: notice for instance how contemporary English pronunciation no longer accommodates the two word-initial *graphemes* <k> and <n> that appear in the spelling of this word. The <kn> sequence – originally spelt <cn> – has become a single /n/ pronunciation, along with equivalent occurrences in other Anglo-Saxon derived lexis in modern English like 'know' and 'knee'. The double consonant pronunciation is however still retained in the vocabulary of cognate languages like modern Dutch; as in 'knie' (meaning 'knee') or 'knoop' (meaning 'knot').

Apart from these fixed features of pronunciation, there is potential for significant variation in much of the *phonetic* detail of the spoken version of example (1). For instance, many speakers of English will not sound in connected speech the 't's of both 'Tha*t*' and 'po*t*plants', but will instead use 'glottal stops' in these positions. This is largely a consequence of the phonetic environment in which the 't' occurs: in both cases it is followed by a /p/ consonant and this has the effect of inducing a change, known as a 'secondary articulation', in the way the 't' is sounded (Ball and Rahilly 1999: 130). Whereas this secondary articulation is not necessarily so conditioned, the social or regional origins of a speaker may affect other aspects of the spoken utterance. A major regional difference in accent will be heard in the realisation of the historic <r> – a feature so named because it was once, as its retention in the modern spelling of a word like 'ove*r*' suggests, common to all accents of English. Whereas this /r/ is still present in Irish and in most American pronunciations, it has largely disappeared in Australian and in most English accents. Finally, the articulation of the 'ing' sequence at the end of the word 'knocking' may also vary, with an 'in' sound indicating a perhaps lower status accent or an informal style of delivery.

The sentence also contains words that are made up from smaller grammatical constituents known as *morphemes*. Certain of these morphemes, the 'root' morphemes, can stand as individual words in their own right, whereas others, such as prefixes and suffixes, depend for their meaning on being conjoined or bound to other items. Thus, 'potplants' has three constituents: two root morphemes ('pot' and 'plant') and a suffix (the plural morpheme 's'), making the word a three morpheme cluster. Moving up from morphology takes us into the domain of language organisation known as the *grammar*, or more appropriately perhaps, given that both lexis and word-structure are normally included in such a description, the *lexico-grammar*. Grammar is organised hierarchically according to the size of the units it contains, and most accounts of grammar would recognise the sentence as the largest unit, with the clause, phrase, word and morpheme following as progressively smaller units (see further A3). Much could be said of the grammar of this sentence: it is a single 'clause' in the indicative declarative mood. It has a Subject ('That puppy'), a Predicator (''s knocking over') and a Complement ('those potplants'). Each of these clause constituents is realised by a phrase which itself has structure. For instance, the verb phrase which expresses the Predicator has a three part structure, containing a contracted auxiliary '[i]s', a main verb 'knocking' and a preposition 'over' which operates as a special kind of extension to the main verb. This extension makes the verb a *phrasal verb*, one test for which is being able to move the extension particle along the sentence to a position beyond the Complement ('That puppy's knocking those potplants over!').

A semantic analysis is concerned with meaning and will be interested, amongst other things, in those elements of language which give the sentence a 'truth value'. A truth value specifies the conditions under which a particular sentence may be regarded as true or false. For instance, in this (admittedly hypothetical) sentence, the lexical item 'puppy' commits the speaker to the fact that a certain type of entity (namely, a young canine animal) is responsible for the action carried out. Other terms, such as the superordinate items 'dog' or even 'animal', would still be compatible in part with the truth conditions of the sentence. That is not to say that the use of a more generalised word like, say, 'animal' will have exactly the same repercussions for the utterance as *discourse* (see further below). In spite of its semantic compatibility, this less specific term would implicate in many contexts a rather negative evaluation by the speaker of the entity referred to. This type of implication is *pragmatic* rather than semantic because it is more about the meaning of language in context than about the meaning of language *per se*. Returning to the semantic component of example (1), the demonstrative words 'That' and 'those' express physical orientation in language by pointing to where the speaker is situated relative to other entities specified in the sentence. This orientational function of language is known as *deixis* (see further A7). In this instance, the demonstratives suggest that the speaker is positioned some distance away from the referents 'puppy' and 'potplants'. The deictic relationship is therefore 'distal', whereas the parallel demonstratives 'This' and 'these' would imply a 'proximal' relationship to the referents.

Above the core levels of language is situated *discourse*. This is a much more open-ended term used to encompass aspects of communication that lie beyond the organisation of sentences. Discourse is context-sensitive and its domain of reference includes pragmatic, ideological, social and cognitive elements in text processing. That means that an analysis of discourse explores meanings which are not retrievable solely through the linguistic analysis of the levels surveyed thus far. In fact, what a sentence 'means' in strictly semantic terms is not necessarily a guarantor of the kind of job it will do as an utterance in discourse. The raw semantic information transmitted by sentence (1), for instance, may only partially explain its discourse function in a specific context of use. To this effect, imagine that (1) is uttered by a speaker in the course of a two-party interaction in the living room of a dog-owning, potplant-owning addressee. Without seeking to detail the rather complex inferencing strategies involved, the utterance in this context is unlikely to be interpreted as a disconnected remark about the unruly puppy's behaviour or as a remark which requires simply a

verbal acknowledgment. Rather, it will be understood as a call to action on the part of the addressee. Indeed, it is perhaps the very obviousness in the context of what the puppy is doing *vis-à-vis* the content of the utterance that would prompt the addressee to look beyond what the speaker 'literally' says. The speaker, who, remember, is positioned deictically further away from the referents, may also feel that this discourse strategy is appropriate for a better-placed interlocutor to make the required timely intervention. Yet the same discourse context can produce any of a number of other strategies. A less forthright speaker might employ a more tentative gambit, through something like 'Sorry, but I think you might want to keep an eye on that puppy . . .'. Here, indirection serves a politeness function, although indirection of itself is not always the best policy in urgent situations where politeness considerations can be over-ridden (and see further thread 9). And no doubt even further configurations of participant roles might be drawn up to explore what other discourse strategies can be pressed into service in this interactive context.

Summary

The previous sub-unit is no more than a thumbnail sketch, based on a single illustrative example, of the core levels of language organisation. The account of levels certainly offers a useful springboard for stylistic work, but observing these levels at work in textual examples is more the starting point than the end point of analysis. Later threads, such as 6 and 7, consider how patterns of vocabulary and grammar are sorted according to the various *functions* they serve, functions which sit at the interface between lexico-grammar and discourse. Other threads, such as 10 and 11, seek to take some account of the cognitive strategies that we draw upon to process texts; strategies that reveal that the composition of a text's 'meaning' ultimately arises from the interplay between what's in the text, what's in the context and what's in the mind as well. Finally, it is fair to say that contemporary stylistics ultimately looks towards *language as discourse*: that is, towards a text's status as discourse, a writer's deployment of discourse strategies and towards the way a text 'means' as a function of language in context. This is not for a moment to deny the importance of the core levels of language – the way a text is constructed in language will, after all, have a crucial bearing on the way it functions as discourse.

The interconnectedness of the levels and layers detailed above also means there is no necessarily 'natural' starting point in a stylistic analysis, so we need to be circumspect about those aspects of language upon which we choose to concentrate. Interaction between levels is important: one level may complement, parallel or even collide with another level. To bring this unit to a close, let us consider a brief illustration of how striking stylistic effects can be engendered by offsetting one level of language against another. The following fragment is the first three lines of an untitled poem by Margaret Atwood:

You are the sun
in reverse, all energy
flows into you . . .

(Atwood 1996: 47)

At first glance, this sequence bears the stylistic imprint of the *lyric poem*. This literary genre is characterised by short introspective texts where a single speaking voice expresses emotions or thoughts, and in its 'love poem' manifestation, the thoughts are often relayed through direct address in the second person to an assumed lover. Frequently, the lyric works through an essentially metaphorical construction whereby the assumed addressee is blended conceptually with an element of nature. Indeed, the lover, as suggested here, is often mapped onto the sun, which makes the sun the 'source domain' for the metaphor (see further thread 11). Shakespeare's sonnet 18, which opens with the sequence 'Shall I compare thee to a summer's day?', is a well-known example of this type of lyrical form.

Atwood however works through this generic convention to create a startling re-orientation in interpretation. In doing so, she uses a very simple stylistic technique, a technique which essentially involves playing off the level of grammar against the level of graphology. Ending the first line where she does, she develops a linguistic *trompe l'oeil* whereby the seemingly complete grammatical structure 'You are the sun' disintegrates in the second line when we realise that the grammatical Complement (see A3) of the verb 'are' is not the phrase 'the sun' but the fuller, and rather more stark, phrase 'the sun in reverse'. As the remainder of this poem bears out, this is a bitter sentiment, a kind of 'anti-lyric', where the subject of the direct address does not embody the all-fulfilling radiance of the sun but is rather more like an energy-sapping sponge which drains, rather than enhances, the life-forces of nature. And while the initial, positive sense engendered in the first line is displaced by the grammatical 'revision' in the second, the ghost of it somehow remains. Indeed, this particular stylistic pattern works literally to establish, and then reverse, the harmonic coalescence of subject with nature.

All of the levels of language detailed in this unit will feature in various places around this book. The remainder of this thread, across to a reading in D2 by Katie Wales, is concerned with the broad resources that different levels of language offer for the creation of stylistic texture. Unit B2 explores juxtapositions between levels similar in principle to that observed in Atwood and includes commentary on semantics, graphology and morphology. In terms of its vertical progression, this section feeds into further and more detailed introductions to certain core levels of language, beginning below with an introduction to the level of grammar.

GRAMMAR AND STYLE

A3

When we talk of the *grammar* of a language we are talking of a hugely complex set of interlocking categories, units and structures: in effect, the *rules* of that language. In the academic study of language, the expression 'rules of grammar' does not refer to prescriptive niceties, to the sorts of proscriptions that forbid the use of, say, a double negative or a split infinitive. These so-called 'rules' are nothing more than a random collection of *ad hoc* and prejudiced strictures about language use. On the contrary, the genuine grammatical rules of a language are *the* language insofar as they stipulate the very bedrock of its syntactic construction in the same way that the rules of tennis or the rules of chess constitute the core organising principles of those games. This makes grammar somewhat of an intimidating area of analysis for the beginning stylistician because it is not always easy to sort out which aspects of a text's many interlocking patterns of grammar are stylistically salient. We will therefore use this unit to try to develop some useful building blocks for a study of grammar and style. The remainder of this thread examines patterns of grammar in a variety of literary texts, culminating, across in D3, with a reading by Ronald Carter which explores patterns of grammar in a 'concrete' poem by Edwin Morgan. But first, to the basics.

A basic model of grammar

Most theories of grammar accept that grammatical units are ordered hierarchically according to their size. This hierarchy is known as a *rank scale.* As the arrangement below suggests, the rank scale sorts units in a 'consists of' relationship, progressing from the largest down to the smallest:

sentence (or clause complex)
clause
phrase (or group)
word
– morpheme

As the rank scale indicates, the *morpheme* (see A2 above) is the smallest unit in grammar simply because it has no structure of its own; if it did, it would not be the bottom-most unit on the scale. Arguably the most important unit on the scale is the *clause*, The clause is especially important because it is the site of several important functions in language: it provides *tense*; it distinguishes between positive or negative *polarity*; it provides the core or 'nub' of a proposition in language; and it is where information about grammatical 'mood' (about whether a clause is declarative, interrogative or imperative) is situated. The clause will therefore be the principal focus of interest in the following discussion.

For our purposes, we can distinguish four basic elements of clause structure. These are the *Subject* (S), the *Predicator* (P), the *Complement* (C) and the *Adjunct* (A). Here are some examples of clauses which display an 'SPCA' pattern:

	Subject	**Predicator**	**Complement**	**Adjunct**
(1)	The woman	feeds	those pigeons	regularly.
(2)	Our bull terrier	was chasing	the postman	yesterday.
(3)	The Professor of Necromancy	would wear	lipstick	every Friday.

(4)	The Aussie actress	looked	great	in her latest film.
(5)	The man who came to dinner	was	pretty miserable	throughout the evening.

These examples highlight grammar's capacity to embed units of different sizes within one another. Notice for example how the elements of clause structure are 'filled up' by other units, like words and phrases, which occur lower down on the rank scale. Indeed, it is a defining characteristic of clause structure that its four basic elements are typically realised by certain types of phrases. For instance, the Predicator is always filled by a *verb phrase*. The Subject is typically filled by a *noun phrase* which is a cluster of words in which a noun forms the central component. The key nouns in the phrases which express the Subjects above are, respectively, 'woman', 'terrier', 'Professor', 'actress' and 'man' . The Complement position is typically filled either by a noun phrase or, as in examples (4) and (5), by an *adjective phrase* where an adjective, such as 'great' and 'miserable', features as the prominent constituent in the cluster. Finally, the Adjunct is typically filled either by an *adverb phrase* or by a *prepositional phrase*. The Adjunct elements in examples (1), (2) and (3) are all of the adverbial type. Prepositional phrases, which form the Adjunct element in (4) and (5), are clusters which are fronted by a preposition and which are normally rounded off by a noun or phrase, as in 'in (preposition) her latest film (noun phrase)'. The rule which stipulates that a verb phrase must fill up the Predicator slot is a hard and fast one, whereas the rules about what sorts of phrases go into the other three slots are less absolute and are more about typical tendencies. Later in this unit, a little more will be said about phrases (also known as 'groups') and their significance in stylistic analysis, but for the moment we need to develop further our account of clauses.

Tests for clause constituents

We can test for the Subject, Complement and Adjunct elements of clause structure by asking various questions around the verb – assuming of course that we can find the verb! Here is a list of useful tests for sorting out clause structure:

Finding the Subject:	it should answer the question 'who' or 'what' placed *in front of* the verb.
Finding the Complement:	it should answer the question 'who' or 'what' placed *after* the verb.
Finding the Adjunct:	it should answer questions such as 'how', 'when', 'where' or 'why' placed after the verb.

Thus, the test for Subject in example (1) – '*who or what?* feeds those pigeons regularly' – will confirm 'The woman' as the Subject element. Alternatively, the test for Complement in example (2) – 'The man who came to dinner was *what?* throughout the evening' – will confirm the adjective phrase 'pretty miserable' as the Complement.

There is another useful test for elements of clause structure which can also be used to adduce further information about grammatical structure. Although this test will feature in a more directed way in unit B3, it is worth flagging it up here. The test involves adding a 'tag question' to the declarative form of a clause. The examples provided thus far are declarative because all of their Predicator elements come after the Subject, in the form that is standardly (though not always) used for making statements. Adding a tag, which may be of positive or negative polarity, allows the speaker or writer to alter the function of the declarative. Thus:

(1a) The woman feeds those pigeons regularly, doesn't she?

(2a) Our bull terrier was chasing the postman yesterday, was it?

There are several reasons why the tag is a useful tool for exploring grammatical structure. For one thing, it will always repeat the Subject element as a pronoun ('she', 'it') and it will do this irrespective of how complicated or lengthy the Subject is. It also draws out an important aspect of the Predicator in the form of an auxiliary verb ('does', 'was') which supplies amongst other things important information about tense and 'finiteness' (see further B3 and C3). The slightly awkward thing about the 'tag test' is that the questioning tag inverts the word order and often the polarity of the original clause constituents. However, if you have the good fortune to be Irish, then the Hiberno-English dialect offers an even more straightforward mechanism for testing elements of the clause. Adding an Hiberno-English emphatic tag (eg. 'so she does'; 'so it was') to the end of a declarative will repeat the Subject as a pronoun without affecting word-order or changing the polarity of the original. Thus:

(3a) The Professor of Necromancy would wear lipstick every Friday, so she would.

The tag test, whether in the questioning or the emphatic form, still works even when the Subject element is relatively 'heavy'. In a sequence like

(6) Mary's curious contention that mackerel live in trees proved utterly unjustified.

the appending of 'did *it*?', 'didn't *it*?' or 'so *it* did' renders down to a simple pronoun the entire sequence 'Mary's curious contention that mackerel live in trees'. This structure, which incidentally contains an embedded clause of its own, is what forms the Subject element in (6).

Activity

The tag test can usefully differentiate between other types of grammatical structures. For example, in each of the following two examples, the Subject element is expressed by *two* noun phrases. If this is your book, write in an appropriate tag after each of the examples in the space provided:

(7) My aunt and my uncle visit the farm regularly, ________

(8) The winner, a local businesswoman, had donated the prize to charity, ________

Clearly, the application of our 'who or what?' test before the verb will reveal the Subject elements in (7) and (8) straightforwardly enough, but what the tag test further reveals is that the Subjects are of a very different order. In (7), the two noun phrases ('My aunt' and 'my uncle') refer to *different* entities which are brought together by the conjunction 'and'. Notice how the tag will yield a plural pronoun: 'don't *they*?' or 'so *they* do'. The grammatical technique of drawing together different entities in this manner is known as *coordination* (and see further B3). In the second example, the tag test brings out a singular pronoun only ('had *she*?', 'so *she* had') which shows that in fact the two phrases 'The winner' and 'a local businesswoman' refer in different ways to the *same* entity. The term for a grammatical structure which makes variable reference to the same entity is known as *apposition.*

Variations in basic clause structure

Whereas most of the examples provided so far exhibit a basic SPCA pattern of clause structure, it is important to note that this configuration represents only one of a number of possible combinations. Other types of grammatical *mood*, for example, involve different types of of clausal patterning. A case in point is the *imperative*, which is the form typically used for requests and commands. Imperative clauses like 'Mind your head' or 'Turn on the telly, please' have no Subject element, a knock-on effect of which is that their verb always retains its base form and cannot be marked for tense. *Interrogatives*, the form typically used for asking questions, do contain Subject elements. However, many types of interrogative position part of the Predicator in front of the Subject thus:

(3b) Would the Professor of Necromancy wear lipstick every Friday?

When there isn't enough Predicator available to release a particle for the pre-Subject position, a form of the pro-verb 'do' is brought into play:

(1b) Does the woman feed those pigeons regularly?

By way of footnote, the use of the verb 'do' for this purpose is a relatively recent development in the history of English language. In early Modern English, the SP sequence was often simply inverted to make an interrogative, as in the following absurdly anachronistic transposition of (4):

(4a) Looked the Aussie actress great in her latest film?

Declarative clauses may themselves display significant variation around the basic SPCA pattern. Pared down to its grammatical bare bones, as it were, a clause may realise S and P elements only, as in 'The train arrived' or 'The lesson began'. Occasionally a clause may contain two Complements. This occurs when one of the C elements is a 'direct object' and the other an 'indirect object', as in 'Mary gave her friend a book' or 'Bill told the children a story'. Notice however that both examples will still satisfy our test for Complement in that the test question is answered *twice* in each case: 'Mary gave *who? what?*', 'Bill told *who? what?*'.

Adjunct elements are many and varied in terms of the forms they take and of the type of information they bring to a clause. They basically describe the *circumstances* (see A6) that attach to the process related by the clause and for that reason they can often be removed without affecting the grammaticality of the clause as a whole. Here is an example of a clause with an SPAAAA pattern. Try to sort out the four Adjuncts it contains by asking the test questions: 'how?' 'where?' 'when?' and 'why?':

(10) Mary awoke suddenly in her hotel room one morning because of a knock on the door.

What the forgoing discussion illustrates is that, strictly speaking, neither the Subject, Complement nor Adjunct elements are essential components of clause structure. The situation regarding the Predicator element is not quite so clear-cut, however, and there has been much debate among grammarians about the status of 'P-less' structures. Impacting on this is the fact that much of our everyday language use involves a type of grammatical abbreviation known as *ellipsis*. For instance, if A asks 'Where are the keys?' and B answers 'In your pocket!', then B's response, while lacking a Predicator, still implicitly retains part of the structure of the earlier question. In other words, even though B's elliptical reply amounts to no more than a simple prepositional phrase, it still presupposes the elements of a full-blown clause. The term *minor clause* is conventionally used to describe structures, like this one, which lack a Predicator element. It is important to acknowledge minor clauses not only because these elliptical structures play an important role in much spoken interaction but also because, as the other units in this thread will argue, they form an important locus for stylistic experimentation. Finally, as a general rule of thumb, when analysing elements which *are* present in a text, there can only be one Subject element and one Predicator element of structure in any given clause. There may however be up to two Complement elements and any number of Adjunct elements.

Quite how clause structure and other types of grammatical patterning function as markers of style will be the focus of attention across the remainder of this strand, and indeed for part of unit C4 also. Next up in this introductory section of the book is the topic of sound and rhythm as it intersects with style in language. The following unit introduces therefore some key concepts used by stylisticians in their investigations of phonology and metrical patterning.

A4 RHYTHM AND METRE

Literature is, by definition, written language. This truism might suggest then that literature is not a medium especially well suited to exploration either at the linguistic level of phonology or in terms of its phonetic substance. However, sound patterning plays a pivotal role in literary discourse in general, and in poetry in particular.

Attention has been given elsewhere (unit C2) to the techniques writers use for representing *accent*, one aspect of spoken discourse, in prose fiction. This unit deals more directly with the issue of sound patterning in literature and it introduces core features, like *rhythm* and *metre*, which have an important bearing on the structure and indeed interpretation of poetry.

Metre

When we hear someone reading a poem aloud, we tend to recognise very quickly that it is poem that is being read and not another type of text. Indeed, even if the listener cannot make out or, as is often the case for young readers, the listener doesn't understand all the words of the text, they still know that they are listening to poetry. One reason why this rather unusual communicative situation should arise is because poetry has *metre*. A pivotal criterion for the definition of verse, metre is, most simply put, an organised pattern of strong and weak syllables. Key to the definition is the proviso that metrical patterning should be *organised*, and in such a way that the alternation between accentuated syllables and weak syllables is repeated. That repetition, into a regular phrasing across a line of verse, is what makes *rhythm*. Rhythm is therefore a patterned movement of pulses in time which is defined both by periodicity (it occurs at regular time intervals) and repetition (the same pulses occur again and again).

Let us now try to work through these rather abstract definitions of metre and rhythm using some textual examples. In metrics, the *foot* is the basic unit of analysis and it refers to the span of stressed and unstressed syllables that forms a rhythmical pattern. Different sorts of metrical feet can be determined according to the number of, and ordering of, their constituent stressed and unstressed syllables. An *iambic* foot, for example, has two syllables, of which the first is less heavily stressed than the second (a 'de-dum' pattern, for want of a more formal typology). The *trochaic* foot, by contrast, reverses the pattern, offering a 'dum-de' style of metre. Here is a well-known example of the first type, a line from Thomas Gray's 'Elegy Written in a Country Churchyard' (1751):

(1) The ploughman homeward plods his weary way

In the following annotated version of (1), the metrical feet are segmented off from one another by vertical lines. Positioned below the text are two methods for capturing the alternation between strong (s) and weak (w) syllables:

(1a) The plough | man home | ward plods | his wea | ry way
w s w s w s w s w s
de dum de dum de dum de dum de dum

As there are five iambs in the line, this metrical scheme is *iambic pentameter*. Had there been six feet, it would have been iambic *hexameter*, four feet, iambic *tetrameter*, three feet . . . well, you can work out the rest by yourself. What is especially important about metre, as this breakdown shows, is that it transcends the lexico-grammar (see A2). Metrical boundaries are no respecters of word boundaries, a consequence of which is that rhythm provides an additional layer of meaning potential that can be developed along Jakobson's 'axis of combination' (see B1). That extra layer can either enhance a lexico-grammatical structure, or rupture and fragment it. In respect of this point, it is worth noting the other sound imagery at work in the line from Gray. *Alliteration* is a type of rhyme scheme which is based on similarities between consonants. Although rhyme is normally thought of as a feature of line endings, the internal alliterative rhyme in (1) picks out and enhances the balancing halves of the line through the repetition of, first, the /pl/ in 'ploughman' and 'plods' and, later, the /w/ in 'weary' and 'way'. In terms of its impact on grammatical structure, the first repetition links both Subject and Predicator (see A3), while the /w/ consolidates the Complement element of the clause; taken together, both patterns give the line an *acoustic punctuation*, to use Carter and Nash's term (Carter and Nash 1990: 120). A rearrangement of the line into a structure like the following

(1b) The ploughman plods his weary way homeward

will make the acoustic punctuation redundant because the Adjunct 'homeward', which had originally separated the Subject and Complement, is simply no longer there. And of course, this rearrangement collapses entirely the original metrical scheme.

Here are some more examples of metrical patterning in verse. The following fragment from Tennyson's *Lady of Shallott* (1832) is a good illustration of a trochaic pattern:

(2) By the margin, willow veiled
Slide the heavy barges trailed

Using our model of analysis, the first line of the couplet can be set out thus

(2a) By the | margin | willow | veiled
s w s w s w s w
dum de dum de dum de dum de

and this will reveal, amongst other things, that (2) is an example of trochaic *tetrameter*.

The following line from W. H. Auden's poem 'The Quarry' represents another, slightly more complicated, type of versification:

(3) O what is that sound that so thrills the ear

This sequence, on my reading of it, begins with an *offbeat*. An offbeat is an unstressed syllable which, depending on the metrical structure of the line as a whole, is normally placed at the start or the end of a line of verse. In the initial position, an offbeat can act like a little phonetic springboard that helps us launch into the metrical scheme proper. Here is a suggested breakdown of the Auden line:

(3a) O | what is that | sound that so | thrills the ear
w s w w s w w s w w
de dum de de dum de de dum de de

Here the three metrical feet contain three beats apiece, and in a strong-weak-weak configuration which is known as a *dactyl.* That makes the line as whole an example of *dactylic trimeter.*

Issues

The example from Auden raises an interesting issue to do with metrical analysis. I am sure that for many readers their scansion of (3) brings out a different metrical pattern, with stress on words other than or in addition to those highlighted in (3a). A strong pulse might for example be preferred on 'ear', giving the line an 'end-weight' focus, or maybe even on 'so' which would allow extra intensity to be assigned to the process of thrilling. In spite of what many metricists suggest, metrical analysis is not an exact science, and these alternative readings are in my view perfectly legitimate. Basically, while conventional phrasing dictates certain types of metrical scheme, readers of poetry have a fair amount of choice about exactly how and where to inflect a line of verse.

A contributing factor in reader choice is that the distinction between strong and weak syllables is relative, and not absolute. Consider again the line from Shakespeare's sonnet 18 which was mentioned briefly in unit A2:

(4) Shall I | compare | thee to | a sum | mer's day?

The line's five metrical feet, with stress falling on the second element, clearly make it iambic pentameter. However, this classification tends to assume that all accentuation is equal, an interpretation which is not necessarily borne out when reading the line aloud. Whereas in the fourth foot ('a sum') the contrast in stress is clear, in the first foot ('Shall I'), the second beat is only marginally more accentuated, if at all, than the first beat. The second foot ('compare') exhibits a degree of contrast somewhere between the fourth and the second, while the third foot seems to have little accentuation on either syllable. In other words, there are about four *degrees* of accentuation in this line, which we might order numerically thus:

(4) Shall I | compare | thee to | a sum | mer's day?
3 4 1 4 1 2 1 4 1 4

Although the degree of contrast within metrical feet may be variable, what is important in metrical analysis is that the contrast itself be there in the first place, whatever the relative strength or weakness of its individual beats. (See further Fraser 1970: 3–7)

Now to a final issue which will wrap up this unit. While verse is (obviously) characterised by its use of metre, it does not follow that all metre is verse; and it is important not to lose sight of the fact that metre has an existence outside literature.

We need therefore to treat this stylistic feature, as we do with many aspects of style, as a common resource which is shared across many types of textual practice. By way of illustration, consider the following short example of 'nonliterary' discourse, an advertisement for a bathroom shower appliance:

(5) Never undress
for anything less!

Example (5) is a jingle; that is, a phonologically contoured text designed by advertisers as an *aide memoire*. A 'simple' text, to be sure, but (5) nonetheless makes use of an interesting metrical scheme. My own 'reading' suggests the following pattern:

(5a)		Nev	er	|	un	dress
		s	w		w	s
		dum	de		de	dum

for	|	an	y	|	thing	less
w		s	w		w	s
de		dum	de		de	dum

Notice how the couplet employs an offbeat at the start of its second line. Line-initial offbeats are commonly used to help galvanise so-called 'four-by-four' sequences, and example (5) does indeed contain two lines of four syllables each. The scheme is also organised into a *chiasmus*, which is a symmetrical 'mirror image' pattern where the strong to weak pulse ('dum de') is paralleled by a weak to strong pulse ('de dum'). Overall, this four syllable pattern resembles a 'pæonic' metre, which is a type of metrical pattern that invites a brisk style of delivery with a 'cantering' tempo of recitation (Leech 1969: 112).

Other issues to do with sound and style will be taken up across this thread. In B4, attention turns to developments in the interpretation of sound symbolism in literary texts. Unit C4 offers a set of activities based on a single poem where particular emphasis is put on patterns of sound. That poem introduces, amongst other things, a different form of versification, known as *free verse*, where strict metrical schemes give way to the inflections of naturally occurring speech. Finally, the reading which rounds off this thread is Derek Attridge's entertaining study of the significance of sound, not in poetry, but in prose.

A5 NARRATIVE STYLISTICS

Narrative discourse provides a way of recapitulating felt experience by matching up patterns of language to a connected series of events. In its most minimal form, a narrative comprises two clauses which are temporally ordered, such that a change in their order will result in a change in the way we interpret the assumed chronology of the narrative events. For example, the two narrative clauses in

(1) John dropped the plates and Janet laughed suddenly

suggest a temporal progression between the two actions described. Indeed, not only do we assume that John's mishap preceded Janet's response, but also that it was his mishap that brought about her response. However, reversing the clauses to form 'Janet laughed suddenly and John dropped the plates' would invite a different interpretation: that is, that Janet's laughter not only preceded but actually precipitated John's misfortune.

Of course, most narratives, whether those of canonical prose fiction or of the spontaneous stories of everyday social interaction, have rather more to offer than just two simple temporally arranged clauses. Narrative requires development, elaboration, embellishment; and it requires a sufficient degree of stylistic flourish to give it an imprint of individuality or personality. Stories narrated without that flourish will often feel flat and dull. On this issue, the sociolinguist William Labov has argued that narratives require certain essential elements of structure which, when absent, render the narrative 'ill-formed'. He cites the following attested story as an illustration:

(2) well this person had a little too much to drink
and he attacked me
and the friend came in
and she stopped it

(Labov 1972: 360)

This story, which is really only a skeleton of a fully formed narrative, was told by an adult informant who had been asked to recollect an experience where they felt they had been in real danger. True, the story does satisfy the minimum criterion for narrative in that it comprises temporally connected clauses, but it also lacks a number of important elements which are important to the delivery of a successful narrative. A listener might legitimately ask, for instance, about exactly where and when this story took place. And who was involved in the story? That is, who was the 'person' who had too much to drink and precisely whose friend was 'the friend' who stopped the attack? How, for that matter, did the storyteller come to be in the same place as the antagonist? And is the friend's act of stopping the assault the final action of the story? Clearly, much is missing from this narrative. As well as lacking sufficient contextualisation, it offers little sense of closure or finality. It also lacks any dramatic or rhetorical embellishment, and so risks attracting a rebuke like 'so what?' from an interlocutor. Reading between the lines of Labov's study, the narrator of (2) seems to have felt some discomfort about the episode narrated and was therefore rather reluctantly lured into telling the story. It may have been this factor which constrained the development of a fully articulated narrative.

There is clearly, then, more to a narrative than just a sequence of basic clauses of the sort evidenced in examples (1) and (2). However, the task of providing a full and rigorous model of narrative discourse has proved somewhat of a challenge for stylisticians. There is much disagreement about how to isolate the various units which combine to form, say, a novel or short story, just as there is about how to explain the interconnections between these narrative units. Moreover, in the broad communicative event that is narrative, narrative *structure* is only one side of a coin of which narrative *comprehension* is the other (see further thread 10). Allowing then that a fully comprehensive description is not achievable, the remainder of this introductory unit will establish the core tenets only of a suggested model of narrative structure. It will point out which type of individual stylistic framework is best suited to which particular unit in the narrative model and will also signal whereabouts in this book each of the individual units will be explored and illustrated.

It is common for much work in stylistics and narratology to make a primary distinction between two basic components of narrative: narrative *plot* and narrative *discourse*. The term *plot* is generally understood to refer to the abstract storyline of a narrative; that is, to the sequence of elemental, chronologically ordered events which create the 'inner core' of a narrative. Narrative *discourse*, by contrast, encompasses the manner or means by which that plot is narrated. Narrative discourse, for example, is often characterised by the use of stylistic devices such as flashback, prevision and repetition – all of which serve to disrupt the basic chronology of the narrative's plot. Thus, narrative discourse represents the realised text, the palpable piece of language which is produced by a story-teller in a given interactive context.

The next step involves sorting out the various stylistic elements which make up narrative discourse. To help organise narrative analysis into clearly demarcated areas of study, let us adopt the model shown in Figure A5.1.

Beyond the plot–discourse distinction, the categories towards the right of the diagram constitute six basic units of analysis in narrative description. Although there are substantial areas of overlap between these units, they nonetheless offer a useful set of reference points for pinpointing the specific aspects of narrative which can inform a stylistic analysis. Some further explanation of the units themselves is in order.

The first of the six is *textual medium*. This refers simply to the physical channel of communication through which a story is narrated. Two common narrative media

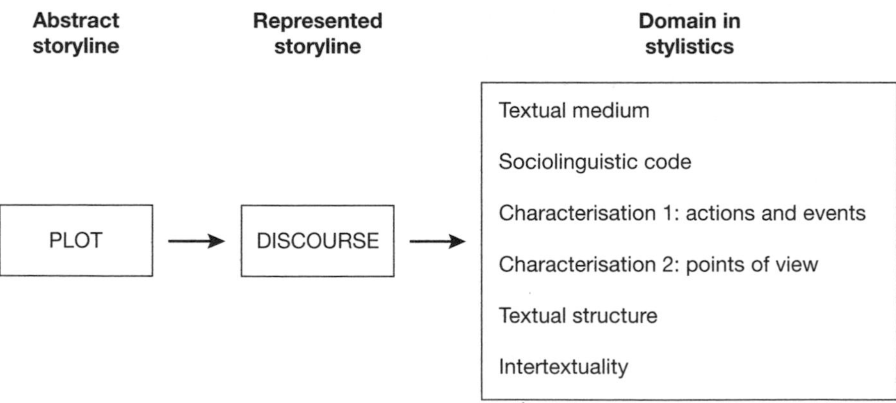

Figure A5.1 A model of narrative structure

are film and the novel, although various other forms are available such as the ballet, the musical or the strip cartoon. The examples cited thus far in this unit represent another common medium for the transmission of narrative experience: spoken verbal interaction. The concept of textual medium, in tandem with the distinction between plot and discourse, is further explored in B5.

Sociolinguistic code expresses through language the historical, cultural and linguistic setting which frames a narrative. It locates the narrative in time and place by drawing upon the forms of language which reflect this sociocultural context. Sociolinguistic code encompasses, amongst other things, the varieties of accent and dialect used in a narrative, whether they be ascribed to the narrator or to characters within the narrative, although the concept also extends to the social and institutional registers of discourse deployed in a story. This particular narrative resource is further explored in C2.

The first of the two characterisation elements, *actions and events*, describes how the development of character precipitates and intersects with the actions and events of a story. It accounts for the ways in which the narrative intermeshes with particular kinds of semantic process, notably those of 'doing', 'thinking' and 'saying', and for the ways in which these processes are attributed to characters and narrators. This category, which approaches narrative within the umbrella concept of 'style as choice', is the main focus of attention across the units in strand 6.

The second category of narrative characterisation, *point of view*, explores the relationship between mode of narration and a character's or narrator's 'point of view'. Mode of narration specifies whether the narrative is relayed in the first person, the third person or even the second person, while point of view stipulates whether the events of story are viewed from the perspective of a particular character or from that of an omniscient narrator, or indeed from some mixture of the two. The way speech and thought processes are represented in narrative is also an important index of point of view, although this stylistic technique has a double function because it relates to actions and events also. Point of view in narrative is examined across strand 7, while speech and thought presentation is explored in strand 8.

Textual structure accounts for the way individual narrative units are arranged and organised in a story. A stylistic study of textual structure may focus on large-scale elements of plot or, alternatively, on more localised features of story's organisation; similarly, the particular analytic models used may address broad-based aspects of narrative coherence or they may examine narrower aspects of narrative cohesion in organisation. Textual structure (as it organises narrative) is the centre of interest across the remainder of this strand (B5, C5, D5).

The term *intertextuality*, the sixth narrative component, is reserved for the technique of 'allusion'. Narrative fiction, like all writing, does not exist in a social and historical vacuum, and it often echoes other texts and images either as 'implicit' intertextuality or as 'manifest' intertextuality. In a certain respect, the concept of intertextuality overlaps with the notion of sociolinguistic code in its application to narrative, although the former involves the importing of other, external texts while the latter refers more generally to the variety or varieties of language in and through which a narrative is developed. Both of these constituents feature in units C1 and C2.

A6 STYLE AS CHOICE

Much of our everyday experience is shaped and defined by actions and events, thoughts and perceptions, and it is an important function of the system of language that it is able to account for these various 'goings on' in the world. This means encoding into the grammar of the clause a mechanism for capturing what we say, think and do. It also means accommodating in grammar a host of more abstract relations, such as those that pertain between objects, circumstances and logical concepts. When language is used to represent the goings on of the physical or abstract world in this way, to represent patterns of experience in spoken and written texts, it fulfils the *experiential* function. The experiential function is an important marker of style, especially so of the style of narrative discourse, because it emphasises the concept of *style as choice*. There are many ways of accounting in language for the various events that constitute our 'mental picture of reality' (Halliday 1994: 106); indeed, there are often several ways of using the resources of the language system to capture the *same* event in a textual representation. What is of interest to stylisticians is why one type of structure should be preferred to another, or why, from possibly several ways of representing the same 'happening', one particular type of depiction should be privileged over another. Choices in style are motivated, even if unconsciously, and these choices have a profound impact on the way texts are structured and interpreted.

The particular grammatical facility used for capturing experience in language is the system of *transitivity*. In the present account, the concept of 'transitivity' is used in an expanded semantic sense, much more so than in traditional grammars where it simply serves to identify verbs which take direct objects. Transitivity here refers to the way meanings are encoded in the clause and to the way different types of *process* are represented in language. Transitivity normally picks out three key components of processes. The first is the process itself, which is typically realised in grammar by the *verb phrase* (see A3). The second is the *participant(s)* associated with the process, typically realised by *noun phrases.* Perhaps less importantly for stylistic analysis, transitivity also picks out the *circumstances* associated with the process. This third element is typically expressed by *prepositional* and *adverb* phrases which, as we saw in A3, fill up the Adjunct element in clause structure.

Linguists working with this functional model of transitivity are divided about how exactly to 'carve up' the experiential function. How many sorts of experience, for example, should the system distinguish? How easy is it to place discrete boundaries around certain types of human experiences when those experiences tend to overlap or shade into one another? In the brief account of transitivity that follows, six types of process are identified, although the divisions between these processes will always be more provisional than absolute.

Material processes, the first of the six, are simply processes of *doing.* Associated with material processes are two inherent participant roles which are the *Actor*, an obligatory role in the process, and a *Goal*, a role which may or may not be involved in the process. The following two examples of material processes follow the standard notation conventions which place the textual example above its individual transitivity roles:

(1)	I	nipped	Daniel.
	Actor	Process	Goal
(2)	The washing machine		broke down.
	Actor		Process

Mental processes constitute the second key process of the transitivity system and are essentially processes of *sensing*. Unlike material processes which have their provenance in the physical world, mental processes inhabit and reflect the world of consciousness, and involve cognition (encoded in verbs such as 'thinking' or 'wondering'), reaction (as in 'liking' or 'hating') and perception (as in 'seeing' or 'hearing'). The two participant roles associated with mental processes are the Sensor (the conscious being that is doing the sensing) and the Phenomenon (the entity which is sensed, felt, thought or seen). Here are illustrations of the three main types of mental process:

(3)	Mary	understood	the story.	(cognition)
	Sensor	Process	Phenomenon	
(4)	Anil	noticed	the damp patch.	(perception)
	Sensor	Process	Phenomenon	
(5)	Siobhan	detests	paté.	(reaction)
	Sensor	Process	Phenomenon	

The roles of Sensor and Phenomenon relate exclusively to mental processes. This distinction is necessary because the entity 'sensed' in a mental process is not directly affected by the process, and this makes it of a somewhat different order to the role of Goal in a material process. It is also an important feature of the semantic basis of the transitivity system that the participant roles remain constant under certain types of grammatical operation. Example (5), for instance, might be rephrased as 'Paté disgusts Siobhan', yet 'Siobhan' still remains the Sensor and 'Paté' the Phenomenon.

A useful check which often helps distinguish material and mental processes is to test which sort of present tense best suits the particular example under analysis. The 'natural' present tense for mental processes is the simple present, so the transformation of the past tense of example (3) would result in 'Mary understands the story'. By contrast, material processes normally gravitate towards the present continuous tense, as in the transposition of (2) to 'The washing machine is breaking down'. When transposed to the present continuous, however, mental processes often sound odd: 'Siobhan is detesting paté', 'Anil is noticing the damp patch' and so on.

There is a type of process which to some extent sits at the interface between material and mental processes, a process which represents both the activities of 'sensing' and 'doing'. *Behavioural* processes embody physiological actions like 'breathe' or 'cough', although they sometimes portray these processes as states of consciousness as in 'sigh', 'cry' or 'laugh'. They also represent processes of consciousness as forms of behaviour, as in 'stare', 'dream' or 'worry'. The key (and normally sole) participant in behavioural processes is the Behaver, the conscious entity who is 'behaving':

(6)	That student	fell asleep	in my lecture again.	
	Behaver	Process	Circumstance	
(7)	She	frowned	at the mess.	
	Behaver	Process	Circumstances	

The role of Behaver is very much like that of a Sensor, although the behavioural process itself is grammatically more akin to a material process. Thus, while both examples above display many of the characteristics of mental processes, our 'tense' test satisfies the criteria for material processes: 'That student is falling asleep . . .'; 'She is frowning . . .'.

Close in sense to mental processes, insofar as they articulate conscious thought, are processes of *verbalisation.* These are processes of 'saying' and the participant roles associated with verbalisation are the Sayer (the producer of the speech), the Receiver (the entity to which the speech is addressed) and the Verbiage (that which gets said). Thus:

(8)	Mary	claimed	that the story had been changed.	
	Sayer	Process	Verbiage	
(9)	The minister	announced	the decision	to parliament.
	Sayer	Process	Verbiage	Receiver

Notice how the Verbiage participant, which, incidentally, is not a term used in any derogatory sense, can cover either the 'content' of what was said (as in 8) or the 'name', in speech act terms, of what was said (as in 9). It is also important to note that the process of saying needs to be interpreted rather broadly, so that even an inanimate Sayer can be accommodated: 'The notice said be quiet'.

Now to an important and deceptively complex category: *relational processes.* These are processes of 'being' in the specific sense of establishing relationships between two entities. Relational processes can be expressed in a number of ways, and not all of the numerous classifications which present themselves can be accommodated here. There is however general agreement about three main types of relational process. An *intensive* relational process posits a relationship of equivalence, an 'x *is* y' connection, between two entities, as in: 'Paula's presentation was lively' or 'Joyce is the best Irish writer'. A possessive relational process plots an 'x *has* y' type of connection between two entities, as in 'Peter has a piano' or 'The Alpha Romeo is Clara's'. Thirdly, *circumstantial* relational processes are where the circumstantial element becomes upgraded, as it were, so that it fulfils the role of a full participant in the process. The relationship engendered is a broad 'x *is at*/*is in*/*is on*/*is with*/ y' configuration, realised in constructions like 'The fête is on all day', 'The maid was in the parlour' or 'The forces of darkness are against you'.

This seemingly straightforward three-way classification is rather complicated by the fact that it intersects with another distinction between *attributive* and *identifying* relational processes. This means that each of the three types come in two modes, yielding six categories in total. The grid shown in Table A6.1 will help summarise this

Table A6.1 Relational processes grid

Type	Mode attributive	identifying
intensive	Paula's presentation was lively	The best Irish writer is Joyce Joyce is the best Irish writer
possessive	Peter has a piano	The Alpha Romeo is Clara's Clara's is the Alpha Romeo
circumstantial	The fête is on all day	The maid is in the parlour In the parlour is the maid

classification. In the attributive mode, the entity, person or concept being described is referred to as the Carrier, while the role of Attribute refers to the quality ascribed to that Carrier. The Attribute therefore says what the Carrier is, what the Carrier is like, where the Carrier is, what it owns and so on. In the identifying mode, one role is identified through reference to another such that the two halves of the clause often refer to the same thing. This means that unlike attributive processes, all identifying processes are reversible, as the grid above shows. In terms of their participant roles, one entity (the Identifier) picks out and defines the other (the Identified). Thus, in the pattern:

(10)	Joyce	is	the best Irish writer
	Identified	Process	Identifier

the sequence 'the best Irish writer' functions to identify 'Joyce' as the key representative of a particular class of individuals. The alternative pattern, 'The best Irish writer is Joyce', simply reverses the sequence of these two participant roles.

Existential processes constitute the sixth and last category of the transitivity model. Close in sense to relational processes, these processes basically assert that something exists or happens. Existential processes typically include the word 'there' as a dummy subject, as in 'There was an assault' or 'Has there been a phone call?', and they normally only contain one participant role, the 'Existent', realised respectively in these examples by 'an assault' and 'a phone call'.

In another sense, the existential process leads us right back to the material process, the category with which we began this review of the system of transitivity. Significantly, both types of process can often accommodate a question like 'what happened?', the response to which results in two possible configurations. Thus, both 'X assaulted Y' and 'There was an assault' would offer a choice of responses to this hypothetical question. However, what happens in the existential version is that no role other than Existent is specified, and that role, moreover, is filled by a *nominalised* element which is created by converting a verbal process into a noun (see C3).

It is worth reemphasising this idea of 'style as choice' in transitivity, and in this respect consider an anecdotal example. When questioned about some rowdiness that

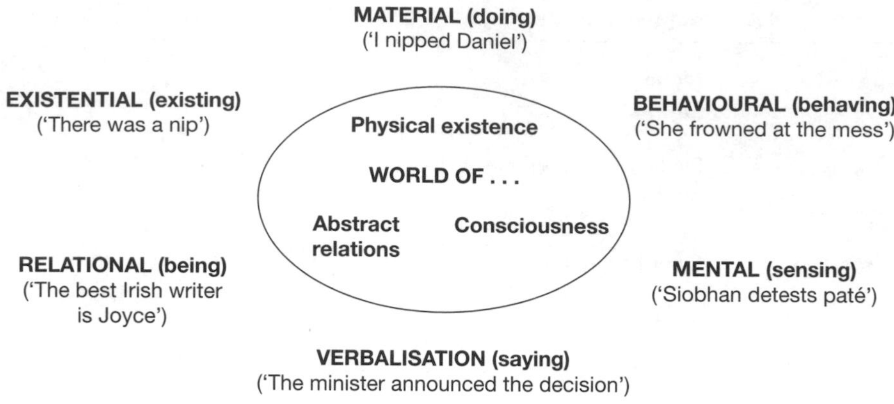

Figure A6.1 A model of transitivity

resulted in a slight injury to his younger brother, my (then five year old) son replied: 'There was a nip'. This is an interesting experiential strategy because it satisfies the question 'what happened' while simultaneously avoiding any material process that would support an explicit Actor role. It manages in other words to sidestep precisely the configuration displayed in example (1) above, 'I nipped Daniel', where the role of Actor is conflated with the speaker. Another strategy might have been to create a passive, as opposed to active, construction, wherein the Goal element is brought into Subject position and the Actor element removed from the clause entirely ('Daniel was nipped'). However, because the passive still supports the question 'by whom?', this configuration retains a degree of *implicit* agency. The general point is that transitivity offers systematic choice, and any particular textual configuration is only one, perhaps strategically motivated, option from a pool of possible textual configurations.

The core processes of transitivity, arranged so as to capture their interrelationship to one another, are summarised in Figure A6.1. The transitivity model has proved an important methodological tool in stylistics and in more general investigations of text. The remainder of this strand surveys some developments in this area and goes on to examine patterns of transitivity in a variety of texts. The thread concludes with a reading by Deirdre Burton (D6) which applies the model to a passage from Sylvia Plath's novel *The Bell Jar.*

A7 STYLE AND POINT OF VIEW

The *perspective* through which a story is told constitutes an important stylistic dimension not only in prose fiction but in many types of narrative text. Much of the feel, colour or texture of a story is a direct consequence of the sort of narrative framework it employs. A story may for instance be told in the first person and from the viewing position of a participating character-narrator whose account of actions and events is the one we must as readers share. Alternatively, the story might be narrated in the third person by a detached, invisible narrator whose 'omniscience' facilitates privileged access to the thoughts and feelings of individual characters. Yet further permutations are possible. We may encounter a kind of 'restricted omniscience' where a third-person narrator, although external to the action of the story, comes across as unable or reluctant to delve at will into the thoughts and feelings of characters. These issues of narrative organisation are very much at the heart of story-telling and, as noted in A5, function as an important index of characterisation in fiction. The umbrella term reserved for this aspect of narrative organisation is *point of view.*

Point of view in fiction

Much has been written on point of view by stylisticians and narratologists, such that there is now a proliferation of often conflicting theories, terms and models. In these circumstances, the best way to develop an introduction to point of view will be by going straight to a textual example from which can be garnered some basic categories and principles. Below is a passage from Iain Banks's novel *The Crow Road* which raises a number of interesting general issues concerning point of view in fiction. Kenneth McHoan, one of the novel's central characters, has just returned from university to his home town of Gallanach, and this episode details his arrival in the rural village station.

> He rested his arms on the top of the wall and looked down the fifty feet or so to the tumbling white waters. Just upstream, the river Loran piled down from the forest in a compactly furious cataract. The spray was a taste. Beneath, the river surged round the piers of the viaduct that carried the railway on towards Lochgilpead and Gallanach.
>
> A grey shape flitted silently across the view, from falls to bridge, then zoomed, turned in the air and swept into the cutting on the far bank of the river, as though it was a soft fragment of the train's steam that had momentarily lost its way and was not hurrying to catch up. He waited a moment, and the owl hooted once, from inside the dark constituency of the forest. He smiled, took a deep breath that tasted of steam and the sweet sharpness of pine resin, and then turned away, and went back to pick up his bags.
>
> (Banks 1993: 33)

Activity 

A good general technique for the exploration of point of view in a piece of narrative is to imagine it as if you were preparing to film it. That is, try to conceive a particular episode, as a director might, in terms of its visual perspective, its various vantage points and viewing positions. There are often clear textual clues about where to point your camera, so to speak, and about how a visual sequence should unfold. This passage works extremely well in this respect insofar as it abounds in point of view markers that work to structure the panoramic sweep of the narrative camera. There will be more on these markers shortly, but a feature of more general interest is the way this passage offers an almost model explication of a core distinction in point of view theory. This is the distinction in a story between *who tells* and *who sees.* It is clear from this passage that whereas a detached, omniscient narrator *tells* the story, it is a particular character who *sees* the unfolding scene described. Although this is not the pattern for the whole of Banks's novel – most of it is written in the first person, in fact – there is a marked limiting of narrative perspective, in this instance at least, to that of an individual character within the story. We see what McHoan sees, and we see it in the gradual and accumulative unfolding of the focal points that are reflected in his visual purview. Following the relevant terminology, that makes the character of McHoan, even if momentarily, the *reflector of fiction*.

Even working from so short an extract, there is much more that can be said on the general dynamic of point of view in narrative fiction. We have established that the third person narrator is external, detached, situated outside the story as such. In the sense that its narrator is 'different' from the exegesis that comprises the story, this makes the narrative *heterodiegetic*. However, had the events described been narrated directly in the first person by McHoan himself, the narrative would be *homodiegetic*. A homodiegetic narrator is one who is internal to the narrative, who is on the 'same' plane of exegesis as the story.

The distinction between heterodiegesis and homodiegesis can be explored by transposing the text between first-person and third-person modes of narration. This is a very useful exercise in terms of what it can reveal about point of view, and it is often surprisingly easy to carry out a transposition in those instances where a third person narrative employs a reflector of fiction. Converting the character of McHoan into an internal, homodiegetic narrator requires very little alteration to the text. Indeed, most of the passage can stay exactly as it is, as this checklist of third-to-first-person transpositions shows:

> **I** rested **my** arms on the top of the wall [. . .] **I** waited a moment [. . .] **I** smiled, took a deep breath [. . .] and went back to pick up **my** bags.

The smoothness and facility of transposition shows just how strongly in the reflector mode the original passage is; in effect, nothing is narrated that has not been felt, thought or seen by McHoan. (Indeed, the passage reverberates with references to its reflector's senses of taste, sight and hearing.) However, a first person version makes for a very different narrative in other respects. For a start, it brings us psychologically much closer to the central character. In consequence, it loses much of the space, the often ironic space, that can be placed by a writer between the narrator of a story and a character within that story. There will be more on this issue later in this strand, but for now it is worth developing yet further features of general interest in the passage.

Throughout the Banks extract, as noted above, there are stylistic cues about the viewing position it privileges. These cues are a result of the combination of two levels of language: the semantic principle of *deixis* (see unit A2; and further B7) and the use of certain types of grammatical *Adjunct* (see units A3 and B3). The first of these, deixis, works primarily by situating the speaking voice in physical space. In the passage, the reflector of fiction forms a deictic centre, an 'origo', around which objects are positioned relative to their relative proximity or distance to the reflector. Notice, for instance, how certain verbs of directionality express movement *towards* the speaking source: eg. '[A grey shape] zoomed . . .'. Alternatively, movement *away* is signalled when, near the end of the passage, the reflector 'turned away' from the scene and when he 'went back' (not 'came back') to pick up his bags. This deictic anchoring is supplemented by groups of Adjuncts which express location and spatial relationship. These units of clause structure are normally expounded by prepositional and adverb phrases indicating place and directionality, of which a selection from the passage includes but is not restricted to:

[looked] down
Just upstream
[piled] down
Beneath
across the view
from falls to bridge
into the cutting
on the far bank of the river
from inside the dark constituency of the forest.

The umbrella term *locative expression* is used to cover grammatical units, such as those listed, which provide an index of location, direction and physical setting in narrative description.

Lastly, there is in the passage an occurrence of a particular, specialised point of view device which merits some comment. The term *attenuated focalisation* refers to a situation where point of view is limited, even if temporarily, to an impeded or distanced visual perspective. Lexical items which signal that such a restricted viewing has occurred are nouns with generalised or unspecific reference like 'thing', 'shape' or 'stuff'. Consider this sequence from the passage:

> A grey shape flitted silently across the view . . .

McHoan sees something which (at that point) he can't make out, and that blurring of vision is relayed as attenuated focalisation. However, the restriction in point of view is only temporary and, as is often the case when this technique is deployed, is soon resolved. Interestingly, whereas most attenuation is resolved when an indistinct object comes into shaper focus visually, the status of the shape is resolved here by recourse to another mental faculty, through auditory and not visual identification:

> . . . the owl hooted . . .

Attenuated focalisation often works subtly in relaying the impression that we are momentarily restricted to the visual range of a particular character. As always in point of view analysis, transposition exercises will accentuate the technique and its stylistic effect. Consider, for example, how the impact would be nullified had the sequence been reversed in the first instance; that is, had the item 'owl' replaced 'shape' thus: 'A grey owl flitted silently across the view'.

In sum, this unit has laid some foundations for a description of point of view in narrative. Working from a single passage, some general categories for a model of point of view have been proposed. Across the thread, the model will be progressively refined and reviewed as further categories are added and further passages analysed. The reading which informs this unit is Mick Short's study of narrative viewpoint in Irvine Welsh, a reading which given its breadth of coverage 'doubles up' for both units 5 and 7.

A8 REPRESENTING SPEECH AND THOUGHT

An important preoccupation of modern stylistics has been its interest in the way in which speech and thought is represented in stories. In other words, stylisticians are keen to examine the methods which writers use for transcribing the speech and thoughts of other people, whether these people be imagined characters in a novel or, in the case of everyday 'social' stories, real individuals. While it is true that a great deal of what makes up a story is action and events (see A6), it is also the case that stories contain a great deal of reported speech and thought. And this is as true of news reporting as it is of prose fiction – much of what makes up the 'news', for instance, is a record of what politicians and other public figures (allegedly) say and think.

The presentation of speech and thought is not straightforward. There is an array of techniques for reporting speech and thought, so it makes sense as stylisticians to be aware of and to have at our disposal a suitable model that in the first instance enables us to identify the modes used, and in the second, enables us to assess the effects in the ways these modes are used. The first step towards the development of this model is taken in the next sub-unit which provides a brief outline of the principal categories of speech and thought presentation.

The speech and thought model

The most influential framework for the analysis of speech and thought representation in narrative fiction is undoubtedly that developed by Mick Short and his co-researchers. Leech and Short's textbook (Leech and Short 1981) contains the first systematic account of this important narrative technique and their account is rich in illustrative examples. More recently, much work has been carried out by stylisticians on the way speech and thought is presented in discourse genres beyond those conventionally classed as literary. As our chief concern here is to develop a set of tools that can be used relatively comfortably by the student of language and stylistics, the brief summary of the model provided in this unit will of necessity be kept as simple as possible. To this effect, reference will be made principally to the introductory treatments of the subject in Leech and Short (1981) and Short (1996).

Beginning with the categories of *speech* presentation, the 'baseline' form against which other forms are often measured is *Direct Speech* (DS). In this mode, the report*ed* clause, which tells us what was said, is enclosed within quotation marks, while the report*ing* clause (which tells us who did the reporting) is situated around it. The following two examples of Direct Speech (DS) illustrate how the reporting clause in this mode may be either put in front of, or, as is more common, placed after the quoted material:

(1) She said, 'I'll come here tomorrow.'

(2) 'I'll come here tomorrow,' she said.

Direct Speech stands in contrast to (though is systematically related to) an altogether more remote form of reporting known as *Indirect Speech* (IS). Here is the equivalent Indirect form of the examples above:

(3) She said that she would go there the following day.

The method for converting Direct forms into Indirect ones requires you to carry out a series of simultaneous grammatical operations. These are summarised as follows:

Stage 1: Make the reported material distant from the actual speech used.
Stage 2: Alter pronouns by shifting 1st and 2nd person pronouns ('I', 'you', 'we') into 3rd person forms ('he', 'she', 'it' or 'they').
Stage 3: Switch deictic words (see A7) from their proximal forms into their distal forms.
Stage 4: Change the direction of movement verbs.
Stage 5: Place tenses in their 'backshifted' forms. For example, if the primary tense is in the simple present (eg. 'know') the backshifted tense will be in the simple past ('knew'). Through this process, a modal verb like 'will' becomes 'would', 'does' becomes 'did', 'must' becomes 'had to', 'is' becomes 'was' and so on. If the primary tense is already in the past ('knew') the backshifted tense will be past perfect ('had known').

When these steps are carried out, the following changes are brought about to the report in our Direct Speech example:

Direct form	*Indirect form*
'I'	'she'
''ll'(will)	'would'
'come'	'go'
'here'	'there'
'tomorrow'	'the following day'

A further operation may be carried out on both the Direct and the Indirect forms above to render them into their corresponding 'Free' variants. This involves removing

the reporting clause and removing, if present, any inverted commas. If this operation is only partially followed through, then various intermediate forms present themselves. Here are the 'Free' versions, along with possible subvarieties, of both the DS and IS forms introduced above:

Free Direct Speech (FDS):

(4) I'll come here tomorrow, she said.

(5) 'I'll come here tomorrow.'

(6) I'll come here tomorrow. (freest form)

Free Indirect Speech (FIS):

(7) She would be there the following day.

(8) She would be there tomorrow. (freest form)

The categories available for presenting *thought* in narrative fiction are formally similar to those for speech. Here are examples of the four main types:

Does she still love me? (Free Direct Thought: FDT)

He wondered, 'Does she still love me?' (Direct Thought: DT)

Did she still love him? (Free Indirect Thought: FIT)

He wondered if she still loved him. (Indirect Thought: IT)

It is important to note that in spite of their formal similarities, there are significant conceptual differences between the speech and thought modes. Whereas speech could be overhead and reported by any bystander to an interaction, the presentation of thought is somewhat 'counterfeit' insofar as it presumes entry into the private consciousness of a character. To this extent, the presentation of thought in stories is ultimately an artifice (see Short 1996: 290).

There is one more important category of speech and thought presentation which we can add to our model. This is manifested in its speech and thought variants as, respectively, Narrative Report of Speech (NRS) and Narrative Report of Thought (NRT). This technique involves a narrator reporting that speech or thought has taken place but without offering any indication or flavour of the *actual* words used. Here are two Narrative Report transpositions, one for speech and one for thought, of the basic examples given above:

(9) She spoke of their plans for the day ahead. (Narrative Report of Speech)

(10) He wondered about her love for him. (Narrative Report of Thought)

Unlike the more explicit modes discussed above, where it is possible to work out the 'words' in which something was said or thought, this mode can be used to summarise whole stretches of reported speech or thought. That is not to say that the NRS and NRT modes are always more 'economical' than their more explicit counterparts – in fact, it is sometimes easier to report verbatim what someone has uttered than to try to look for alternative ways of capturing what they have said.

Practice

Activity 

The practical work suggested in unit C8 of this thread is very detailed, requiring some fine distinctions to be drawn between various modes of speech and thought presentation, so this is a good place to begin firming up your knowledge of how the basic speech and thought categories work. Admittedly a departure from the overall format of this introductory section, the remainder of this unit therefore develops a short transposition exercise which is designed to test the categories introduced thus far.

Examples a–e listed below are all written in the Direct mode of speech or thought presentation. Working from these base forms, try to convert the five examples into their equivalent Free Direct, Indirect and Free Indirect modes. Some suggestions on how to proceed are offered below the examples:

a 'I know this trick of yours!' she said. [said to a male addressee]
b 'Can you get here next week?' he asked. [said to a female addressee]
c 'Why isn't John here?' she asked herself.
d She said, 'We must leave tonight.'
e 'Help yourselves,' he urged them.

It is probably most straightforward if you convert them into their Free Direct counterparts first of all. Then, going back to the Direct forms, convert these into their Indirect variants using the five sets of criteria provided in the sub-unit above. It should also be possible to get from the Free Direct variants to their equivalent Free Indirect forms by following these same criteria. That said, there are certain types of grammatical patterns which block some transpositions and you may come up against some them here. If so, try to account for any problems you encounter. Can you construct some NRS and NRT forms for a–e also? For solutions and commentary, go to unit D8.

Across the remainder of this strand, we will see how speech and thought presentation can be aligned with broader issues to do with narrative communication. In B8, additional refinements are made to the speech and thought model. Further along the strand, unit C8 offers a workshop programme which is designed to develop awareness of the way speech and thought presentation can be used in literary narrative. Unit D8 provides solutions relating to the practice material developed in this unit, which is why there is not the space for a selected reading to accompany this strand.

A9

DIALOGUE AND DISCOURSE

The late 1970s and early 1980s witnessed a new interest among stylisticians in the role of *dialogue* in literature. This interest was paralleled by a concern with literature's status as *discourse*; that is, as a form of naturally occurring language use in a real social context. Thus, the emerging field of *discourse stylistics* was defined largely by its use of models that were interactive in their general bearing and which situated the units of analysis for literary discourse in a framework of utterances as opposed to sentences (see A2). The concept of the 'literary speech situation' (see D9) required for its exploration the methods of pragmatics, politeness theory, conversation analysis and speech act theory. Given this new orientation in research method, it was no coincidence that there developed in parallel a particular interest in the interactive dynamic of drama dialogue, and for this reason much early work in discourse stylistics has come to be associated with the study of dialogue in plays (See Burton 1980; Short 1989; Simpson 1989). To reflect these trends in stylistics, this thread focuses generally on *dialogue*, and more particularly, on dialogue in plays.

Dialogue in drama

It is important to think carefully about what we mean when we talk of literature as *interaction.* We need for instance to separate out the types of interaction that go on between characters within a text from the sort of higher-order interaction that takes place between an author and a reader. In the context of drama dialogue, Short argues that interaction works mainly on two levels, with one level of discourse embedded inside another. He suggests the schema shown in Figure A9.1 as a way of configuring the structure of dialogue in plays. Short's schema is useful in a number of ways. It shows how the utterances that pass from one character to another become part of what the playwright 'tells' the audience. It also differentiates two sets of interactive contexts: the fictional context surrounding the characters within the world of the play, and the 'real' context framing the interaction between author and reader. From this, it holds that the features that mark social relations between people at the character level become messages *about* those characters at the level of discourse between author and reader/audience.

This is not to say the levels of discourse portrayed by the schema are absolutely rigid. For example, reported speech (see A8), where one character reports the words of another on stage, opens up a further, third layer of embedding. By contrast, the use

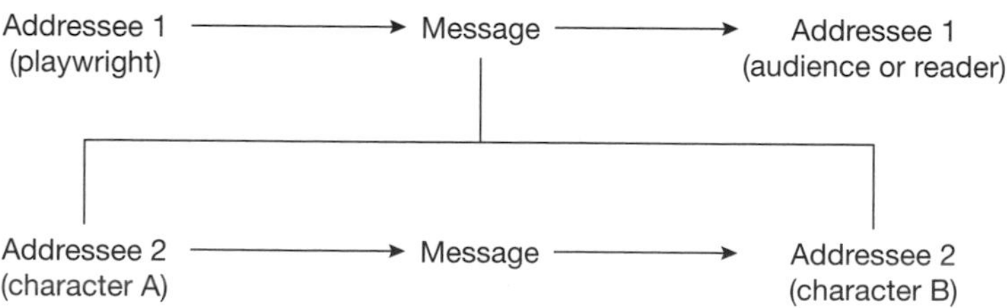

Figure A9.1 Dialogue in plays: from Short (1989: 149)

of soliloquy tends to break down the layering pattern because the words of a character, while remaining 'unheard' by other interlocutors on the stage, are relayed directly to the reader/audience. Whatever the precise characteristics of its embedding, verbal interaction in plays nonetheless requires for its understanding and interpretation the same rules of discourse that govern everyday social interaction. In other words, the assumptions we make about dialogue in the world of the play are predicated upon our assumptions about how dialogue works in the real world (see further B9).

Understanding dialogue in drama: context, structure, strategy

It was observed in unit A2 that *discourse* is a relatively fluid and open-ended level of language organisation that encompasses aspects of communication that go beyond the structure of words and sentences. In this respect, it is not that easy to find a compact, workable model of discourse that can be readily pressed into service for the exploration of dramatic dialogue. However, one principle that is common to many models of discourse analysis is the understanding that all naturally occurring language takes place in a *context* of use. We can divide up the notion of context into three basic categories:

Physical context: This is the actual setting in which interaction takes place. Physical context may be constituted by the workplace, the home environment or by a public area. In face-to-face conversation, speaker and hearer share the same physical context, although in some forms of spoken interaction, such as broadcast or telephone talk, speaker and hearer are physically separated.

Personal context: This refers to the social and personal relationships of the interactants to one another. Personal context also encompasses social networks and group membership, the social and institutional roles of speakers and hearers, and the relative status and social distance that pertains between participants.

Cognitive context: This refers to the shared and background knowledge held by participants in interaction. Cognitive context, which is susceptible to change as interaction progresses, also extends to a speaker's world-view, cultural knowledge and past experiences (see further A10).

Against this sketch of interactive context, we can begin to plot some principles of dialogue. One approach that I have found to be reasonably effective, though in no way a canonical or definitive method of analysis, is to conceptualise dialogue in terms of two axes. These intersecting axes – let us call them *structure* and *strategy* – are organised along the lines of the Jakobsonian 'axis of combination' and 'axis of selection' introduced in unit B1. From this perspective, an utterance can be analysed either in terms of its linear placement along an axis of combination or in terms of its status as a strategic choice from the axis of selection. Put another way, the axis of combination forms a structural frame along which units of dialogue are strung in an 'a *and* b' relationship, while the axis of selection connects elements of discourse in an 'a *or* b' relationship.

To illustrate more clearly how this conceptual model works, consider the following hypothetical exchange in which a speaker, who for the sake of argument needs to get a taxi home, decides to borrow some money from a close acquaintance:

(1) A: Could you lend me five pounds, please?
B: Umm, OK. [hands money to A]

The two utterances in (1) combine to form a jointly produced unit of discourse called an *exchange*. Here the speaker's request prompts a reaction from the hearer, expressed through both a verbal act ('Umm, OK') and the non-verbal act of handing over the money. This 'request and reaction' pattern is a common exchange type, as are other familiar two-part pairings like 'question and answer' and 'statement and acknowledgement'.

Of course, this simple exchange pattern may have been realised through other structural permutations, through other variations along the axis of combination as it were. For instance:

(2) A: Could you lend me five pounds, please?
B: What d'ye wannit for?
A: I need to get a taxi home.
B: Umm, OK. [hands money to A]

Here, the progress of the exchange is delayed by speaker B's request for clarification. This utterance prompts a little mini-exchange, known as an *insertion sequence*, which, until it is completed, holds up the progression of the main exchange.

The axis of selection, with its focus on strategy, emphasises the 'tactical' nature of discourse. In this respect, the form of A's utterance represents just one choice from a pool of options that are available to speakers. More direct choices present themselves, as do more indirect ones:

Choice 2 [more direct]: Lend me five pounds.
Choice 1: Could you lend me five pounds, please?
Choice 3 [less direct]: Er, I think I might have a bit of a problem getting home . . .

This three-way pattern of options says much about the ways in which we make strategic choices in utterance selection. We tend to balance the need for directness, whose principal pay-off is clarity and conciseness, with the need for indirectness, whose principal pay-off is politeness. Much of our everyday linguistic practice involves instant on-the-spot calculations of this sort. Choice 2, for example, is a maximally direct speech act because it matches up a grammatical form with the function of the utterance: it uses an imperative structure to make a request. However, while this tactic is unquestionably efficient and clear as a directive, its forthrightness will be interpreted as peremptory and rude in many contexts. Choice 3 is, by contrast, a more oblique gambit, the content of which is rather more tangential to the task it asks of the hearer. It is a *hint*, so defined because the body of the utterance makes no direct lexical link to what it implicitly refers. The pay-off is that the speaker is seen to be politely non-coercive, although the down-side is that the relative obscurity of the utterance means that it stands less chance of successfully accomplishing its goal.

It is interesting, then, that the middle sequence, choice 1, would seem to be the default option for most interactive contexts. This strategy exhibits *conventionalised indirectness* because it draws on the grammatical form used for asking questions and not the one anticipated for commands or requests. Nevertheless, this sort of indirectness is normal in situations where we want to mitigate what we say with a degree of politeness (see further below). Also, the utterance's particular speech act status – its *illocutionary force* – is made clear by the particle 'please'. As well as consolidating the politeness function, this particle confirms the utterance's function as a request for action, and not, say, as a polite inquiry about the addressee's hypothetical ability to carry out the action referred to.

As with the elements arranged along the structural continuum, variations in the strategic continuum are also possible. In respect of choice 1, we can supplement the main request with extra markers of politeness that make use of additional pragmatic tactics. For example, a common technique when making requests is to indicate pessimism about the intended outcome of your utterance:

(3) I don't suppose you'll be able to do this, but could you lend me five pounds, please?

Alternatively, it is always a good idea to state the overwhelming reasons that led you to carry out the request:

(4) The cash machine wasn't working, so could you lend me five pounds, please?

Then again, perhaps a formal declaration of indebtedness might be the best gambit:

(5) I'd really be eternally grateful to you for this – could you lend me five pounds, please?

Finally, it normally helps to downplay the degree of imposition you are making on your interlocutor, throwing in a few hedges for good measure:

(6) Er, I've just a tiny wee favour to ask you . . . umm . . . I was wondering . . . umm . . . could you lend me five pounds, please?

Leaving aside for the moment the more fine-tuned politeness tactics in examples (3) to (6), the three basic choices from the axis of selection – the unmitigated command, the routinely indirect default form and the 'hint' embodied by choice three – all mark a broad shift in politeness, ranging from the least polite to the most polite form.

Speakers are normally acutely aware of what sort of strategy can be used in which circumstances, which is why the idea of context can never be divorced from the analysis of dialogue. Whereas there may be little interactive risk in using choice 2 with friends and social equals in an informal setting, its use in a formal setting with an interlocutor who is an acknowledged social superior may have damaging interactive consequences. A speaker's communicative strategies are thus sensitive to the perceived context, so in this respect, context, in its three aspects outlined above, operates as a key strategy-framing device in discourse. This knowledge of what to say, and when and where to say it, is called *communicative competence* (Hymes 1972). Communicative competence is the skill involved in matching an utterance to an appropriate context of use; in other words, knowing when to be familiar and when to be formal, knowing when to be direct and when to be indirect, or simply knowing when to talk and when to keep quiet.

Summary

This unit has established some basic categories and concepts for the analysis of dialogue. Developing the strand further, unit B9 looks at some of the directions that have been taken within this branch of stylistics while unit C9 suggests a practical activity based around the theoretical constructs developed here. The thread is concluded in D9 with a reading by Mary Louise Pratt which explores the concept of the literary speech situation. In A10, the notion of cognitive context is developed further as attention is focussed on a movement in stylistics which followed in the wake of discourse stylistics. This movement has become known as *cognitive stylistics*.

A10 COGNITIVE STYLISTICS

It is part of the natural development of modern stylistics constantly to enrich and update its methods of analysis. In the previous strand, we saw how ideas about dialogue, discourse and social interaction have found their way into stylistics, both as a tool for exploring the interactive dimension of literary discourse in the broader sense and as a method for examining patterns of dialogue between fictional characters in the narrower. In this unit, attention focusses on a yet further development in stylistics which has had a profound impact on the direction the discipline has taken in the twenty first century. This development has come to be known as the 'cognitive turn' in stylistics, and its broad rationale is the basis of this unit.

Cognitive models in and for stylistic analysis

As highlighted by the Fowler-Bateson debate (D1), stylistics has since its earliest days set great store by the use of detailed linguistic analysis as a basis for the interpretation of literary texts. This focus on the methods of compositional technique has tended to make stylistics *writerly* in its general theoretical orientation. However, what has largely been missing from this approach has been any account of the mental processes that inform, and are affected by, the way we read and interpret literary texts. Stylistics has in other words lacked a *readerly* dimension. In the last decade of the previous century, stylisticians began to redress the 'writerly bias' in stylistics by exploring more systematically the cognitive structures that readers employ when reading texts. In doing so, they borrowed heavily from developments in cognitive linguistics and Artificial Intelligence, and this new emphasis in research method saw the emergence of *cognitive stylistics* or *cognitive poetics.* While cognitive stylistics is intended to supplement, rather than supplant, existing methods of analysis, it does aim to shift the focus away from models of text and composition towards models that make explicit the links between the human mind and the process of reading.

A further stimulus to the cognitive turn was provided by the object of analysis itself, literature. As noted from strand 1 onwards, a core assumption in much stylistic work has been that there is simply no such thing as a 'literary language'. This ground rule has been important polemically because it positions stylistics in direct counterpoint to the sort of literary criticism that places 'the language of literature' beyond the reach of ordinary users of ordinary language. It does, however, come at a price in that it tends to make harder the task of finding out what it is that makes literature *different* from other forms of social discourse. With its focus on the process of reading rather than writing, cognitive stylisticians have addressed precisely this problem in their work, arguing that literature is perhaps better conceptualised as a way of reading than as a way of writing. Furthermore, exploring fully this way of reading requires a thorough overhaul of existing models of stylistic analysis.

This search for new models was to go beyond even those models of pragmatics and discourse analysis that had become a familiar part of the stylistics arsenal since the 1980s. Moving away from theories of discourse, the new orientation was to models which accounted for the stores of knowledge which readers bring into play when they read, and on how these knowledge stores are modified or enriched as reading progresses. To bring this discourse-cognitive interface into sharper focus, let us consider the following seemingly rather banal utterance whose full significance will emerge shortly:

(1) Could I have a pint of lager, please?

Across the previous thread, we looked at how spoken utterances might be interpreted in terms of either discourse strategy or discourse structure. An example like this was developed in A9, where observations were made on its various tactical functions in verbal interaction. We might indeed make a number of similar inferences about the pragmatic function of the utterance above. For instance, the utterance, with its conventionally indirect form-to-function pattern, is of the 'choice 1' variety on the strategic continuum (see A9). Furthermore, its illocutionary force as a request is confirmed by the particle 'please', which, along with the reference to a quantity of alcoholic drink within the utterance, would lead to the fairly unexceptional deduction that it is uttered by a single speaker in some kind of public house.

However, what an analysis of discourse would *not* account for is the way we are able to store a mental picture of a 'pub' which can be activated for the understanding of this utterance in context. This mental picture develops out of past experience of such places, experience gathered either through direct contact or through indirect sources. In other words, even if the pub as a social phenomenon does not feature in your own culture, your experience of, say, Western film, television and literature may have provided sufficient input to form an image schema which, if only weakly held, is still susceptible to ongoing modification as more new information comes in.

Whatever the precise type of primary input, it is clear that we can form a mental representation which will specify what a certain entity is, what it is for, what it looks like and so on. This image has been rendered down from multiple experiences into a kind of idealised prototypical image, an image which we might term an *idealised cognitive model*. An idealised cognitive model (ICM) contains information about what is typical (for us) and it is a domain of knowledge that is brought into play for the processing and understanding of textual representations. These domains of knowledge are also accompanied by conceptual slots for the things that routinely accompany the mental representation; the mental representation for the pub would, for instance, include an entry for 'roles' like barman, customer, waiter, bouncer and so on, as well as one for 'props' like tables, optics, chairs, a bar and so on (Schank and Abelson 1977: 43; and see B10). Of course, ICMs differ between subjects, so the props for one individual prototypical representation of a pub might include, say, traditional carved panelling and old oak tables while, for another, the inventory could contain a pool table, a wide-screen television or a games machine. Importantly, ICMs are subject to modification in the course of an individual subject's experience and development. For example, I once had cause to visit a pub in the west of Ireland which doubled up both as a grocery shop, and, more improbably, as a funeral parlour. Amongst other things, this experience caused me to revise my mental model of the pub: the less typical representation interacted with the prototype leading to a modified ICM. Yet I was still able to 'make sense' of the newly experienced pub-cum-funeral-parlour because I was able to structure the new knowledge in terms of the older, familiar ICM. In a dynamic process of conversion, transference between concepts leads us constantly to modify our ICMs as new stimuli are encountered.

When it comes to reading and interpreting texts, it is important to bear in mind that ICMs may be activated often by only the most minimal syntactic or lexical marker in a text. This is not surprising. After all, it would be odd indeed if, for every time we heard the word 'pub', we required for its understanding the provision of a contextualising text like the following:

(2) The term 'pub' is a contraction of 'public house'. Pubs are premises licensed for the consumption of alcohol and soft drinks. In Western cultures which have no prohibition on alcohol, pubs are establishments which are open to the public, although localised restrictions apply to the admission of minors. Licensed premises may be housed in a variety of building designs which vary in character and theme, although most contain a bar across which drinks, and possibly light snacks or meals are served . . .

There is simply no end to the amount of context that could be provided here, but the point is that such context is unnecessary because the domains of knowledge that comprise ICMs allow us to take cognitive short-cuts when we interpret language. We do not, in other words, need to have a fully elaborated *textual representation* of a concept in order to set in motion a *cognitive representation* of that concept.

Summary

This unit has addressed the broad tenets of a cognitive approach to style. Coverage has however been rather sketchy because little explicit information has been provided either on key models of cognitive stylistic analysis or on the main practitioners in the field. To address this, the cognitive theme will be elaborated further in two different directions. Horizontally, unit B10 surveys some of the key developments in this branch of stylistics and introduces a variety of models of analysis. Further across the strand, C10 develops some practical activities for cognitive stylistic analysis which take account of the ideas introduced both here and in B10. The strand concludes with a reading by Margaret Freeman which offers a rigorous cognitive stylistic analysis of Emily Dickinson's poetry. Vertically, the cognitive theme is developed in A11 where attention focusses on one of the most important devices we use to transfer, modify or blend mental constructs. This device is metaphor which, along with the related concept metonymy, plays a pivotal role in contemporary cognitive stylistic analysis.

METAPHOR AND METONYMY

A11

An important feature of cognitive stylistics has been its interest in the way we transfer mental constructs, and especially in the way we map one mental representation onto another when we read texts. Stylisticians and cognitive poeticians have consistently drawn attention to this system of conceptual transfer in both literary and in everyday discourse, and have identified two important tropes, or figures of speech, through which this conceptual transfer is carried out. These tropes are *metaphor* and *metonymy* and this unit will introduce these core concepts in cognitive stylistics.

Metaphor

A metaphor is a process of mapping between two different conceptual domains. The different domains are known as the *target* domain and the *source* domain. The target domain is the topic or concept that you want to describe through the metaphor while the source domain refers to the concept that you draw upon in order to create the metaphorical construction. Thus, in an expression like:

(1) She really blew her lid.

the target domain is our understanding of the concept of anger because it is the concept we wish to describe through the metaphor. The source domain for the metaphor can be conceptualised as 'heated fluid in a container' because that is the concept which provides the vehicle for the metaphorical transfer. The metaphor as a whole can represented, using the standard notation of small capital letters, by the formula: ANGER IS A HEATED FLUID IN A CONTAINER. This type of formulation is useful because it abstracts out of the particular linguistic structure of the metaphor its underlying organisation.

Importantly, the relationship between metaphor and linguistic form is an indirect one, which means that we can express the same conceptual metaphor through a variety of constructions. Consider, for instance, an alternative version of example (1):

(2) Talk about letting off steam . . . She really blew her lid, I mean really blew her top. She just exploded!

Although this example comprises four grammatical clauses, this is not to say that it contains four metaphors. All of the clauses in fact express the same source and target domain, which means that the single underlying conceptual metaphor ANGER IS A HEATED FLUID IN A CONTAINER is being played out through a variety of linguistic constructions.

In his influential study of the poetic structure of the human mind, Gibbs (1994) highlights the important part metaphor plays in our everyday conceptual thought. Metaphors are not some kind of distorted literal thought, but rather are basic schemes by which people conceptualise their experience and their external world. Figurative language generally, which also includes irony (see A12), is found throughout speech and writing; moreover, it does not require for its use any special intellectual talent or any special rhetorical situation (Gibbs 1994: 21). Indeed, the fact that many metaphors pass us by in everyday social interaction is well illustrated by this unwitting slip by a venerable British sports commentator:

(3) We didn't have metaphors in my day. We didn't beat about the bush.

Metaphor is simply a natural part of conceptual thought and although undoubtedly an important feature of creativity, it should not be seen as a special or exclusive feature of literary discourse. For instance, examples (4) to (6) below, which embody the same conceptual metaphor, are from a variety of print and broadcast media covering the conflict in Iraq in 2003:

(4) The third mechanised infantry are currently clearing up parts of the Al Mansur Saddam village area.

(5) The regime is finished, but there remains some tidying up to do.

(6) Official sources described it as a 'mopping up' operation.

Examples (4) to (6) rehearse the same basic metaphor through three different linguistic realisations. The experience of war, which is the topic that forms the target domain of the metaphor, is relayed through the idea of cleaning, which is the concept that provides the source domain. The metaphor might thus be represented as: WAR IS CLEANING. Given its context, the ideological significance of this metaphor is worth commenting on. It suggests that the conflict is nothing more than a simple exercise in sanitation, a perspective which, it has to be said, is unlikely to be shared by military personnel on the opposing side. In an effort presumably to allay domestic worries about the progression of the conflict, the British and American press are playing down both the extent and intensity of the conflict through this strategically motivated metaphor.

If we accept that metaphors are part and parcel, so to speak, of everyday discourse, an important question presents itself. Are there any qualitative differences in the sorts of metaphors that are found in different discourse contexts? An important criterion in this respect is the degree of *novelty* exhibited by a metaphor. As with any figure of speech, repeated use leads to familiarity, and so commonplace metaphors can sometimes develop into idioms or fixed expressions in the language. The commentator's reference to 'beat about the bush' in (3) is a good example of this process. However, what arguably sets the use of metaphor in literature apart from more 'idiomatised' uses of the trope is that in literature metaphors are on the one hand typically *more novel* and on the other typically *less clear* (Kövecses 2002: 43). Writers consciously strive for novelty in literary expression and this requires developing not only new conceptual mappings but also new stylistic frameworks through which these mappings can be presented. This theme of novelty in metaphor is taken up in B11.

Metonymy

In contrast with metaphor, *metonymy* is based on a transfer within a single conceptual domain. Staying within the boundaries of the same domain, metonymy involves transpositions between associated concepts and this commonly results in transfer between the part and the whole, a producer and the produced, an institution and its location and so on. Metonymy in which the part stands for the whole – a trope known as *synecdoche* – is found in expressions like 'hired hand' or 'a fresh pair of legs'. Alternatively, constructions where a location substitutes for the particular institution which it houses can be found in expressions like 'Buckingham Palace is thought to be furious' or 'The Pentagon refused to comment on the story'. Metonymies where the producer of something is associated with what is produced occur in expressions like 'Have you read the new Kate Atkinson?' or 'There's a good Spielberg on tomorrow night'.

Other metonymies are more contextually dependent for their interpretation, as in, say, 'The lead guitar has gone AWOL' where a more contingent 'stands-for' relationship pertains between the musician and the particular instrument played. In general, whereas a metaphor assumes a certain distance between the concepts it embodies, between its target and source, a metonymy upgrades certain salient characteristics from a single domain to represent that domain as a whole.

It is not always easy to spot the difference between metaphor and metonymy but a useful test to distinguish one trope from the other is to try to convert the expression into a *simile*. A simile makes an explicit connection between two concepts

through the use of the IS LIKE formula. Applying the test serves therefore to draw attention to the conceptual space between a target and a source domain in metaphor, but the same test will collapse when applied to metonymy. For example, (1) and (4) to (6) convert easily into similes, as in, respectively:

(1′) ANGER IS LIKE A HEATED FLUID IN A CONTAINER

(4′) to (6′) WAR IS LIKE CLEANING

By contrast, the metonymy 'hired hand' cannot support the parallel simile 'A worker is like a hand', nor does 'a fresh pair of legs' convert to 'A substitute is like a pair of legs'. The same restriction blocks the conversion of the other metonymies noted above, as in: 'A musician is like a lead guitar', 'A monarchy is like Buckingham Palace', 'Spielberg is like a film' and so on.

Like metaphors, metonymies find their expression in everyday discourse practices. A metonymy that became briefly popular in Britain some years ago began life when a notoriously combative midfielder, employed by a wealthy English football club, criticised certain of that club's fans for their less than committed support of the team. He described them as the sort of people who would eat prawn sandwiches during the half time interval, behaviour which he at least considered unworthy of real soccer fans. The British sports pundits quickly seized on this figure of speech, and within a few months, a novel metonymy had found its way into media and popular discourse. The term 'prawn sandwich' had come to stand for any effete or whimpish football fan, while expressions like 'They're just a bunch of prawn sandwiches' could be said of any set of supporters, and not just those who comprised the original referents of the phrase.

Metonymy has an important stylistic function. In unit B6 it can be seen how *meronymic agency* is a type of transitivity process which involves the part 'standing for' the whole in such a way as to place a human body part, rather than a whole person, in the role of an Actor, Sensor, Sayer and so on. Metonymy also plays an important role in the technique of *caricature*. Caricature is a form of metonymic distortion, much favoured by satirical humorists, which involves the distortion of some aspect of human appearance, normally physiognomy, such that this exaggerated body part assumes a prominence sufficient to symbolise the whole being. For example, most caricatures of former British Prime Minister Margaret Thatcher played, according to Garland (1988: 77), on her bouffant hair and pointed nose. This gradually shaded into ever more grotesque representations until the nose and hair themselves became the visual embodiment of the politician (and see further chapter five of Simpson (2003)).

Summary

This introductory unit is developed further in B11, where amongst other things the important issue of novelty as a feature of literary metaphor is explored. Unit C11 offers a range of practical suggestions covering both metaphor and metonymy, while the thread concludes, in D11, with a reading by Peter Stockwell on the theory of metaphor.

STYLISTICS AND VERBAL HUMOUR

In various places in the book, connections have been drawn between patterns of style and verbal humour (see for example units B9, C1, C5 and C9). This concluding unit to section A offers the opportunity to review some of the principles which inform the stylistic analysis of humorous discourse. Although there are no corresponding B and C units in this thread, the theme of style and humour is explored further in reading D12, by Walter Nash.

Puns and verbal play

Two key theoretical principles underpin the language of humour, the first of which is that humour requires an *incongruity*. The principle of incongruity is mooted in B9 and C9 in respect of absurdism in drama dialogue, but the concept applies more generally to (i) any kind of stylistic twist in a pattern of language or (ii) any situation where there is a mismatch between what someone says and what they mean. The second principle is that incongruity can be situated in any layer of linguistic structure. Just as style is a multilevelled concept (A2), the humour mechanism can operate at any level of language and discourse, and it can even play one level off against another. The stylistic analysis of humour therefore involves identifying an incongruity in a text and pinpointing whereabouts in the language system it occurs. Of course, not all incongruities are funny but the complex reasons as to why this is so will have to be left aside for now (see further Attardo 2001).

One of the most commonly used stylistic devices for creating humour is the *pun*. In its broadest sense, a pun is a form of word-play in which some feature of linguistic structure simultaneously combines two unrelated meanings. Whereas the unrelated meanings in a pun are often situated in individual words, many puns cut across different levels of linguistic organisation and so their formal properties are quite variable. Clearly, the pun is an important part of the stylistic arsenal of writers because it allows a controlled 'double meaning' to be located in what is in effect a chance connection between two elements of language. It is however a resource of language that we all share, and it is important, as emphasised throughout this book, not to sequester away literary uses of language from everyday language practices. Let me provide a simple illustration of the commonality of punning as a language resource, which comes, of all things, from the names of various hairdressing salons in the south of the city of Belfast. Such emporia are now but a distant memory for your follically challenged author, and so the examples and commentary that follow are offered strictly from the vantage point of the dispassionate outsider:

(1) Shylocks
Curl up n Dye
Shear Luck
Streaks Ahead
Hair Affair

Although a variety of individual punning strategies are used here, all of the names play on a chance similarity between two or more unrelated aspects of language. My own favourite, 'Shylocks', plays on an intertextual connection with Shakespeare's famous character by exploiting the phonological similarity between 'locks' (of hair) and the morphology of the personal name. Other names make use of 'homophones' which are words with the same sound but different spellings: thus, 'dye' versus 'die', 'Shear' versus 'sheer' and so on. Interestingly, these puns are framed in the context of familiar idioms and fixed expressions in the language ('curl up and die', 'sheer luck') and they provide good illustrations of how foregrounding takes its source material from the commonplace in language (see B1). Especially clever is the multiple punning in 'Streaks Ahead'. Projected into the discourse domain of hairdressing, this fixed expression not only gives a new resonance to the word 'streaks' but the morphology of 'a*head*' facilitates an allusion to the relevant feature of anatomy. The last name on the list, if not strictly a pun, contours a sequence of sounds to create an internal rhyme scheme. It thus works by projecting the Jakobsonian axis of selection onto the axis of combination – a good example of the poetic principle in operation if ever there was one!

Moving onto puns in literature, the technique is illustrated by the following lines from the fourth book of Alexander Pope's *Dunciad* (1743):

(2) Where Bentley late tempestuous wont to sport
In troubled waters, but now sleeps in port.

Although this is just an isolated example from what is undoubtedly an enormous pool of possibilities in literature, it does illustrate well the basic principle of punning. The form *port* embraces two lexical items: both obvious, one refers to a harbour and the other an alcoholic beverage. In the context of Pope's couplet, Bentley (a boisterous Cambridge critic) is described through a nautical metaphor, as someone who has crossed turbulent seas to reach a tranquil safe-haven. Yet the second sense of *port* makes for a disjunctive reading, which, suggesting a perhaps drunken sleep, tends to undercut comically the travails of Bentley. This is the essence of punning, where an ambiguity is projected by balancing two otherwise unrelated elements of linguistic structure.

Parody and satire

Parody and satire are forms of verbal humour which draw on a particular kind of *irony* for the design of their stylistic incongruity. Irony is situated in the space between what you say and what you mean, as embodied in an utterance like 'You're a fine friend!' when said to someone who has just let you down. A particularly important way of producing irony is to *echo* other utterances and forms of discourse. This is apparent in an exchange like the following:

(3) A: I'm really fed up with this washing up.
B: *You're fed up!* Who do you think's been doing it all week?

In this exchange, the proposition about being fed up is used in a 'straight' way by the first speaker, but in an ironic way by the second. This is because the proposition is explicitly *echoed* by the second speaker during their expression of their immediate reaction to it. The status of the proposition when echoed is therefore not the same as when it is used first time out.

We have already seen in this book an example of the echoic form of irony at work. In unit C1, it was observed how the greater part of Dorothy Parker's poem 'One Perfect Rose' echoed ironically the lyric love poem of the seventeenth or eighteenth century. This principle of ironic echo is absolutely central to the concept of *parody*. Once echoed, a text becomes part of a new discourse context so it no longer has the illocutionary force (A9) it once had in its original context. Parody can take any particular anterior text as its model, although more general characteristics of other genres of discourse, as we saw in the case of 'One Perfect Rose', can also be brought into play. This broad capacity of parody to function as a 'discourse of allusion' is the substance of Nash's reading at the end of this thread, and readers will find there some further illustrations of this technique.

The distinction between parody and satire is not an easy one to draw, but it is commonly assumed that satire has an aggressive element which is not necessarily present in parody. How this translates into stylistic terms is that satirical discourse, as well as having an echoic element, requires a further kind of ironic twist or distortion in its textual make-up. This additional distortion means that while parodies can remain affectionate to their source, satire can never be so. Consider, for example, Jonathan Swift's *A Modest Proposal* (1729) which lays good claim to being the most famous piece of satire ever written. Swift's text echoes the genre of the early eighteenth-century pamphlet, and more narrowly the proliferation of pamphlets offering economic solutions to what was then perceived as the 'Irish problem'. The opening of the Proposal reviews various schemes and recommendations to alleviate poverty and starvation, but it is only after about nine hundred words of text that its mild-mannered speaker eventually details his 'proposal':

> (4) I shall now therefore humbly propose my own thoughts, which I hope will not be liable to the least objection.
>
> I have been assured by a very knowing American of my acquaintance in London, that a young healthy child well nursed is at a year old a most delicious, nourishing, and wholesome food, whether stewed, roasted, baked, or boiled; and I make no doubt that it will equally serve in a fricassee or a ragout.
>
> (Swift 1986 [1729]: 2175–6)

While Swift's text echoes the conventions of a particular genre of discourse, it contains the requisite distortion that marks it out as satire. This distortion comes through the startling sequence where the persona proposes to alleviate the burden of overpopulation in Ireland by eating that country's children. This twist is both brutal and stark, and marks an abrupt shift from a seemingly moral framework to a framework of abnormality and obscenity. Just how 'humorous' this particular brand of satire is, where the sense of opposition between what is morally acceptable and what is not is very wide, is difficult to assess (see further Simpson (2003)). What it does show is how satire is created through both an echo of another discourse *and* an opposition or distortion within its own stylistic fabric.

Summary

This unit has introduced some of the basic principles of punning and other forms of verbal humour. Although no more than a snapshot of an enormous area of inquiry, it should have demonstrated both how techniques in stylistics are well suited to the exploration of verbal humour and why stylisticians have shown a continued interested over the years in this area of study. One such stylistician is Walter Nash, whose essay on the techniques of parody and allusion, complete with some entertaining self-penned parodies, is reproduced as reading D12.

SECTION B

DEVELOPMENT

DOING STYLISTICS

VELOPMENTS IN STYLISTICS

is unit looks at some of the important influences on stylistics that have helped to ıpe its development over the years. From the Classical period onwards there has been continued healthy interest among scholars in the relationship between patterns of language in a text and the way a text communicates. The Greek rhetoricians, for example, were particularly interested in the tropes and devices that were used by orators for effective argument and persuasion, and there is indeed a case for saying that some stylistic work is very much a latter-day embodiment of traditional rhetoric. However, there is one particular field of academic inquiry, from the early twentieth century, that has had a more direct and lasting impact on the methods of contemporary stylistics. This field straddles two interrelated movements in linguistics, known as Russian Formalism and Prague School Structuralism. Of the former movement, key figures include Viktor Shklovsky and Boris Tomashevsky; of the the latter, Jan Mukarovsky and Wilhem Mathesius. One scholar, whose work literally links both movements, is Roman Jakobson, who moved from the Moscow circle to the Prague group in 1920. Many of the central ideas of these two schools find their reflexes in contemporary stylistics and two of the more durable theoretical contributions are the focus of this unit. These are the concept of *foregrounding* and the notion of the *poetic function* in language.

Foregrounding

Foregrounding refers to a form of textual patterning which is motivated specifically for literary-aesthetic purposes. Capable of working at any level of language, foregrounding typically involves a stylistic distortion of some sort, either through an aspect of the text which deviates from a linguistic norm or, alternatively, where an aspect of the text is brought to the fore through repetition or parallelism. That means that foregrounding comes in two main guises: foregrounding as 'deviation from a norm' and foregrounding as 'more of the same'. Foregrounding is essentially a technique for 'making strange' in language, or to extrapolate from Shklovsky's Russian term *ostranenie*, a method of 'defamiliarisation' in textual composition.

Whether the foregrounded pattern deviates from a norm, or whether it replicates a pattern through parallelism, the point of foregrounding as a stylistic strategy is that it should acquire salience in the act of drawing attention to itself. Furthermore, this salience is motivated purely by literary considerations and as such constitutes an important textual strategy for the development of images, themes and characters, and for stimulating both effect and affect in a text's interpretation. Foregrounding is not, therefore, the simple by-product of this or that writer's idiosyncratic predilections in style. For example, Jonathan Swift, a writer with much to say about language and style, was reputedly never very fond of words which were made up of only one syllable. Whereas the relative scarcity of monosyllabic words in Swift's work might therefore be noticeable or salient, it is rather more a consequence of the personal stylistic foibles of the writer than of a carefully modulated design in literary foregrounding. In sum, if a particular textual pattern is not motivated for artistic purposes, then it is not foregrounding.

The theory of foregrounding raises many issues to do with the stylistic analysis of text, the most important of which is probably its reliance on the concept of a 'norm' in language. Given the functional diversity of language, it is very difficult – if not impossible – to say what exactly a 'normal' sentence in English actually is. This constitutes a substantial challenge to foregrounding theory because the theory presupposes that there exists a notional linguistic yardstick against which a particular feature of style can be measured. A related issue concerns what happens when a once deviant pattern becomes established in a text. Does it stay foregrounded for the entire duration of the text? Or does it gradually and unobtrusively slip into the background?

One way of addressing these important questions is through a short illustration. Unit C8 of this book develops a workshop in practical stylistics which is based on a passage from Ernest Hemingway's novella *The Old Man and the Sea* (1952). That passage arguably typifies Hemingway's written style, a style which literary critics have described with epithets like 'flat', 'dry', 'restrained', 'journalistic' or even 'tough guy' (see C8). These observations are largely based on a perceived scarcity of adjectives in the writer's work, which is correlated with the 'machismo' feel of much of his narrative style. It is indeed true that in the first few lines of the passage analysed in C8, almost all of the nouns receive *no* adjectival modification at all: 'the tuna', 'the stern', 'the gaff', 'the line' and 'the fish'. Let us accept for the moment, then, that this marked non-adjectival pattern is foregrounded because it deviates from our expectations about the 'normal' style of twentieth-century prose fiction.

Such an interpretation immediately raises two interconnected problems. The first, as noted above, concerns the degree to which the 'no-adjective' pattern is able to stay foregrounded before it gradually slips into the background. The second is about what would happen should a phrase that *did* contain adjectives suddenly appear in the text; that is, should a structure occur whose very use of adjectives goes against the foregrounded pattern. As it happens, there is elsewhere in the novella a rather startling example of such a deviation. When a poisonous jellyfish approaches the old man's boat, the narrative refers to it as 'the purple, formalised iridescent gelatinous bladder of a Portuguese man-of-war' (Hemingway 1960 [1952]: 28). This is stylistically somewhat of a quantum leap insofar as the simple article-plus-noun configuration gives way here to a sequence of not one but *four* adjectives which are built up before the main noun ('bladder'). The old fisherman's superstitious mistrust of this dangerous animal, this 'whore of the sea' as he puts it, is captured in a stylistic flourish and with a type of hyperbole that would not be out of place in a D. H. Lawrence novel. The upshot of this is that foregrounding can be seen to work on two levels, both across and within texts. Whereas Hemingway's so-called 'flat' noun phrases may be foregrounded against the notional external stylistic backdrop of the twentieth century novella, their repetition in the text develops a norm which is itself susceptible to violation. This type of secondary foregrounding, known as *internal foregrounding,* works inside the text as a kind of deviation within a deviation. Moreover, it is clear that foregrounding does not stand still for long and that a writer's craft involves the constant monitoring and (re)appraisal of the stylistic effects created by patterns in both the foreground and in the background. The concept of foregrounding will be further explored and illustrated in B2.

Jakobson's 'poetic function'

Activity

In a famous paper, that still reverberates in much of today's stylistic scholarship, the structuralist poetician Roman Jakobson proposes a model of language which comprises six key functions (Jakobson 1960). These are the *conative, phatic, referential, emotive, poetic* and *metalingual* functions of language. Alongside the referential function (the content carrying component of a message) and the emotive function (the expression of attitude through a message), there is one function that stands out in respect of its particular appeal to stylisticians. This is the poetic function, which Jakobson defines thus: 'the poetic function projects the principle of equivalence from the axis of selection into the axis of combination' (Jakobson 1960: 358). This rather terse formula is not the most transparent definition you are likely to come across in this book, so some unpacking is in order. As a short demonstration of the formula at work, consider first of all the following example which is the opening line of W. H. Auden's elegiac poem 'In Memory of W. B. Yeats' (1939). A key verb in the line has been removed and you might wish to consider what (sort of) word would make an appropriate entry:

> He ________ in the dead of winter

There are clearly many items that might go into the slot vacated in the line. That said, some words, if semantically compatible, can be ruled out on the grounds of inappropriateness to the context: the euphemistic cliché 'passed away' or the crudely informal idiom 'kicked the bucket' are unlikely to be strong contenders in the context of an poetic elegy. You may instead prefer to settle on a verb like 'died', a contextually neutral form which is more in keeping with the poem's obvious funereal theme. However, the missing verb is actually 'disappeared', reinstated here for clarity:

> He disappeared in the dead of winter

The technique of blanking out a word in a line, a *cloze test* in stylistics parlance, is to force us to think about the pool of possible lexical entries from which a choice is ultimately made. This pool of available words is what Jakobson means by his term 'axis of selection'. What is significant about Auden's selection, one word taken from many possibilities, is that it engenders a series of resonances across the line as a whole. Notice for example, how the three syllable word 'disappeared' creates associative phonetic links with other words in the line. Most obviously, its initial and final consonant /d/ alliterates with those in the same position in the word 'dead' later in the line. Possibly more subtly, its third, stressed syllable (disapp*ea*red) contains a diphthong, the first element of which is the vowel /i:/, the same as the vowel in 'H*e*'. This type of vowel harmony, known as *assonance*, further consolidates points of equivalence across the poetic line.

However, there are also semantic as well as phonetic transferences in the line. Notice how it is the season, winter, which takes over the semantic quality of death and, when positioned together in the same grammatical environment, the words 'dead' and 'disappeared' enable new types of signification to emerge. More specifically, the parallel drawn between the words opens up a *conceptual metaphor* (A11), where the concept of death is represented in terms of a journey. In fact, we commonly invoke this DEATH IS A JOURNEY metaphor in everyday interaction when we talk of the 'dearly departed', or of someone 'passing away' or 'going to a final resting place'. The point about Auden's technique, though, is that this is a novel metaphor (B11), suggesting the sense of being lost or of straying from a journey, and this is brought about subtly by the implied connection between the process of disappearing, and the references to death and the seasons elsewhere in the same line. In sum, the way Auden uses language is a good illustration of Jakobson's poetic function at work: the particular language patterns he develops work to establish connections (*a principle of equivalence*) between the words he chooses from the pool of possible words (*the axis of selection*) and the words that are combined across the poetic line (*the axis of combination.*)

Summary

It is important to footnote the foregoing discussion with a rider. Whereas many of the precepts of both the Formalist and Prague School movements have had a significant bearing on the way stylistics has developed, this is not for a moment to say that stylisticians have embraced these ideas unequivocally, unanimously or without debate. We have already touched upon some of the theoretical problems associated with the theory of foregrounding, and in this context, stylisticians like van Peer (1986) and Cook (1994) have made advances in solidifying the foundations of this generally useful concept. Amongst other things, their work has incorporated cognitive and psychological models of analysis to explain how text-processors perceive foregrounding in texts (see further B10).

Application of the concept of the poetic function in language also brings with it an important caveat. Although not articulated especially clearly by Jakobson, it is essential to view the poetic function not as an exclusive property of literature but rather as a more generally creative use of language that can pop up, as it were, in a range of discourse contexts. One consequence of seeing the poetic function as an exclusively literary device is that it tends to separate off literature from other uses of language, and this is not a desired outcome in stylistic analysis. This latter issue will come more to the fore in the next unit along this strand, C3, while the unit below provides an opportunity, through the analysis of a short poem, to investigate and illustrate further the concept of foregrounding.

LEVELS OF LANGUAGE AT WORK: AN EXAMPLE FROM POETRY

B2

This unit, which investigates patterns of language in a single short text, forms a useful intersection between the two areas of interest raised in units B1 and A2. On the one hand it offers a chance to illustrate some basic principles of foregrounding in the context of literary discourse; on the other it develops further the main remit of this thread by exploring how different levels of language can be pressed into service in stylistically significant ways. These themes will be worked through jointly as the unit progresses.

On e e cummings's 'love is more thicker than forget'

The following untitled poem was published in 1939 by the American poet e e cummings:

love is more thicker than forget
more thinner than recall
more seldom than a wave is wet
more frequent than to fail

it is most mad and moonly
and less it shall unbe
than all the sea which only
is deeper than the sea

love is less always than to win
less never than alive
less bigger than the least begin
less littler than forgive

it is most sane and sunly
and more it cannot die
than all the sky which only
is higher than the sky

(cummings 1954 [1939]: 381)

This text – a love poem, of sorts – shall in the absence of a formal title be referred to from now on as 'love is more thicker'. It certainly bears many of the familiar stylistic imprints of its author, notable among which is the conspicuous spelling and orthography resulting from the removal of standard punctuation devices such as commas, full stops and capital letters. It also contains a number of invented words, *neologisms*, such as the adjectives 'sunly' and 'moonly', as well as the verb 'unbe' which suggests a kind of reversal in sense from 'being' to 'not being'. Perhaps even more markedly, the poem treats existing words in the English lexicon, especially adjectives and adverbs, in a striking and colourful way. In counterpoint to this more 'deviant' strand of textual structure, there is nonetheless a high degree of regularity in the way other aspects of the poem are crafted. Observe, for example, the almost mathematical symmetry of the stanzaic organisation, where key words and phrasal patterns are repeated across the four verses. Indeed, all of the poem's constituent clauses are connected grammatically to the very first word of the poem, 'love'.

Choosing models for analysis

In order for a solid basis for interpretation to be built, we need to be both clear and precise about what resources of language cummings uses, so the preceding rather informal description needs to give way to a more rigorous account of linguistic technique. To do this requires that we step back from the text for a moment in order to pinpoint more narrowly which aspects of language, in particular, the poet is manipulating. *Adjectives*, for a start, have already been highlighted as one of the main sites for stylistic experimentation in the poem. Constituting a major word class in the vocabulary of English, adjectives ascribe qualities to entities, objects and concepts, familiar examples of which are words like *large*, *bright*, *good*, *bad*, *difficult* and *regular*. A notable grammatical feature of adjectives, and one which cummings exploits with particular stylistic force, is their potential for *gradability*. Many English adjectives can be graded by extending or modifying the degree or intensity of the basic quality which they express. A useful test for checking whether or not an adjective is gradable is to see if the intensifying word 'very' can go in front of it. Indeed, all of the adjectives cited thus far satisfy this test: 'a *very bright* light', 'the *very good* decision', 'this *very regular* routine' and so on. The test does not work for another group of adjectives, known as *classifying adjectives*, which specify more fixed qualities relative to the noun they describe. In the following examples, insertion of 'very' in front of the classifying adjectives 'former' and 'strategic' feels odd: 'the *very former* manager', 'those *very strategic* weapons'.

A special feature of gradable adjectives, whose significance to 'love is more thicker' is shortly to become clear, is their capacity to compare objects and concepts through expressions of *comparative*, *superlative*, *equal* and *inferior* relationships. Thus, a comparative form of the regular adjective *large* can be formed by adding the inflectional morpheme *er* to form 'larger', while a superlative form adds *est* to form 'largest'. Comparative and superlative gradation of irregular adjectives involves a change in the whole stem of the word: thus, 'good' becomes respectively 'better' and 'best'. If on the other hand the adjective contains more than one syllable, then the comparative and superlative forms normally require the introduction of a separate word, as in '*more* regular' or '*most* difficult'. Finally, adjectives may be graded to signal equal relationships ('as bright as . . .', 'as difficult as . . .') as well as inferior or negative, as opposed to positive, relations ('less/least large', 'less/least regular').

Another notable feature of adjectives, again pertinent in the present context, is the way the grammar of English allows for material to be placed *after* the adjective in order to determine more narrowly its scope of reference. Compare for instance the following sentences:

(1) The pilot was *conscious*.

(2) The pilot was *conscious of his responsibilities*.

Clearly, very different meanings can be assigned to the adjective *conscious* in the two examples. Whereas the adjective on its own in (1) suggests (mercifully) a general state of being awake, in the second example the appended phrase targets more specifically a special kind of awareness on the part of the pilot. Thus, in a sentence like 'Mary is now *much better at maths*' the main adjective signalling Mary's general improvement ('better') is bounded on *both* sides by other elements. These elements comprise the intensifier 'much' and the scope defining element 'at maths':

intensifier	adjective	scope
much	better	at maths

Notice here how the loss of this final scope element would invite a very different interpretation, or at least a much less specific interpretation, for the clause as whole.

Exploring levels of language in 'love is more thicker'

Let us return now to the cummings text, and in particular, to his manipulation of the features of grammar and vocabulary pinpointed above. To some extent, 'love is more thicker' is an object lesson in how *not* to form adjective phrases in English. Much of what the poet does is arguably either grammatically redundant or semantically anomalous. Not intended as a sleight on this style of writing, this comment requires some explanation. For a start, cummings constantly 'reduplicates' the grammatical rules for comparative and superlative gradation. In spite of their one-syllable status, adjectives like 'thick' and 'thin' receive *both* the inflectional morpheme *and* the separate intensifier ('*more* thick*er*'). However, no sooner is this pattern introduced in the poem, than it is thrown off course by a number of secondary operations which constitute good examples of *internal foregrounding* (see B1). For a start, superlative forms of other one-syllable adjectives like 'mad' and 'sane' do *not* receive the inflectional morpheme (as in 'maddest' or 'sanest') but are instead fronted, more unusually, by separate words: 'most mad' and 'most sane'. Thereafter, a further variation on the pattern emerges where markers of both positive and inferior relations are mixed together in the *same* adjective phrase. Notice how, for example, 'big' is converted to 'less bigger' and, even more oddly, 'little' to 'less littler'. It is as if many of the grammatical structures in the poem are designed to push in two different directions simultaneously, creating a textural frame which, the more it advances, the more it tends to self-nullify.

These are by no means all of the lexical and grammatical operations cummings employs, nor indeed are they even all of the tweaks performed on the structure of adjective phrases. The scope element, introduced above as the device that 'rounds off' the meaning of the adjective phrase, also comes in for particular enhancement in the poem. Take first of all the conventional usage of the structure, as embodied in the proverb 'Blood is thicker than water'. Here the comparative adjective 'thicker' connects up the entity 'blood' with the key item in the scope element, 'water'. Moreover, so that the adjective can, as it were, do its job, the entities thus compared need to be compatible at least in some measure – both blood and water are liquids, for example, and it is their relative viscosity that forms the nub of the comparison. A comparison of 'love' might therefore reasonably anticipate another noun element which derives from the broad compass of human emotion, yet nothing of the sort is offered by cummings. Instead, it is verbs, of all things, which often fill the position reserved for the compared entity. Consider the opening sequence of the poem in the context of the structural formula set up in B2:

intensifier	adjective	scope
more	thicker	than forget

Here the adjective phrase works ostensibly to develop a comparison of the noun 'love'. That noun represents the abstract domain of human experience, yet the grammatical relationship into which it is projected involves a comparative adjective standardly used to describe solids and liquids. Odder again is that the scope of reference of that adjective is specified not by another noun from the same broad set as 'love' but by a verb referring to a mental process.

Other eye-catching patterns litter the poem, one of which emerges in the second and third lines of the first stanza and is sustained for the remainder of the poem. Eschewing adjectives completely in this case, cummings inserts *adverbs of time-relationship*, like 'seldom', 'always' or 'never', into the main slot in the adjective phrase frame. Adverbs have a markedly different grammatical function from adjectives. Whereas adjectives describe qualities, adverbs normally describe circumstances. The adverbs employed here are of a specific type in that they provide circumstantial information about the duration and time-frame in which a verbal process did or did not take place. Furthermore, many of these adverbs function to communicate *negative* time relationships, and when piled up on one another, words like this can make a text very hard to unravel conceptually. For example, if someone were to remark of the book you are currently reading that 'This is a book you must not fail to miss', you might initially interpret this as a solid endorsement of the work in question. However, closer scrutiny will reveal that the remark means precisely the opposite, that is, that you should endeavour at all costs to avoid this book. In terms of discourse processing, then, the cumulative build up of words like 'fail', 'seldom', 'forget' and 'less' – words denoting a kind of negative semantic space – creates a complex interpretative framework which makes the text in certain respects almost impenetrable as a unit of meaning.

This framework is further problematised by other semantic devices in the poem. One such technique is *tautology* which in common parlance means saying the same thing twice and which is embodied in everyday phrases like 'War is war' or 'If she goes, she goes'. Many of cummings's comparative and superlative structures are full-blown logical tautologies simply because they replicate the basic premises of the proposition. Notice how the *same* entities are positioned either side of the adjectival structure in 'the sea is . . . deeper than the sea' or 'the sky is . . . higher than the sky'. In the strictest sense, these comparisons aren't comparisons at all because their underlying logical structures fail to establish new propositions. Other features embedded in the semantic fabric of the text include *lexical antonyms*, words of opposite meaning like the adjectives 'thicker' and 'thinner', the adverbs 'never' and 'always' and even the adjectival neologisms 'sunly' and 'moonly'. Antonyms are one way of establishing cohesion in a text, and perhaps rather ironically here, these opposites help shore up the poem's cohesive organisation when, so to speak, chaos is breaking out elsewhere in the grammatical system. Through its interplay between the levels of semantics, lexis and grammar, then, 'love is more thicker' is a poem which is strongly cohesive on the one hand but which still seems to resist interpretation on the other.

Stylistic analysis and interpretation

It is admittedly not easy, when faced with complex language like this, to discuss either *what* a text means or indeed *how* a text means. However, it is important to stress that, in spite of the veritable semantic labyrinth that is 'love is more thicker', the poem still does *communicate*. Indeed, a case could be made for arguing that it is the very opacity, the very indeterminacy of its linguistic structure which acts out and parallels the conceptualisation of love that cummings seeks to capture and portray. The individual stylistic tactics used in the poem, replicated so vigorously and with such consistency, all drive towards the conclusion that love is, well, incomparable. Every search for a point of comparison encounters a tautology, a semantic anomaly or some kind of grammatical *cul de sac*. Love is at once more of something and less of it; not quite as absolute or certain as 'always' but still more than just 'frequent'. It is deep, deeper even than the sea, and then a little bit deeper again.

Perhaps more contentiously, a case might be made for suggesting that many localised stylistic features hint at the struggle of an innocent trying to find some resource in the language system that adequately captures this aspect of felt emotion. Notice for example how the grammatical reduplication echoes the expressions of a child trying to come to grips with the irregularities of English; 'worsest', 'more badder' and 'baddest' are, after all, common developmental errors and these have close stylistic analogues in the poem. In many respects, this is a 'meta-poem', a poem about trying to write a poem. It seeks on the one hand to capture the world of human understanding and relationships, although the difficulty of the linguistic exercise draws attention in turn to the difficulty in mediating that world through language. This lack of reconciliation between form and content is mirrored in the way the resources of the language system are deployed. Buried in the semantics of the poem is its central enigma, acted out in the very contradictions ascribed to the poem's central theme, the experience of love.

Much of the internal dynamic of cummings's poem is sustained by the subversion of simple and everyday patterns of language, and it is the distortion of these commonplace routines of speech and writing that deliver the main stylistic impact. In a sense, there is nothing to be scared of in a text like 'love is more thicker' simply because, as analysis reveals, the grammatical patterns of English upon which it is based are in themselves straightforward. That is why it is important to be precise in stylistic analysis, and indeed, as noted in A1, it is an important part of the stylistic endeavour that its methods probe the conventional structures of language as much as the deviant or the distorted. In any case, to say that the language of this particular poem is 'deviant' is both a sweeping and contingent categorisation. Foregrounding never stays still for long, and once a striking pattern starts to become established in a text, so, by imputation, it begins to drift towards the background as new patterns take its place. There is also, as noted, a high level of symmetry in the poem, which means that the technique of foregounding-through-deviation is supplemented by foregounding-through-more-of-the-same (B1). Finally, I hope this exercise has demonstrated the importance of making the analysis retrievable to other students of style, by showing how not just one level, but multiple levels of language organisation simultaneously participate, some in harmony and some in conflict, in creating the stylistic fabric of a poem.

SENTENCE STYLES: DEVELOPMENT AND ILLUSTRATION

B3

This unit sets out to achieve two main goals. Focussing exclusively on grammar, it narrows down the broader perspective adopted in B2, which was principally interested in how various levels of language function in textual patterning. This unit also dovetails with other units in this strand both by offering a number of extensions to the model of grammar developed in A3 and by paving the way for the practical stylistic exercise that will be undertaken in C3.

Sentence types

The principal focus of attention thus far in our study of grammar and style has been on the clause and on the units which are situated beneath it on the rank scale (see A3, and also B2). So far, little attention has been paid to the highest unit of organisation in grammar, the sentence. Also known as the 'clause complex', the sentence is a far from straightforward category. Grammarians are divided about its importance with some arguing that it is really only an extension of the clause and others that it comprises a genuine unit with its own elements of structure. Whatever its precise theoretical status, the sentence is nonetheless a significant feature in the organisation of style and is worth elaborating upon in a little more detail here.

The most 'simple' type of sentence structure is where the sentence comprises just *one* independent clause. Here are two sentences, each containing a single clause apiece:

(1) He ate his supper. He went to bed.

Not surprisingly, the term for sentences which are so constructed is *simple sentence.* A good technique for conceptualising sentence structure (and this will come more to the fore as we look at other types) is to imagine a sentence as a box whose housing forms a grammatical boundary and whose contents are variable. The conceptual structure of (1) would therefore be as two boxes placed side-by-side but without any formal linkage between them:

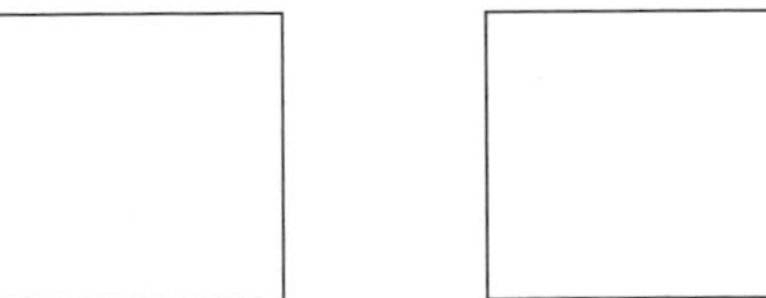

Although circumspection is always advised in generalisations about the effects of grammatical patterns, one of the stylistic functions of the simple sentence is often to engender a frenetic or fast-paced feel to a passage of description. Consider to this effect the following extract from Jerome K. Jerome's novel *Three Men in a Boat.* The novel's first person narrator has just been perusing a medical encyclopaedia only to convince himself that he suffers from all but two of the numerous ailments listed therein:

> I tried to examine myself. I felt my pulse. I could not at first feel any pulse at all. Then, all of a sudden, it seemed to start off. I pulled out my watch and timed it. I made it a hundred and forty-seven to the minute. I tried to feel my heart. I could not feel my heart. It had stopped beating.
>
> (Jerome 1986 [1889]: 5)

Most of the sentences in this short passage are made up of a single independent clause. In this narrative context, their sense of speed and urgency helps deliver a melodramatic mock tension as the hypochondriac narrator's self-examination unfolds.

The term *compound sentence* is used to describe structures which have more than one clause in them, and where these clauses are of equal grammatical status. Compound sentences are built up through the technique of coordination (see A3) and they rely on a fixed set of coordinating conjunctions like *and, or, but, so, for,* and *yet.* Each of examples 2–4 are *single* compound sentences which contain within them *two* coordinated clauses:

(2) He ate his supper and he went to bed.

(3) He ate his supper so he went to bed.

(4) He ate his supper but he went to bed shortly after.

The best way of conceptualising the structure of compound sentences, using the 'boxes' analogy, is to imagine them as linked together like square beads on string, thus:

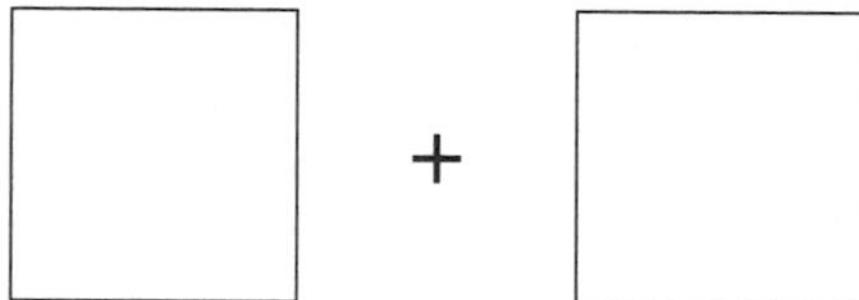

Compound sentences can perform a variety of functions, and the symmetrical nature of the connection between their units makes them a favoured style in material designed for junior readers. This fragment from a popular nursery rhyme is a compound sentence containing three coordinated clauses:

(5) He huffed and he puffed and he blew the house down.

A similar technique of coordination is at work in this sequence from Hemingway's *The Old Man and the Sea*:

> They sat on the terrace and many of the fishermen made fun of the old man and he was not angry.
>
> (Hemingway 1960: 3)

Notice how this is coordination of the most basic sort. The direct coordinator *and* takes precedence over an 'adversative' conjunction like *but*, even when one might expect the latter. The adversative would after all impart some sense of contrast between the last two conjuncts – 'many of the fishermen made fun of the old man *but* he was not angry' – yet the narratorial perspective is kept almost wilfully non-interpretative here (see further C8).

Complex sentences involve two possible structural configurations, but their main informing principle is that the clauses they contain are in an asymmetrical relationship to one another. The first configuration involves *subordination*, where the subordinate clause is appended to a main clause. To form this pattern, subordinating conjunctions are used and these include *when, although, if, because* and *since*. As further variations on the sample sentences used so far, consider the following examples which are all two-clause complex sentences:

(6) When he had eaten his supper, he went to bed.

(7) Having eaten his supper, he went to bed.

(8) Although he had just eaten his supper, he went to bed.

(9) If he has eaten his supper, he must have gone to bed.

The conceptual structure for the subordinate relationship is to imagine that one box leans on another thus:

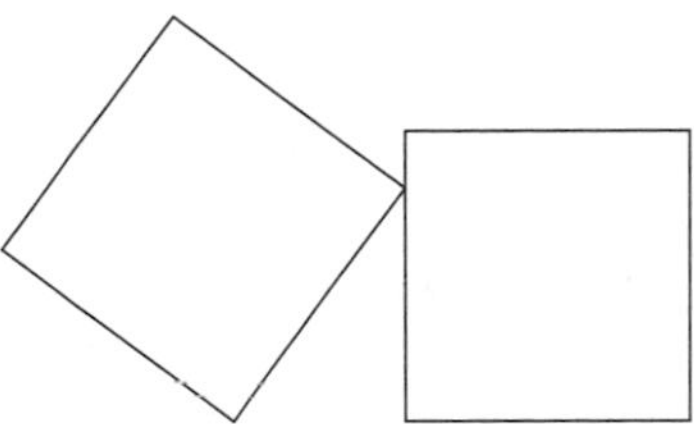

The main clause is the supporting box which, if taken away, will cause the (subordinate) box leaning on it to topple.

The second type of complex sentence involves the *embedding* of one structure inside another. To put it another way, this pattern involves taking a unit at the rank of clause and squeezing it inside another clause. This means that the embedded clause has had to be pulled down a rank ('downranked') in order to fit inside a structure of equal size. Here are some examples of complex sentences containing downranked clauses:

(10) Mary realised he had eaten his supper.

(11) She announced that he had gone to bed.

(12) That he had eaten his supper was obvious to everyone.

Highlighting the capacity of grammar to embed units within other units of varying sizes, the 'boxes' analogy conceives this structure conceptually as:

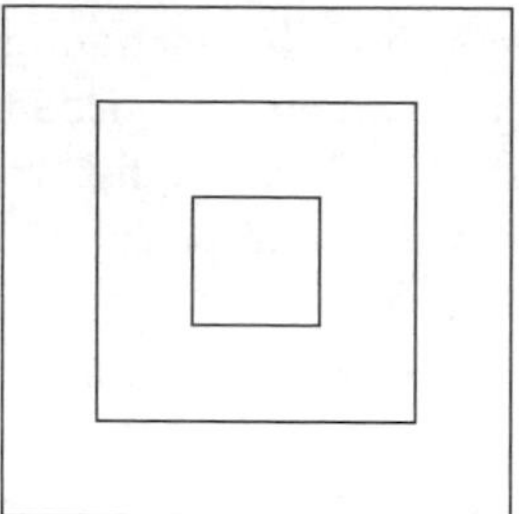

The outside box is the main clause and nested inside it is any number of downranked clauses. You can test for the main elements in each of examples (10) to (12), sorting out which is the matrix clause and which is the embedded, by using the various grammatical tests provided in A3.

Trailing constituents and anticipatory constituents

Although coordination between clauses is a founding principle of compound sentences, the same operation can be performed on other grammatical ranks. For example, words and phrases, as opposed to clauses, may be coordinated, as indicated by the following well-known couplet from Shakespeare's *Macbeth:*

> Tomorrow, and tomorrow, and tomorrow,
> Creeps in this petty pace from day to day.
> (*Macbeth,* V.v.19–20)

Here, three occurrences of the temporal adverb 'tomorrow' are tied together with the coordinating conjunction 'and' to form an Adjunct. As the play draws to its conclusion, the grim inevitability of its denouement is signalled in this sequence of repetition, delivered here with an almost laboured monotony. The inexorability of the passage of time is picked up again at the end of the sequence with the repetition of another temporal adverb in the Adjunct 'day to day'. Thus, grammatical structure works to create temporal 'book-ends' around the main Predicator ('Creeps in') and Subject ('this petty pace') elements. The stylistic effectiveness of this configuration can be tested simply by pulling it apart; the following 'unravelled' version has little impact and nor does it seem to make much sense:

> This petty pace creeps in from day to day
> Tomorrow, and tomorrow, and tomorrow

This point leads to another issue about grammatical patterning which concerns the positioning of various elements of clause structure in a particular text. Imagine the Subject, Predicator and Complement elements of a main clause as the hub around which satellite structures, principally Adjuncts and subordinate clauses, can be placed. In the Shakespeare example, Adjuncts are placed on either side of that hub. In such situations, where the weighting of elements on either side of a Subject and Predicator is balanced, we use the term *equivalent constituents* to explain this stylistic technique. However, the following sequence, which is the opening two lines of Michael Longley's poem 'The Ghost Orchid' displays a rather different pattern:

> You walked with me among water mint
> And bog myrtle when I was tongue-tied . . .
>
> (Longley 1995)

The two Adjunct elements, filled by the prepositional phrases 'with me' and 'among water mint and bog myrtle', along with the subordinate clause ('when I was tongue tied'), come after the hub of the clause. *Trailing constituents* is the term used in stylistics for units which follow the Subject and Predicator in this way.

Finally, to the reverse technique, where Adjuncts and subordinate clauses are placed before the main Subject-Predicator matrix. When this occurs, the initial elements are known as *anticipatory constituents.* Here is good illustration of the principle at work in a piece of narrative description from Joseph Conrad's novella *The Secret Sharer.* The anticipatory constituents have been highlighted:

> *On my right hand* there were lines of fishing-stakes resembling a mysterious system of half submerged fences . . . *To the left* a group of barren islets had its foundations set in a blue sea . . . *And when I turned my head to take a parting glance,* I saw the straight line of the flat shore . . . *Corresponding in their insignificance to the islets of the sea,* two small clumps of trees . . .
>
> (Conrad 1995 [1912]: 1)

These initial elements serve to orientate each sequence of unfolding description within the spatial perspective of the first person narrator. In their analysis of the grammar of this same passage, Leech and Short (1981: 83–9) note how the description is etched with meticulous detail in such a way that we are able to construct in our mind's eye the whole topography as perceived by the passage's lone human observer.

Illustrating grammar in action: Dickens's famous fog

Thus far in our developing model of grammar, short illustrations from literary texts have been used to illustrate each of the various categories introduced. In order to show how a range of devices of grammar can work simultaneously in a text, it will be useful to close this unit by focussing on a slightly longer passage. Much beloved of stylisticians because of its foregrounded patterns of language, this text is the second paragraph of Charles Dickens's novel *Bleak House,* reproduced here with sentences numbered for convenience:

> (1) Fog everywhere. (2) Fog up the river, where it flows among green aits and meadows; fog down the river, where it rolls defiled among the tiers of shipping, and the waterside pollutions of a great (and dirty) city. (3) Fog on the Essex Marshes, fog on the Kentish heights. (4) Fog creeping into the cabooses of collier-brigs; fog lying out on the yards, and hovering in the rigging of great ships; fog drooping on the gunwales of barges and small boats. (5) Fog in the eyes and throats of ancient Greenwich pensioners, wheezing by the firesides of their wards; fog in the stem and bowl of the afternoon pipe of the wrathful skipper, down in his close cabin; fog cruelly pinching the toes and fingers of his shivering little 'prentice boy on deck. (6) Chance people on the bridges peeping over the parapets into a nether sky of fog, with fog all round them, as if they were up in a balloon, and hanging in the misty clouds.
>
> (Dickens 1986 [1853]: 49)

Rather than attempt to tease out every significant stylistic feature of this famous paragraph – such an undertaking would on its own take up a whole unit and more – we shall restrict ourselves to analysis of just five noteworthy grammatical patterns in this text. Commentary on these patterns will be kept brief.

Feature 1

A key stylistic feature is the way the central noun 'fog' is elaborated (or perhaps more accurately, 'un-elaborated') throughout the passage. It is a resource of grammar that nouns commonly enter into combinations with other words so that any particular or special quality they possess can be identified and picked out. Thus, in a phrase like 'the thick grey fog nearby', the grammatical slots around the word 'fog' are filled up by a determiner ('the'), two adjectives ('thick grey') and an adverb ('nearby'). However, none of the available slots are thus filled in the passage and this marked absence of grammatical modification makes the central noun, 'fog', emerge as stark, undifferentiated and (literally) undetermined. Its characterless quality is reinforced by comparison, in that many other nouns in the passage receive precisely this sort of grammatical modification: eg. 'green aits', 'waterside pollutions' and 'a great (and dirty) city'.

Feature 2

A popular interpretation of this passage is to see it as a text with 'no verbs'. This is not strictly accurate, however, because only in the first three sentences and in part of sentence (5) have verbs been excised completely. In any case, there are plenty of verbs in the numerous subordinate clauses in the passage. A more rigorous stylistic description would therefore stipulate that the passage displays a restricted verbal development in its main clauses. In the opening sentences, the Predicator element has been ellipsed completely, and this takes with it all sense of verbal process. Later in the passage, from sentence (4), part of the Predicator element is offered, but significantly, one key element is omitted. This element, known as the *finite*, is often expressed by auxiliary verbs and it serves to provide, among other things, tense, polarity and grammatical agreement with the Subject. By offering only the main verbal component in 'lying', 'creeping' and 'pinching', Dickens effectively splits the Predicator in two so that we get a sense of ongoing process, but no indication of tense. Trying out the tag tests developed in unit A3 is revealing in this respect. Applied to the sequence 'Fog creeping into the cabooses of collier-brigs', the tag test would pick out 'Fog' as Subject without any trouble, but the absence of a finite verbal particle creates problems in choosing a tense for the tag:

> Fog creeping into the cabooses of collier-brigs [wasn't it?/isn't it?]
>
> Fog creeping into the cabooses of collier-brigs, [so it is/so it was]

So while these clause patterns indicate both a basic verbal process and the location of that process, they offer no indication of tense, a consequence of which is that it is difficult to establish a time frame for the events narrated. Whereas the fog's omnipresence in the spatial context is well grounded, there is little sense of concrete anchoring in the corresponding temporal context.

Feature 3

The passage abounds in 'trailing constituents' in which grammatical build-up takes place towards the right of the main Predicator position. These clauses contain numerous subordinate clauses and Adjuncts of location, so again, and sustaining feature 2, the narrative is rich in detail about place but low in detail about time. The amount of information contained in these trailing constituents also brings into sharper relief the very sparseness of the material that is positioned to the left of the Predicator slot. Furthermore, the grammatical 'sprawl' that is bought about by these trailing constituents also facilitates an interesting textual ambiguity. In the sequences '. . . it flows . . .' and '. . . it rolls defiled . . .' (2), the pronoun 'it' serves a possible dual reference with respect to its two potential antecedents in the main clause. Is it the fog that flows and rolls, or is it the river? My own interpretation is that the ambiguity is motivated, and that it works to underscore the very blurring and indeterminacy that is ascribed to the core visual elements in the scene.

Feature 4

There is a gradual narrowing of spatial focus as the passage progresses. Whereas the first Adjunct declares that the fog is, well, everywhere, subsequent Adjunct elements move progressively right down into the localised, even microscopic, environment of the stem and bowl of the skipper's pipe. In tandem with this progressive narrowing through Adjuncts, the processes embodied by the related verbs in the main clauses also undergo an interesting change. In experiential terms (see unit A6), the processes associated with 'fog' are initially intransitive in that they do not impact upon a Goal. Here are four such examples, piled up in parallel in the fourth sentence: '. . . *creeping* into the cabooses . . . *lying* out on the yards . . . *hovering* in the rigging . . . *drooping* on the gunwales . . .'. However, just as the overall spatial focus narrows, so the transitivity pattern shifts to a Goal-directed one, as in 'fog cruelly *pinching* the toes and fingers . . .' (5). It is notable that the adverb 'cruelly' is the only instance where a grammatical element (here an Adjunct) is wedged between the 'Fog' and its following Predicator. It seems that the longer the passage goes on, the more menacing and spiteful the fog becomes.

Feature 5

The final sentence of the passage offers a good illustration of *internal foregrounding* (see B1). The pattern established from sentence 1 through to 5 gradually forms its own text-internal norm, so to keep us on our interpretative toes, as it were, Dickens subverts the pattern in the sixth sentence. This he does by creating a different Subject element and by shifting the lexical item 'fog' to the right of the Predicator. That said, 'fog' still receives no grammatical modification and therefore still maintains its undefined, indefinite feel. By showing how a pattern initially built through parallelism and repetition can ultimately be turned on its head, this fifth stylistic feature illustrates well the fluid and dynamic properties of foregrounding.

Summary

As one works through a text like the *Bleak House* passage, it is always important to remember that style comes from the totality of interrelated elements of language rather than from individual features in isolation. While it is not feasible to cover every aspect of language in an analysis, a useful way of dealing with this problem is to make up some sentences that you feel would be at odds with the stylistic techniques used in the passage under examination. This exercise, used extensively in a number of other units, helps tease out through contrast the features that *are* in the text. Here for example is a sample of utterly 'non-fog' language which unravels several of the five features identified above. You can work out which ones by yourself:

> Across the Essex Marshes, a thick choking fog of indistinct proportion was sweeping in.

In the context, a thoroughly un-Dickensian sentence to be sure.

A number of the features addressed here and in unit A3 are explored further in the practical activity developed in C3. In the following unit, attention focuses on another of the core levels of language as it applies to stylistic analysis. This is the level of sound.

B4 INTERPRETING PATTERNS OF SOUND

Unit A4 established a set of basic principles for the analysis of metre and rhythm in poetry. Continuing this theme, the present unit will raise and explore some issues concerning the significance of patterns of sound for stylistic analysis. In particular, this unit should encourage us to think about how, as stylisticians, we make connections between, on the one hand, the physical properties of the sounds represented *within* a text and, on the other, the non-linguistic phenomena situated *outside* a text to which these sounds relate.

Onomatopoeia

Onomatopoeia is a feature of sound patterning which is often thought to form a bridge between 'style' and 'content'. It can occur either in a *lexical* or a *nonlexical* form, although both forms share the common property of being able to match up a sound with a nonlinguistic correlate in the 'real' world. Lexical onomatopoeia draws upon recognised words in the language system, words like *thud, crack, slurp* and *buzz*, whose pronunciation enacts symbolically their referents outside language. Nonlexical onomatopoeia, by contrast, refers to clusters of sounds which echo the world in a more unmediated way, without the intercession of linguistic structure. For example, the mimicking of the sound of a car revving up might involve a series of nonlexical approximations, such as *vroom vroom*, or *brrrrm brrrrm*, and so on. As nonlexical onomatopoeia is explored in depth in reading D4, the remainder of this unit will concentrate mainly on the stylistic importance of lexical onomatopoeia.

The role that lexical onomatopoeia plays in the stylistic texture of poetry makes for an important area of study. The lexicon can be exploited for its imitative potential, with individual words being pressed into a kind of onomatopoeic service on the basis of their particular phonetic profiles. Random or happenstance sequences of sound can thus acquire a mimetic function in particular discourse contexts. Let us develop these observations by considering two short fragments of poetry, both of which display marked sound symbolism. The first is from Stephen Spender's poem 'Pylons' and the second from Gerard Manley Hopkins's 'The Windhover'. In both examples, the relevant sequences are highlighted:

(1) [The valley . . . and the green chestnut . . .]
Are mocked dry like the parched bed of a brook.

(2) Brute beauty and valour and act, *oh, air, pride, plume, here*
Buckle! [. . .]

In the sense that patterns of sound palpably evoke the visual elements of their respective descriptions, both examples are, to my ear, good illustrations of poetic onomatopoeia at work. The example from 'Pylons' is *alliterative* (see A4) because it foregrounds a certain type of consonant in order to ascribe a quality of aridity to the entity it describes. Note the dominance of the voiceless stops /k/ and /t/ in this line, supplemented by voiced stops /b/ and /d/ and the voiceless affricate consonant /tʃ/ in 'par*ch*ed'. Note also that because of their immediately preceding phonetic environment, the spelled 'd's at the end of both 'mocked' and parched' are, when read aloud, assimilated to the voiceless variant /t/. (This is a good illustration, worth noting in passing, of the sometime disparity between written language and spoken language.) Notably absent from the line are the conventionally 'softer' sounds like the fricatives /s/ and /z/, or 'slushier' sounds like the fricative /ʃ/ which is (significantly) found in a word like 'lu*sh*'. My point is that Spender foregrounds a particular set of consonant sounds in order to embody the dryness, the very desiccated quality of the empty brook that his poetic line describes.

The example from Hopkins represents a different kind of onomatopoeia, built not through consonant harmony but by a kind of vowel 'disharmony'. The highlighted words in (2) are describing the path of the windhover (a species of falcon) as it flies at speed through the air. If you try to sound out these words you may notice that the vowel progression between them is almost discordant, with the articulation of each new vowel representing a different place and manner of articulation in the oral cavity. Although accents of English vary, an informal approximation of the six relevant vowels would be: oh – eh – aye – oo – eea – uh. This sequence is a nexus of phonetic contrasts, between front and back vowels (eh/oo), between open and close vowels (uh/*ee*a), between lip-rounded and unrounded vowels (oo/eh) and between shorter monophthongs (oh and uh) and longer diphthongs (aye and eea). My interpretation is that the constant shift in type of articulation, from high to low, back and forth and so on, follows the movement of the bird itself, such that the crisscrossing in phonetic space becomes a mirror of the angles, the spiralling and the swooping, that the windhover makes as it flies through the air. In sum, vowel mimesis works onomatopoetically by mediating with the nonlinguistic world. And because examples (1) and (2) both use sound symbolism to invite from the reader an affective response to a text, they can be said to express poetic *phonaestasia*.

The 'phonaesthetic fallacy'

Did you find my interpretation of sound symbolism in (1) and (2) convincing? Can phonetic detail be matched up with a text in such a way? Or perhaps the interpretation reads too much into a few simple vowels and consonants? So were my views mere hunch?

The simple truth of the matter is that in phonetics there is simply no such thing as a 'dry' consonant or a 'flying' vowel, and such impressionistic labels have no place whatsoever in the systematic study of speech sounds. If such direct connections could be made, it would mean that every time we encountered a consonant configuration like that in (1) we would instantly think 'dry', or every time we came across a sequence of vowels like that in (2) we would think of a bird's flight through the air. We need look no further than the preceding paragraph of this sub-unit for proof of this point. In the second sentence, beginning 'Can phonetic detail . . .', there were actually more of the so-called dry /k/, /t/ and /tʃ/ consonants than there were in the Spender line. You can go back and count them yourself, but the point is that you are unlikely, even when reading this sentence again, to conclude that it is a particularly 'dry' piece of prose. More tellingly, the final sentence of the previous paragraph has exactly the same progression of vowels as the Hopkins line:

oh	eh	aye	oo	eea	uh
so	were	my	views	mere	hunch?

You may have experienced a number of reactions to my sentence – what poor prose style, what a lame rhetorical question and so on – but I would be very surprised indeed if you felt that its sound structure mirrored the shimmering flight path of the European falcon as it flies, spectacularly and fleet of wing, across the horizon.

Clearly, there is a certain risk in trying to connect up directly a particular feature of sound in a text with nonlinguistic phenomena outside the text, and the sort of interpretative practice which does make such direct connections might be termed the *phonaesthetic fallacy*. This is not to say that my feelings or intuitions about examples (1) and (2) were in any sense wrong; it is rather that my analysis drew an uncomfortably direct parallel between these intuitions and the raw linguistic material of the text. In other words, the fallacy lies in the assumption that language functions unproblematically as a direct embodiment of the real world.

The phonaesthetic fallacy, if not articulated in precisely the same terminology as here, is a serious issue for stylistic analysis. Nash talks of it as something that teachers of language and literature have come to dread when dealing with the interpretation of phonetic features in literary texts (Nash 1986: 130). Attridge notes as a failing in much traditional literary criticism that it uses aspects of sound to evoke directly the meaning of the text: a practice evident in common critical comments like 'rhythmic enactment' or 'appropriate sound-patterns' (Attridge 1988: 133). So let me try then to set out some basic principles about the interpretation of sound symbolism that will help avoid the interpretive pitfall that is the phonaesthetic fallacy.

We need first of all to make the assumption that a particular piece of language is *intended* to be performed mimetically. If this function is not understood, then we simply do not seek out sound symbolism. The conventions of reading textbooks differ from those governing the reading of poetry, which is why (I assume) you were not primed to search out mimetic sound patterns in the earlier paragraph. Second, we should never lose sight of the text immediately surrounding the particular feature of style under consideration, the *co-text* in other words. In the Hopkins example, for instance, the salient items are preceded by a very different stylistic pattern, where coordination ('Brute beauty *and* valour *and* act') suggests a perhaps more languid precursor to the contrasting brisker and more strident delivery invited of the highlighted sequence. Related to this point, and echoing units A2 and B2, we need also to think about how a relevant feature is paralleled by other levels of language. In Hopkins, again, note how the disharmony at the phonetic level is underscored by the mixture of grammatical forms that carry these sounds, a mixture which comprises an uncoordinated sequence of nouns, verbs and adverbs and which is even fronted by a nonlexical expressive particle, 'oh'.

There are also conventions for reading sound imagery, such that certain types of sounds are conventionally interpreted in certain ways. Moreover, onomatopoeia works on the reader's familiarity with the entity described which means that we need to know that we are being told about, say, a dry brook or the flight path of a falcon, before we can search out a correspondence in sound. Attridge adopts the useful phrase *heightened meaning* to explain how onomatopoeic conventions work (Attridge 1988: 150). Phonetic and semantic properties interact with one another, and in a way that mutually reinforces and intensifies both aspects of language. Thus, the so-called 'dry' consonants in Spender are conventionally understood as heightening the semantic quality of aridity. This explains why a word like 'waterless', which contains 'softer' consonants like /w/, /l/ and /s/, would not have had the same impact even though it is semantically compatible in the context. It would simply not *heighten* meaning in the way that the word 'parched' does.

We cannot cut sound symbolism adrift from its overall discourse context because – and this is a point that extends to all stylistic practice – the linguistic system does not embody the real world directly. Meanings are signalled only indirectly, so it is a guiding principle of stylistic analysis to be cautious about treating any aspect of language as if it bears an inherent relationship with a given or felt experience. Taking these cautionary observations on board, unit C4 offers a programme for the analysis of a short poem by Michael Longley, in which sound symbolism is one of various levels of language explored. In the reading by Derek Attridge which supplements this unit, the emphasis on patterns of sound is maintained, with the focus on nonlexical as opposed to lexical onomatopoeia.

B5 DEVELOPMENTS IN STRUCTURAL NARRATOLOGY

In unit A5, a distinction was drawn between the concepts of narrative *plot* and narrative *discourse*. It should be noted that this distinction, like many terms developed in this book, mirrors and to some extent simplifies a number of various parallel categories available in the stylistics literature. With particular respect to narrative analysis, my ordering of the elements *plot* and *discourse* is designed to correspond to other comparable pairings like *fabula* and *sjuzhet*, *histoire* and *discours*, and *story* and *discourse*. Whatever the precise terminology, the main point is that the first term in each pair captures the abstract chronological configuration of the core elements of plot and the second the discourse in and through which that plot is realised. The many and varied linguistic-stylistic permutations that are afforded by narrative discourse are covered in strands 6, 7 and 8, but in this unit the emphasis will be strictly on narrative *plot*. The unit begins by reviewing an important *structuralist* model of narrative and then continues with an application of it to two narrative texts.

An important feature of the narrative schema set out in A5 was its acknowledgment that narrative may be encoded in a variety of textual media, which include but are not restricted to film, cartoon, ballad, comic strip, prose fiction and oral vernacular. The two narrative texts that are to come under scrutiny here are 'celluloid' narratives, one film and the other animation, although both narratives have direct counterparts in prose fiction. There will be more to say on these texts shortly, but first to the model of analysis.

Propp's morphology of the folktale

In what became an influential study in structuralist narratology, the Russian scholar Vladimir Propp published in 1928 a 'morphology' of the fairy tale (or the 'folktale', in his terms). Propp's interest is principally in extrapolating out of a corpus of 115 actual stories a kind of blueprint for the folktale as a whole. Although this blueprint does not constitute an analysis of any individual story, its categories are designed so as to capture all of the possible elements available to *any* fairy story. The result of the study is a finite list of *thirty-one* narrative functions, no less, and these functions are undertaken by *seven* basic types of character roles.

The way Propp sets about developing his list of narrative functions is to isolate from his corpus the recurring components of each fairy tale. Acknowledging that the names of the particular 'dramatis personae' may change from story to story, Propp argues that it is the question of *what* a tale's characters do that is important, not so much *who* does it or *how* it is done (Propp 1966 [1928]). This orientation therefore requires the rendering down of narratives into their raw, basic constituents, producing a kind of grammar of narrative which is indeed indicated by the reference to 'morphology' in the title of Propp's study.

According to Propp, a tale usually begins with some sort of initial situation after which some or all of the thirty-one narrative functions follow. The first function, for example, is where one of the members of a family, normally the character role of 'Hero', absents himself from home. This 'absentation' (*sic*) may be precipitated by the death of parents or by some similar calamity, whereupon the Hero may go to war, to the forest or even, curiously, to work. The second narrative function involves an interdiction being addressed to the Hero, normally taking the form of a warning that danger is present and including some instruction about what *not* to do. Following from the interdiction is the narrative function: 'violation of the interdiction'. For example, in the Walt Disney cartoon *Beauty and the Beast*, the Beast warns Beauty not on any account to go into the west wing of the castle (the interdiction), whereupon Beauty, er, goes into the west wing of the castle. The fourth of Propp's functions sees the arrival of the character role of 'Villain'. The Villain attempts to make 'reconnaissance' on the Hero, finding out about his whereabouts or about some vulnerability or weakness. And thus the pattern of the model develops, up to a total of thirty-one possible narrative plot functions.

Now, the point of Propp's model is not to imply that *all* narratives realise *all* functions. Nor is it to suggest that all narratives, in their manifestation as discourse, follow a straightforwardly linear chronology. Suffice it to say, there are numerous stylistic devices which give a stamp of originality to narrative as far as the actual telling of the story is concerned (see strands 6, 7 and 8). However, what Propp's model does is to try to define a genre of narrative discourse, the fairy tale, through a circumscribed set of core organisational parameters. How those parameters might be applied to more contemporary narratives is the focus of the next sub-unit.

The morphology of contemporary narrative

Thus far, the Proppian morphology may look at first glance like a rather antiquated analytic model, a model whose scope of reference embraces nothing more than the quaint oral narratives of a then fledgling Soviet Union. True, contemporary narratives do seem a long way off from the Russian folk story of the 1920s. However, as with any sound theoretical model, it is a central precept of the Proppian framework that it should have universal relevance. That means that it is designed to have the explanatory power to account for folk narratives beyond the specific corpus used in the design of the model, and even for narratives that had not even come into being at the time the model was developed.

Let us consider, in turn, two cases where the application of the Proppian model offers some interesting insights about narrative structure. Both film narratives, the first is Disney's cartoon *The Jungle Book* which is based, rather loosely it has to be said, on Rudyard Kipling's 'Mowgli stories'. The second is Chris Columbus's feature film *Harry Potter and the Philosopher's Stone* which is based, more closely this time, on the first instalment of J. K. Rowling's hugely successful series of 'Harry Potter' novels. What follows is a short exploration of the types and degree of coalescence that there is between the core categories of Propp's model and the key plot advancing functions of both films.

First of all, to Disney's animated film *The Jungle Book* which was released in 1967. Realising the first of Propp's functions, absentation, Mowgli the 'mancub' is displaced from his parents and home and is found wandering in the jungle. Mowgli, clearly fulfilling the character role of 'Hero', then acquires a Helper, a character role dually occupied by Bagheera the panther and later by Baloo the bear. Both friends warn Mowgli of the dangers of being in the jungle on his own (the 'interdiction' function), advice which of course Mowgli ignores (violation of the interdiction). Numerous other Proppian functions are realised thereafter. In a famous and hugely comic scene from the film, the Villain, Shere Khan the tiger, carries out reconnaissance on the Hero by interrogating the snake, Kaa. The Villain then attempts to take possession of the Hero (the sixth of Propp's functions) but in the course of the struggle injures Baloo, Mowgli's protector. This second event realises the eighth function of the model where the Villain hurts a member of the Hero's circle of family and friends. Hero and Villain eventually join in combat (function sixteen), and in the course of the struggle Mowgli uses fire (function twelve, the intercession of a magical agent) in order to scare off Shere Khan (function eighteen, the Villain is vanquished). Mowgli, having been enticed by the 'water girl' and her song, eventually goes back to the 'man village', and so the film concludes with the realisation of function twenty, the Hero returning home, and with perhaps the suggestion that the Hero will eventually be married or crowned (function thirty-one).

Clearly, not all of the thirty-one plot advancing functions are present in Disney's cartoon, but those that are realised square very closely indeed with the key Proppian categories. This is not to suggest that the makers of Disney's film worked to any kind of explicit blueprint of narrative structure – a copy of Propp is unlikely to have been to hand in the production process! The main issue is really about what makes a good story. Disney's cartoon draws out, from a finite list of universalised functions, a specific selection of plot advancing devices. What is interesting is that even though their particular settings, 'dramatic personae' and historical periods may change, a great many Disney films work to the same basic plot typology.

Columbus's film *Harry Potter and the Philosopher's Stone* (2000) is some fifty minutes longer than *The Jungle Book* and is pitched at older viewers, so its even fuller display of Proppian functions is perhaps no surprise. A running commentary on all realisations in the film would be rather dull, so Table B5.1 shows the main connections between Propp's model and the narrative functions realised in *Harry Potter*. The left of the table displays a category of the model, numbered in accordance with Propp's own sequence of functions, and on the right of the table is a short summary

Table B5.1 Propp's model and *Harry Potter and the Philosopher's Stone*

Propp's function	Narrative event in *Harry Potter and the Philosopher's Stone*
1. Hero absents himself	Harry Potter [Hero] has been orphaned and is forced to live in the home of his cruel aunt and uncle, the Dursleys.
2. Hero receives interdiction	Harry is told by the Dursleys *not* to go to Hogwart's school of wizardry
3. Interdiction is violated	Harry goes to Hogwart's school of wizardry
6. Villain attempts to deceive or to take possession	Unknown to all, Voldemort [Villain] has taken over the body of Professor Quirrel.
8. Villain harms member of Hero's family	Harry learns that Voldemort has killed his parents.
9. This harm made known: Hero goes/ is sent on a mission	Harry embarks on a mission to recover the philosopher's stone.
12. Hero gets helper and/ or magical agent	Harry receives (unexpectedly) a top-of-the-range broomstick, a Nimbus 2000.
25. Difficult task set for Hero	Harry is charged with retrieving the 'golden snitch' in a game of Quidditch.
14. Hero uses magical agent.	Harry uses the Nimbus 2000 in the Quidditch game.
26. Task is accomplished.	Harry successfully retrieves the golden snitch.
16. Hero and Villain join in combat	Harry and Voldemort join combat.
17. Hero is branded	Harry has acquired a lightning-shaped scar through an earlier encounter with Voldemort.
28. False Hero is exposed	Quirrel exposed as the host of Voldemort.
29. False Hero is transformed	Quirrel transformed into dust during the combat.
18. Villain is defeated	Voldemort is defeated.
30. Villain is punished	Voldemort forced to leave the body of his dead host.
19. Initial misfortune is set right.	In the Hogwart's school competition, Harry's house Gryffindor is reinstated above their cheating rivals Slytherin.
20. Hero returns home	Harry leaves Hogwart's for the summer recess.

of the relevant plot development and character role as realised in the film. It is noticeable that certain of the narrative functions in the film are slightly out of kilter with the sequence developed in Propp. For example, Harry's parents have been killed by Voldemort prior to the first action of the film, yet Harry only later discovers this and to some extent relives the episode through flashback. Nonetheless, the sometime reordering and indeed repetition of the core narrative functions is precisely what the Proppian model seeks to accommodate, and in actual narrative discourse the use of flashback, prevision and other devices are markers of individuality in the story (see B7). It is interesting also that in neither of the two films are *all* of Propp's thirty-one functions drawn upon, but as we have seen, not all functions are needed to create a coherent narrative. What the identification of features shows, especially in the context of the *Harry Potter* checklist, is that many of the archetypical patterns that inform fairy stories are alive and well in certain genres of contemporary narrative. Admittedly, both film texts examined here are magical, mythical adventures much in the vein of the folktale, so the success with which the Proppian model can accommodate *all* narrative genres remains to be proven. Nonetheless, a narrative genre like the Western, whether embodied in film or prose media, seems an obvious candidate for scrutiny, as might the romance, the detective story or the science fiction story. If anything, the import of Propp's model is not to suggest that all narratives are the same, but rather to explain in part why all narratives are different.

The focus in the next unit along this thread explores narrative through another type of textual medium, the narrative of everyday spoken interaction. The unit below concentrates on narrative as discourse and assesses some of the developments that have taken place in the use of transitivity for narrative analysis.

B6 STYLE AND TRANSITIVITY

Writing about narrative, the American novelist Henry James once posed a pair of rhetorical questions: 'What is character but the determination of incident? What is incident but the illustration of character?'. The integration of 'character' and 'incident' may at first glance seem a curious alignment, but closer scrutiny suggests that James's formula serves very much as a template for the analysis of *transitivity* in narrative. In the model proposed in unit A5, it was suggested that a principal mode of narrative characterisation is the transmission of 'actions and events'. This mode refers to the way character is developed through and by the semantic processes and participant roles embodied in narrative discourse. Character may for instance be determined by degree of influence on narrative incidents, by degree of active involvement in the forward momentum of the plot. Alternatively, character may be determined by detachment from narrative incident, by the positioning, say, of an individual as a passive observer of the events that unfold around them. As noted here and elsewhere, the linguistic framework which encompasses this aspect of narrative organisation is transitivity and this unit will review two of the various applications this model has received in narrative stylistics.

Developments in the analysis of style and transitivity

Over the years, stylisticians have returned regularly to the transitivity model in their analyses of text, and especially in their analyses of narrative text. One particular study, recognised as one of the key early essays in modern stylistics, was conducted by the eminent functional linguist M. A. K. Halliday (1971), architect of the very model of transitivity which informs this strand. In that now classic paper, Halliday applies the framework to William Golding's novel *The Inheritors* and explores, amongst other things, the linguistic patterns which encode the 'mind-styles' of the various Neanderthal peoples who inhabit the story. Whereas the bulk of the novel is narrated from the perspective of Lok, one of a primitive group of Neanderthals, the later stages of the book see Lok and his people supplanted by a more advanced tribe. Halliday argues that choices in transitivity reflect this transition. The behaviour of Lok's tribe is depicted as discontinuous and rather aimless, where physical action rarely affects objects in the immediate environment. In more explicitly experiential terms (see A6), 'Lok language' is marked consistently by material processes which realise an Actor element but no Goal element, in clauses like: 'A stick rose upright' or 'The bushes twitched'. Significantly, these Goal-less processes make the action specified seem self-engendered, even when it is clear from the narrative context that they are brought about by the external agency of Lok's enemies. Lok's failure to see a 'joined up' world of actions and events is therefore conveyed through systematic choices in transitivity, although no such failure in understanding is embodied by the transitivity patterns of the more advanced tribe whose way of configuring the world is, according to Halliday, more like our own.

Halliday's study is important in a number of respects. By using narrative discourse as a test site for a particular model of language, it illustrates well the usefulness of stylistic analysis as a way of exploring both literature *and* language. It also shows how intuitions and hunches about a text (and yes, stylisticians rely on intuitions and hunches) can be explored systematically and with rigour using a retrievable procedure of analysis. That is not to say, however, that Halliday's pioneering analysis was entirely flawless in its design or uncontroversial with respect to the scholarly reception it received. By suggesting that the text's linguistic structure embodies its meaning as discourse, Halliday does make a very strongly 'mimetic' (see B4) claim about the explanatory power of the transitivity model. He argues for instance in respect of 'Lok language' that it is no doubt 'a fair summary of the life of the Neanderthal man' (1971: 350). The methods employed in his study, and this sentiment in particular, are what stimulated Stanley Fish's well-known critique of stylistics, facetiously entitled 'What is stylistics and why are they saying such terrible things about it?', which followed in the wake of Halliday's analysis (Fish 1981: 59–64). Although this is not the place to review that debate in detail, Fish's attack continues to attract rebuttals from stylisticians to the present day, and the polemic has proved important in helping shape the way stylisticians think about the connections between analysis and interpretation (see the further reading suggestion for this unit given at the end of the book).

Several years after Halliday's study, Kennedy used the transitivity model to explore a key passage from Joseph Conrad's novel *The Secret Agent* (Kennedy 1982). In this climactic scene of the story, Mrs Verloc, who has just discovered that her husband has been involved in the death of her brother Stevie, kills a seated Mr Verloc with a carving knife. What is of particular interest to Kennedy is the manner by which Mr Verloc's death is described. For example, in over four hundred words of narrative description, it is striking that no mental processes at all are attributed to Mrs Verloc, giving little if any indication of what this character feels, thinks or perceives. Moreover, although one would anticipate that Mrs Verloc would feature in some material processes – she is after all the 'doer' of the killing – very few of the processes that are realised are Goal-directed. Instead, Goal-less patterns like the following are common: 'She started forward . . .', 'she had passed on towards the sofa . . .'. Mrs Verloc is thus represented as a character whose actions are done seemingly without reflection and without directly affecting the entities (including her husband) that surround her.

The pattern of transitivity which defines Mr Verloc is rather different. He participates in a few non-Goal directed material processes, such as 'He waited . . .' or 'He was lying on his back . . .'. In fact, some of these sequences, like 'He stared at the ceiling', would be coded in the later version of the transitivity model (see A6) as *behavioural* processes insofar as they tend to straddle the interface between material and mental processes. However, the overwhelming majority of the processes ascribed to Verloc are full-blown mental processes which feature him in the role of Sensor and which normally include a Phenomenon element. Patterns like the following are the norm: 'Mr Verloc heard the creaky plank in the floor'; 'He saw partly on the ceiling and partly on the wall the moving shadow of an arm'; 'Mr Verloc [recognised] the limb and the weapon.'. Thus, Verloc is portrayed as someone who is thoroughly aware of everything that is going on around him, yet in spite of his mental acuity, paradoxically, is unable to instigate the action necessary to prevent his own death. By contrast, his wife is portrayed as an insensate being, and as a being whose physical actions rarely influence any external objects in her environment.

The question which these two different characterisations-in-transitivity raise, then, is how is it that Mr Verloc comes, as it were, to be dead? One technique Conrad uses is simply to push the narrative forwards by using material processes with non-human Actors. In this respect, the sequence 'the carving knife had vanished' is especially revealing. A similar technique is the use of the passive (see A6) which allows the deletion of any human Actor that might be responsible for a process: 'The knife was already planted in his breast' is, again, a telling sequence. So, while Mrs Verloc may in the strictest sense be the killer of Mr Verloc, that is not what the transitivity profile of Conrad's text asks us to see.

Conrad employs a further stylistic technique known as *meronymic agency*, the use of which to some extent unites the interests of both Kennedy and Halliday. A slightly misleading term in that 'metonymy' (A11) is the concept which informs it, meronymic agency involves the part 'standing for' the whole in such a way as to place a human body part, rather than a whole person, in the role of an Actor, Sensor, Sayer and so on. This technique stands in contrast to the default position, known as *holonymic agency*, where the participant role is occupied by a complete being. Although not articulated explicitly in either paper, much of what Mrs Verloc does and most of what Lok does is, in experiential terms, carried out through the intercession of their body parts. For instance, it is Mrs Verloc's hand, never 'Mrs Verloc', which acts in key Goal-directed processes in the passage like 'Her right hand skimmed lightly the end of the table' and 'a clenched hand [was] holding a carving knife'. By contrast, Lok's nose and ears seem to do most of the work for him: 'His nose smelled this stuff', 'His ears twitched' and so on. Although these meronyms do different stylistic jobs in their respective narrative contexts, this type of agency is a recurring feature in the transitivity profile of many types of prose fiction. The (literal) disembodiment of a character often makes what they do, say or think appear involuntary, cut adrift from conscious intervention. It can also serve to differentiate the character experientially from other characters who are portrayed, say, in holonymic terms. Importantly, the technique sometimes connects a style of writing with a particular literary genre. This particular theme is resumed across the way in unit C6 where some observations are made on how the transitivity model can be extended to account for these broader dimensions of style. In the unit below, attention turns to the concept of point of view, which is a facet of narrative characterisation which complements well patterns of transitivity.

APPROACHES TO POINT OF VIEW

B7

The first unit along this thread introduced some basic terms and categories for the study of point of view in narrative. It was noted in that unit that a great deal has been written on, and various models have been proposed for, the stylistic analysis of point of view in prose fiction. This unit provides an opportunity to review some important developments in point of view studies as well as to 'tidy up' theoretically some of the competing models of analysis.

Planes of point of view in narrative fiction

In an influential publication on prose composition, the narratologist Boris Uspensky proposed a four-way model for the study of point of view in fiction (Uspensky 1973). This model was later revised and refined by Roger Fowler (Fowler 1996 [1986]: 127–47) so it is probably best to refer to this composite framework of analysis as the 'Fowler-Uspensky model'. The four components identified by the Fowler-Uspensky model of point of view are as follows:

(i) point of view on the *ideological* plane
(ii) point of view on the *temporal* plane
(iii) point of view on the *spatial* plane
(iv) point of view on the *psychological* plane

The broad compass of the model has proved significant in shaping much stylistic work on point of view because it helps sort out different components in narrative organisation. However, certain aspects of it are rather confusing and the review which follows will suggest some simplification and realignment of its four categories. But first, to definitions of the four categories themselves.

Point of view on the ideological plane

The term *ideology* has a wide scope of reference. It refers to the matrix of beliefs we use to comprehend the world and to the value systems through and by which we interact in society. It follows then that the concept of point of view on the ideological plane refers to the way in which a text mediates a set of particular ideological beliefs through either character, narrator or author. Of authorial ideology, Fowler notes how Tolstoy's Christianity, Lawrence's celebration of sexuality and Orwell's hatred of totalitarianism shape respectively the ideologies articulated in their work. Narratives also manifest ideology at the level of character, where the ideas expressed by fictional characters serve as vehicles for ideologies which may or may not accord with those of the real author. For example, the character of 'the Citizen' in the 'Cyclops' episode of Joyce's *Ulysses* is portrayed as a republican ideologue whose short-sighted and philistine outlook cuts across the other ideological positions set up in and by the text. Indeed, it is a tenet of the Fowler-Uspensky model that the more the different value systems articulated in a work compete with one another then the richer and more interesting becomes the work itself.

In the course of his adaptation of Uspensky's ideas on ideological point of view, Fowler makes the telling comment that a novel 'gives an interpretation of the world it represents' (1996: 130). This immediately begs the question: what sort of narrative, whether prose fiction or oral story of everyday experience, does *not* give an interpretation of the world it represents? Furthermore, what type of text – drama, poetry or prose – is *not* ultimately enshrined in some framework of ideology? These are important questions and they highlight the problems that are attendant on trying to align a particularised narrative technique like point of view with an all-embracing concept like 'ideology'. Indeed, the domain of ideology is so broad that just about any aspect of narrative can be brought within its compass, whether it be a facet of narrative 'voice' like author, narrator, character or persona, or an element of narrative 'preoccupation' like emblem, theme, motif, and most important of all, characterisation. What has tended to happen in much narrative stylistics is that ideological point of view has become an all too accommodating 'bucket category' into which more narrowly defined elements of narrative organisation are placed. A result of this practice is that some of the more subtle nuances of textual meaning are glided over. In sum, the concept of ideological point of view, if tempting as an analytic tool, needs to be treated with some caution because it is simply too wide to have much explanatory power. A good case for a fully workable category of ideological point of view remains to be made.

Point of view on the temporal plane

If the first category of the point of view model tends to be rather too broad to be usefully serviceable, the second tends arguably to be somewhat misplaced in the overall context of narrative. Point of view on the temporal plane, in the terms of the

Fowler-Uspensky model, is about the way relationships of time are signalled in narrative. Temporal point of view envelops a whole series of stylistic techniques such as *repetition*, *analepsis* (flashback) and *prolepsis* (prevision or flashforward). In the reading which comprises unit D5, Mick Short examines a number of these aspects of temporal point of view in Irvine Welsh's novel *Marabou Stork Nightmares*. Welsh's narrative exploits narrative time relationships in challenging ways; beginning in the narrating present, it relives the bulk of the story, including a parallel fantasy narrative, as flashback. Another temporal technique, known as *duration* (Genette 1980: 86), relates to the temporal span of a story and accounts for our impression of the way certain events may be accelerated or decelerated. Whereas the entire sweep of, say, Joyce's *Ulysses* is confined to a single day, one paragraph of Virginia Woolf's *To the Lighthouse* marks a twenty-year interval – two extremes of the concept of duration. Temporal point of view basically covers any kind of manipulation of time sequence in narrative, explaining how certain events might be relayed as remote or distant, others as immediate or imminent.

Temporal point of view is certainly an important narrative category, but the question is still begged as to where precisely it should be situated in a multi-dimensional narrative model of the sort proposed in A5. In fact, if we think through the organisation of that model, temporal point of view seems to be less about focalisation and viewpoint and rather more about narrative structure; it does after all encompass the structural segments and sequential progression of the time-line of a narrative. Much of what is analysed under the umbrella term 'temporal point of view' is to do with temporal organisation as it relates to narrative structure. My suggestion is, again, to approach this admittedly useful concept with some caution.

Point of view on the spatial and psychological planes

If the first two categories of the Fowler-Uspensky model are not exactly watertight theoretically, the goods news, so to speak, is that the remaining two, spatial and psychological point of view, really do embody the core characteristics of the concept. Exploration of these two categories will take us through to the end of this unit. Spatial point of view, as demonstrated in unit A7, is about the narrative 'camera angle' and is a device which has palpable grammatical exponents in deixis and in locative expressions. The passage from Iain Banks's *The Crow Road*, where the character of McHoan acted as reflector, illustrated well how these linguistic markers work to establish spatial point of view in a text. However, there were in addition to those indices of physical viewpoint a number of other stylistic markers, such as references to the reflector's senses, thoughts and feelings, which suggested that a more internalised, psychological perspective had been adopted. Uspensky classifies such cases where 'the authorial point of view relies on an individual consciousness (or perception)' as point of view on the *psychological* plane (Uspensky 1973: 81). This formula also hints (in its reference to 'perception') that spatial viewpoint is really one dimension of the broader technique of psychological point of view.

To develop further this idea of the interplay between spatial and psychological point of view, consider by way of illustration the following passage from Ian McEwan's novel *Amsterdam*. In this episode Rose Garmony, an eminent surgeon whose politician husband has just become embroiled in a political scandal, awakes to find nine members of the press outside her London apartment:

> . . . she stared down at the group – there were nine of them now – with controlled fascination. The man had collapsed his extendable pole and had rested it against the railings. One of the others was bringing a tray of coffees from the takeaway shop on Horseferry Road. What could they ever hope to get that they didn't already have? And so early in the morning. What sort of satisfaction could they have from this kind of work? And why was it they looked so alike, these doorsteppers, as though drawn from one tiny gene puddle of humanity?
>
> (McEwan 1998: 94–5)

What happens in this passage is that spatial perspective dovetails with and indeed shades into psychological perspective. Rose Garmony is clearly the reflector of fiction throughout the passage, and her viewing position is established early on with locative expressions like 'down at the group' and deictic markers referring, for instance, to one member of the group 'bringing' (as opposed to 'taking') a tray of coffees. Like an establishing shot in visual film narrative, Rose's demeanour is caught as she stares down at the group; thereafter, a point of view shot shows us what she sees. However, the overall dynamic of point of view development does not stop there. The sequence beginning 'What could they ever hope . . .' marks a further shift into the conscious thought processes of Rose Garmony as she watches the paparazzi outside her home, a pattern which is sustained for the remainder of the passage. Her thoughts are tracked by means of a special mode of thought presentation known as Free Indirect Thought, on which there will be more in the unit below.

It is important to stress that the type of point of view development identified in the McEwan passage, where a spatial perspective shifts almost seamlessly into the cognitive field of a character, is an extremely common progression in prose fiction. Whereas the passage is focalised entirely from Rose's point of view, the slip from her role as anchor for spatial viewpoint into her role as conscious thinker is almost imperceptible, and is in part achieved through the particular device employed for representing her thoughts. This suggests that there are good grounds for subsuming the category of spatial point of view into the broader category of psychological point of view. In fictional narrative, psychological point of view is an extremely rich site for stylistic creativity and this issue will explored more fully along this strand in C7. The unit below considers some of the key techniques of speech and thought presentation, one of which has already been hinted at in this unit.

B8 TECHNIQUES OF SPEECH AND THOUGHT PRESENTATION

Unit A8 introduced a basic model for assessing how speech and thought is represented in narrative while in B7, some observations were made on different planes of point of view in prose fiction. This unit offers, amongst other things, an opportunity to 'marry' both topics by examining the way both narratorial viewpoint and character perspective can be mediated through techniques of speech and thought presentation. The following sub-unit will look at the more indirect techniques, dealing particularly with the special category of Free Indirect Discourse. Then, attention focuses on some of the more direct forms of speech and thought presentation, with particular emphasis on the Free Direct mode, in both its speech and thought guises. The final sub-unit offers a short commentary on the connections between point of view and speech and thought presentation.

Indirect discourse presentation

Whatever the particular category used, all of the techniques of speech and thought presentation represent a shift away from basic narrative structure towards the discourse of a particular character. The external narrative structure onto which the modes of speech and thought are grafted is referred to as Narrator's Representation of Action (NRA). It describes the actions, perceptions and states that occur in the world of the fiction; it basically encompasses all non-speech and non-thought phenomena (see Short 1996: 292). As noted in the first unit of this strand, the most 'minimal' transition into a character's speech or thought is where a narrator reports that speech or thought has taken place but offers no indication or flavour of the *actual* words used. Narrative Report (of speech/thought) thus marks the first step away, as it were, from NRA and although it is often used to summarise whole stretches of reported speech or thought, that is not the only narrative function it serves. Consider the following episode from Henry Fielding's novel *Tom Jones*. Here the eponymous hero, although required to leave the room midway through the encounter, finds himself momentarily in the company of some 'great personages':

> . . . the conversation began to be, as the phrase is, extremely brilliant. However, as nothing past in it which can be thought material to this history, or indeed, very material in itself, I shall omit the relation; the rather as I have known some very fine polite conversation grow extremely dull, when transcribed into books [. . .]
>
> He [Tom Jones] was no sooner gone, than the great personages who had taken no notice of him present, began to take much notice of him in his absence; but if the reader hath already excused us from relating the more brilliant part of this conversation, he will be very ready to excuse the repetition of what may be called vulgar abuse . . .
>
> (Fielding 1970 [1749]: 277–8)

Fielding rather subtly uses the Narrative Report of Speech (NRS) mode both as a mechanism for compressing a sequence of extended dialogue and as an ironising device to critique the 'great personages'. With characteristically false modesty, Fielding's narrator politely demurs from transcribing such reputedly 'fine' talk thereby portraying as arid and effete the conversation of the assembled socialites.

Of all the categories of the speech and thought framework, there is one mode that has come under particular scrutiny from a stylistic perspective. This mode is Free Indirect Discourse (FID), a term which usefully subsumes both its speech (FIS) and thought (FIT) variants. The importance of this narrative technique is evidenced in the existence of numerous other terms for it, such as *erleßte rede*, 'indirect interior monologue' and *style indirect libre.* What is of especial interest to stylisticians is the impression this mode gives of both a character and narrator speaking simultaneously, through a kind of 'dual voice' (yet another term for FID!). Recalling the definition offered in A8, this mode displays all the features of indirectness but, crucially, it lacks a reporting clause and inverted commas. Consider the following brief example of the technique 'at work'. In this passage from Malcolm Lowry's novel *Under the Volcano*, M. Laruelle is contemplating his future in Mexico just before, in the second paragraph, his thoughts turn abruptly and rather more trivially towards the weather:

> Yet in the Earthly Paradise, what had he done? He had made few friends. He had acquired a Mexican mistress with whom he quarrelled, and numerous beautiful Mayan idols he would be unable to take out of the country, and he had –
>
> M. Laruelle wondered if it was going to rain . . .
>
> (Lowry 1984 [1947]: 16)

To give some idea of how effective this first paragraph of FIT is and of how smoothly it blends, or gives the impression of blending, both narrator and character voices, it is worth rewriting it in another mode. A useful technique in stylistic analysis, the transposition of a passage into other structural possibilities often sheds light on the subtleties of its textual composition. If for example the passage were written as Direct Thought (see the criteria in A8), the result would be rather more stilted and contrived in feel:

> 'Yet in the Earthly Paradise, what have I done?' he wondered. 'I have made few friends', he thought to himself. He pondered, 'I have acquired a Mexican mistress with whom I quarrel . . .'

Alternatively, a Free Direct version (see A8), which would dispense with both reporting clauses and inverted commas, would certainly add some immediacy to the narrative representation:

> Yet in the Earthly Paradise, what have I done? I have made few friends. I have acquired a Mexican mistress with whom I quarrel . . .

With respect to Lowry's original, however, the stylistic force of the Free Indirect mode inheres in its seeming coalescence of the thoughts of the character with the structural framework, including deixis and tense, of a third-person heterodiegetic narrative. This coalescence results in an apparent blurring of focus where it is often difficult to distinguish whether the thoughts relayed are to be attributed to a participating character or to the external third-person narrator. This explains to some extent the jolt delivered by the second paragraph as it shifts into the Indirect Speech mode: the dual voice of FIT evaporates as the narrative thread is brought more tightly under the control of the narrator. In fact, such is the schism between the IS and FIT modes here that it even suggests that M. Laruelle is someone other than the reflector of fiction in the paragraph preceding.

These general principles of FID apply to third-person narratives, narratives which offer the opportunity to fashion a seeming split between the voices of character and narrator. What, then, of first-person narratives where narrator and character may be one and the same entity? In other words, how does FID work in *homodiegetic* as opposed to heterodiegetic fiction? To answer these questions, consider first of all the following extract from a homodiegetic narrative written in the first person:

> Wednesday. In the afternoon, Haze (Common-sensical shoes, tailor-made dress) said she was driving downtown to buy a present for a friend of a friend of hers, and would I please come too because I have such a wonderful taste in textures and perfumes. 'Choose your favourite seduction,' she purred.
>
> (Lolita; Nabokov 1986 [1955]: 50)

Here, in what is a very common type of staged progression in narrative, a sequence begins in Indirect Speech ('Haze said she was driving downtown'), then 'slips' into more free and more direct forms, before culminating in Direct Speech ('Choose your favourite seduction', she purred.'). This sequence contains a transitional sequence of FIS: 'Would I please come too because I have such a wonderful taste in textures and perfumes.' Now, the criteria for identifying FID in a first-person, as opposed to third-person, narrative are slightly different because of a variation in the overall pronoun system of the homodiegetic narrative. In reported speech, any second person pronouns used to address the character-narrator are switched, not to the third person, but to the *first* person. Whereas the FIS sequence highlighted does *not* capture the exact words that would have been said to the narrator, a Direct Speech rendition of it would ('Will *you* please come too . . .'), thereby bringing it into line with the actual DS sequence following ('Choose *your* favourite seduction'). So although much of its stylistic import remains the same, Free Indirect Discourse in first-person narratives behaves structurally rather differently from that used in third-person narratives.

Direct discourse presentation

The Free Direct modes of speech and thought presentation have a very different kind of stylistic currency compared to their counterparts in the Free Indirect modes. For example, Free Direct Thought (FDT) is the mainstay of the so-called 'stream of consciousness' technique of prose writing. This technique involves supplementing FDT with a type of grammatical abbreviation known as *ellipsis*, to produce a fast-paced flow of sometimes fragmentary or partial thoughts as they enter the consciousness of a character or narrator. Here is a brief example of the method at work. Taken from 'The Lotus Eaters' episode of Joyce's *Ulysses*, this fragment details Bloom's encounter with Bantam Lyons outside a chemist's:

> Shaved off his moustache again, by Jove! Long cold upper lip. To look younger. He does look balmy. Younger than I am.
>
> (Joyce 1980 [1922]: 86)

It is the highly elliptical quality of the Free Direct Thought here, often pared down to its grammatical bare bones, which engenders the 'stream of consciousness' effect.

By imputation, then, this means that not all uses of FDT constitute stream of consciousness. For example, the earlier transposition of the Lowry extract into FDT took it only part of the way towards a fully fledged stream of consciousness style. Although that short passage seems not to lend itself especially well to ellipsis, here is an attempt to push it that little bit further towards stream of consciousness:

> In the Earthly Paradise. But what have I done? Few friends.
> Mexican mistress, acquired. We quarrel.

Further discussion of the stream of consciousness technique, with a more cognitively driven account of its stylistic impact, is developed in C10.

It is a simple rule of thumb of speech and thought presentation that the more free and/or direct the mode of presentation, the more a narrator's control over what was thought or said diminishes; so much so that a character is permitted ultimately to express thoughts or speech in a seemingly unmediated way. In the speech presentation mode, the freest and most direct form is Free Direct Speech, which is characterised by the loss of reporting clauses or inverted commas, or both. In prose fiction, one of the stylistic functions of FDS is to give an impression of untrammelled, free-flowing dialogue between characters. Here is a second example from Ian McEwan's novel *Amsterdam* (see B7) involving one of the novel's central characters, newspaper editor Vernon Halliday. Arriving late to his office, Halliday finds that a queue of subeditors and secretaries awaits him:

> . . . Everyone moved with him. Ball was saying, 'This Middlesbrough photo. I'd like to avoid the trouble we got into over the wheelchair Olympics. I thought we'd go for something pretty straightforward . . .'
>
> 'I want an exciting picture, Jeremy. I can't see them in the same week, Jean. It wouldn't look right. Tell him Thursday.'
>
> 'I had in mind an upright Victorian sort of thing. A dignified portrait.'
>
> 'He's leaving for Angola. The idea was he'd go straight out to Heathrow as soon as he'd seen you.'
>
> 'Mr Halliday?'
>
> 'I don't want dignified portraits, even in obits. Get them to show us how they gave each other the bite marks. OK, I'll see him before he leaves. Tony, is this about the parking?'
>
> (McEwan 1998: 39–40)

When narrated in the Free Direct Speech mode, the sheer weight of the multiple and varied requests to Vernon Halliday makes it very difficult both to follow the topic switches in this interaction and to ascertain which interlocutor is asking which question. After the opening sequence of Direct Speech, reporting clauses disappear altogether as the dialogue picks up momentum. True, there are some clues in the form of *vocatives* which help identify who is speaking at certain times. These terms of address, such as 'Jeremy', 'Jean', 'Tony' and 'Mr. Halliday', serve a deictic function by pointing out the intended addressee of a particular utterance. Aside from that, however, the use of FDS gives a kind of 'meaningful incoherence' to this dialogue insofar as it consolidates the impression of a busy newspaper editor who, on entering his office, is subject to a rapid-fire question and answer routine involving disparate and numerous topics.

Character viewpoint and speech and thought presentation

As a broad principle, when a character's speech or thought processes are represented, we see things, even if momentarily, from that character's point of view. However, the reverse does not necessarily apply, which is to say that it is possible to be located within a character's viewpoint without any of the formal modes of speech and thought presentation being employed. Consider again the passage from McEwan's *Amsterdam* which was examined in B7. It was noted that the first part of this passage anchors spatial point of view within the perspective of a particular character while the second part relays the active and (self)conscious thought processes of that same character through Free Indirect Thought. The FIT strand 'kicks in' in the second sentence of this sequence

> One of the others was bringing a tray of coffees from the takeaway shop on Horseferry Road. What could they ever hope to get that they didn't already have?

and continues right to the end of the passage (and it can be tested by transpositions of the sort suggested here and elsewhere). However, the point at issue is that only in the latter half of the passage is Free Indirect Thought used even though the character of Rose Garmony has consistently been the reflector of fiction for the entire passage. Thus, whereas the psychological point of view adopted is hers throughout, it is only in part delivered by a formal mode of thought presentation.

This unit is developed along its horizontal axis in unit C8, which offers some further extensions and applications of the speech and thought model elaborated in A8. Along the vertical axis, the interactive dimensions of speech and dialogue are developed. Unit B9 uses techniques in discourse analysis to explore fictional dialogue, although the focus switches from speech in novels to interaction between characters in plays.

DIALOGUE IN DRAMA

B9

Across in A9, a model for the analysis of dialogue was suggested which comprised two principal methodological orientations. The first of these involves a focus on the way spoken discourse is *structured*; on how it is organised in a linear fashion and how its various components are bolted together. A structural analysis of discourse thus seeks to explore the connection (or sometimes, lack of connection) in dialogue between questions and answers, statements and acknowledgements, requests and reactions, and so on. The second orientation involves the study of discourse in terms of *strategy*. Here attention is focussed on the way speakers use different interactive tactics at specific points during a sequence of talk. As observed in A9, the axis of selection forms a strategic continuum ranging from 'direct' to 'indirect', along which different types of utterances can be plotted in terms of their varying degrees of politeness.

If not always signalled in precisely these terms, most stylistic research on drama dialogue over the years has focussed on one or the other planes of organisation. The main thrust of this work, again not always flagged up explicitly, has been both to explain how characterisation is created through patterns of language and to highlight the points of departure and/or intersection between the discourse world of the play and the discourse situation of the world outside the play. This short unit surveys some of the issues and developments arising from this research in discourse stylistics.

The strategies of dialogue

Analysing play dialogue in terms of discourse *strategy* often involves cross-reference between the character level and the higher-order interactive level of playwright and audience/reader (see A9). Not surprisingly, many interesting insights have come from studies of the 'Theatre of the Absurd' where particularly rich comparisons can be drawn between the discourse worlds inside and outside the play. The tradition of absurd writing is characterised by a preoccupation with the apparent futility of human existence, and this often manifests in play talk that, when compared to the socio-linguistic routines of everyday verbal interaction, stands out as deviant, anti-realist or just plain daft.

Here is a brief and relatively straightforward example of how our expectations about discourse routines can act as a context-framing device for interpreting play dialogue. In the following scene from N. F. Simpson's absurdist play *One Way Pendulum*, a courtroom has been hastily assembled inside a domestic living room to facilitate Mr. Groomkirby's 'swearing in' ceremony:

> *The Usher enters followed by Mr. Groomkirby, whom he directs into the witness box. Mr. Groomkirby takes the oath.*
>
> Mr. Groomkirby: (*holding up a copy of 'Uncle Tom's Cabin'*)
> I swear, by Harriet Beecher Stowe, that the evidence I shall give shall be the truth, the whole truth, and nothing but the truth.
>
> Judge: You understand, do you, that you are now on oath?
>
> Mr. Groomkirby: I do, m'lord.
>
> (N. F. Simpson 1960: 60)

A courtroom is institutionally sanctioned to deal exclusively with legal proceedings, and is manifestly not the sort of thing that can be set up by anybody in, for example, a domestic living room. Furthermore, there are established procedures for ritualised activities such as the swearing-in of witnesses, and shared assumptions between participants about the way these routines are conducted thus form part of the cognitive context of the courtroom. Although Mr. Groomkirby's 'swearing-in' contains many instantly recognisable formulaic structures such as ' . . . the truth, the whole truth and nothing but the truth . . .', the use of *Uncle Tom's Cabin* clearly violates the pragmatic conditions which govern this ritual. These conditions, known as *felicity conditions* (Austin 1962: 39), proscribe the swearing in of a witness by anything other than a designated religious text – irrespective of its literary merit. What operates in the discourse world inside the play, then, is thoroughly at odds with the sanctioned routines of the world *outside* the play.

As a footnote to this commentary, it is worth noting how the judge expresses no surprise at the general procedures of Groomkirby's swearing-in ceremony. Were the judge to have outlawed *Uncle Tom's Cabin* and declared the swearing-in inadmissible, as presumably any judge in the 'real' world would do, then this appeal to everyday modes of conduct would have lessened greatly the absurdity of the sequence. The responses of interlocutors at the character level to something that is unanticipated at the higher-order interactive level, such as the Judge's reaction to Mr. Groomkirby's use of *Uncle Tom's Cabin*, is often an important index of dramatic genre. Absurdist, as opposed to realist, drama tends to make use of a special kind of incongruity that comes from a mismatch between communicative strategy and discourse context, often deriving from fictional speakers *not* observing the familiar or expected routines that are cued by everyday discourse contexts. And these incongruities often have humorous outcomes (see further A12).

The structure of dialogue

One of the most significant studies of the structures of play talk is Deirdre Burton's book on dialogue and discourse (Burton 1980). Burton investigates a number of play texts using a variety of different models in conversation analysis and speech act theory (see for example C5). Her book culminates with a lengthy breakdown of Harold Pinter's play *The Dumb Waiter* (1960) using a single model of discourse structure, although it has to be said that the more eclectic chapters leading up to this analysis offer rather more stylistic insight than this longer analysis. That aside, the thrust of her structural analysis is very much in keeping with the rationale of stylistics in that it seeks to base interpretation on rigorous and retrievable methods of analysis.

As an illustration of the sorts of issues Burton's study raises, consider the following short extract from *The Dumb Waiter*:

GUS: I want to ask you something.
BEN: [no response]
BEN: What are you doing out there?
GUS: Well I was just -
BEN: What about tea?
GUS: I'm just going to make it.
BEN: Well go on, make it.
GUS: Yes, I will.

(cited in Burton 1980: 161–2)

The point of Burton's structural breakdown of this passage is to uncover patterns of dialogue which serve to delineate character. For example, in 'I want to ask you something', Gus attempts to initiate an exchange (see A9), although Ben fails to provide the anticipated second part to this. Furthermore, Gus's initiation is couched in the form of a discourse act known as a *metastatement.* Metastatements work as organising devices, but function more as 'language about language' than as information-carrying units of discourse in their own right. This request for permission to hold the floor is of course rebuffed by his interlocutor, who immediately initiates his own 'question and answer' exchange which this time does elicit a reply from his interlocutor. It is noticeable that Gus is prevented from finishing his reply before Ben opens up a new 'request and reaction' type exchange with 'What about tea?'. And so, across many speaker turns in the play, this pattern of exchanges becomes established into a consistent design in discourse structure.

Burton draws a number of conclusions from this design, but the most important, as noted earlier, is to do with characterisation. The unequal statuses of the participants, she argues, are reflected in the structure of dialogue (1980: 70). On the one hand, Ben is the dominating interactant, the confident director of operations and persons, although there are occasional sequences of talk where his frailer side comes to the fore. Gus, in spite of the odd battle for superiority, is the inferior interactant who as 'victim' gains audience sympathy by the end of the play. Interestingly, Burton makes a number of connections between the structure of Pinter's dialogue and that of adult-to-child interaction. The means by which Ben for example asserts his conversational dominance bears much similarity to the patterns other researchers have uncovered for the way adults interact with children. Gus's attempts at initiation, by contrast, resemble those of children who also tend to be less successful initiators of conversational exchanges. The overall point is that, in keeping with the schema developed in A9, the structures Burton uncovers in play talk become messages about those characters at the level of discourse between playwright and audience.

Summary: recent developments

Published over two decades after Burton's study, Culpeper's study of language and characterisation continues the tradition of exploring plays using stylistic and pragmatic models of discourse (Culpeper 2001). Concentrating particularly on the language of Shakespearean plays, Culpeper criticises traditional approaches to characterisation in literary criticism which tend to 'humanise' fictional characters as if they were real people in the real world. He argues that the discussion of characterisation in literature needs to be conducted with a firm grasp both of stylistic research on dialogue and also of relevant aspects of social psychology. It is this orientation towards social psychology that takes the study of discourse into a new territory, where the sorts of analyses undertaken across this thread are supplemented with ideas from cognitive linguistics. Culpeper points out for example that the process of inferring character from text relies in part on the cognitive structures and inferential mechanisms that readers have already developed for real-life people (2001: 10). This emphasis on the cognitive dimension in textual interpretation reflects a more recent general trend in modern stylistics, a trend which is the focus of the next unit.

DEVELOPMENTS IN COGNITIVE STYLISTICS

This unit offers an opportunity to firm up the broad ideas sketched in A10 by targeting more specifically some important developments in cognitive stylistics. Shortly, we will look at one of the main models in Artificial Intelligence (hereafter AI) to have found its way into this branch of stylistics. This theory has provided an insightful method for accounting for how we draw on stores of knowledge, and how we make conceptual transfers between these stores, when reading literary texts. Later, the emphasis shifts away from conceptual transfer to the idea of conceptual tracking. With specific reference to narrative, attention focusses on how we organise, retain and follow certain types of mental representation when reading fiction. Across the thread in C10, a range of activities are developed which apply and test these models of analysis.

Schema theory and discourse deviation

The adaptation by stylisticians of the AI model known as *schema theory* represents a significant landmark in cognitive stylistic research. Schema theory is an umbrella term covering a range of individual cognitive models at the heart of which are situated the core concept *schema* and the attendant concepts *frame*, *scenario* and *script*. One of the most significant developments in this field is Schank and Abelson's influential script-based model of human understanding and memory (Schank and Abelson 1977). In their terms, a script (and by imputation a schema) is a chunk of knowledge which describes 'a predetermined, stereotyped sequence of actions that defines a well-known situation' (Schank and Abelson 1977: 41). Scripts are expectation-based, preexisting knowledge stores, but they are also subject to modification in the course of an individual subject's experience and development. In other words, fresh incoming information interacts with what we already know, thereby causing us to modify our mental representations. This cognitive process was implicit in the development of the 'pub' scenario in A10.

The importance of the script-based framework lies mainly in its capacity to explain how we can understand texts without having to rely on explicit linguistic signals *in* the text (again, see A10). In respect of this issue, Schank and Abelson develop the famous, and now ubiquitous, 'restaurant script' (Schank and Abelson 1977: 42–9). The restaurant script is a knowledge structure which is activated by an essential precondition – that is, wanting to eat. The script is sustained further as a 'giant causal chain' by accompanying conceptual slots such as *roles*, which include sub-entries like WAITER and CUSTOMER, or *props*, with entries like TABLE and MENU (Schank and Abelson 1977: 43; and see A10). Importantly, scripts allow for new conceptualisations of objects within them just as if these objects had been previously mentioned, such that 'objects within a script may take 'the' without explicit introduction because the script itself has already implicitly introduced them' (Schank and Abelson 1977: 41). The precise nature of conceptualisations varies from one individual to another, and there is no obvious upper limit to the number of conceptualisations that can be invoked for every script. This potentially endless list of specifiable features has resulted in some criticism of the Schank and Abelson model, the theoretical implications of which must be left aside for now (see Stockwell 2002: 75–89 for a useful survey of the model).

Although superseded to some extent by more recent developments in AI, application of the schema model represented an important move in stylistics, away from a linguistic and text-based approach and towards a cognitive and expectation-based approach to literary discourse. One of the most significant of these applications is Cook's (1994) assimilation of schema theory with Formalist and Structuralist concepts like *deviation* and *foregrounding* (see B1). An important assumption of the AI approach is that we draw on schemata to help establish coherence in textual interpretation. However, according to Cook, the primary function of certain kinds of discourse is to effect a change in the schemata of their readers, and preeminent among these is literary discourse which often works to *disrupt* and then *refresh* schemata (1994: 191). Cook accepts that other forms of discourse, such as jokes and advertisements, can also refresh schemata. He even gives an example from Stephen Hawking's *A Brief History of Time* as an illustration of 'extreme schema disruption' in which the remarkable suggestion that time can go backwards is expressed in lucid and unremarkable prose. Discourse like this, which disrupts and refreshes schemata, stands in direct contrast to discourse in which schemata are *preserved*. For example, in the outline in A10 of the *pub schema* (for that is what it was), reference was made to the way this ICM might be modified and revised in the wake of new incoming information. But the addition of, for example, a new prop to the schema (such as an entry for WIDE-SCREEN TELEVISION) is more an extension to the schema rather than a disruption. Cook's general point is that because literary texts affect our schemata in special ways and on a number of levels, traditional stylistic concepts like *foregrounding* and *defamiliarisation* are better located in a framework of cognition than in a framework of language.

Text worlds and narrative comprehension

Let us begin with a seemingly tangential observation. British television runs a popular hospital drama called *Casualty* in which stories about the professional and personal entanglements of the medical staff are intermingled with stories of various emergencies that befall ordinary members of the public. Many episodes begin with a series of unrelated mini-narratives involving assorted luckless characters whose actions will lead inexorably towards the accident that takes them to the casualty department. What is intriguing is how, as viewers of the programme, we are able to track the progress of these various mini-narratives, which are patched together through a technique called 'parallel editing', when only one of the stories is in frame at any one time. It is also intriguing that we expect *not* to be returned to any of these stories at the same point at which we left – it would be thoroughly disorientating if we were. Clearly, we have some cognitive faculty that not only allows us to track the progression of character and narrative, but also to make inferences about the forward development of a plot even when it is, so to speak, un-narrated. This sub-unit will focus on two developments in cognitive stylistics that are linked by an interest in narrative, character and plot, and which, if only implicitly, address the sorts of issues just raised about narrative understanding.

The first model derives from the pioneering work on *text worlds* by Paul Werth (Werth 1999; and see Gavins (in press) for a compact introduction). Werth seeks to account for the conceptual space that links narrative levels, and to this effect he proposes three 'worlds' of discourse. The first is the *discourse world* which is the immediate, higher-order conceptual space that is inhabited by an author and a reader. Understanding of this world by the reader is founded on 'real' external circumstances and requires direct perception backed up by knowledge of the elements perceived (Werth 1999: 17). Through the discourse world is constructed a *text world.* A text world is a 'total construct' which requires for its understanding memory and imagination, rather than direct perception. Text worlds as conceptual spaces are defined *deictically* and *referentially*, and are anchored by references to the world depicted by the discourse (Werth 1999: 52). For instance, in the opening of Samuel Beckett's *Molloy* (1950):

(1) I am in my mother's room. It is I who live there now.

deictic references pick out spatial location ('in', 'there') and temporal location ('now'), while referential information identifies the entities present in the text world ('I', 'my mother's room') and signals their relationship to one another.

The third type of conceptual space in Werth's typology is a *sub-world.* Sub-worlds are established when a character projects thoughts and reflections, perhaps through a flashback or prolepsis (B7), to create another conceptual space inside the text world. This projection forms a distinct situation of its own, because it sets up a reality outside the parameters of the existing text world. Some practical suggestions about how to identify text world and sub-world defining elements are set out in unit C10.

The second key model of conceptual tracking is the framework of narrative comprehension developed by Emmott (1997). Emmott, as with Werth, is interested in the way the reader can hold more than one context at once while concentrating on one context in particular. Emmott develops the term *binding* to describe how episodic links between people and places are established in a text, and how these links create a context which is monitored by the mind. Characters are bound into a mental frame at the point at which they enter a fictional place. This process is distinguished in Emmott's model from the process of *priming* which describes the process by which one particular contextual frame becomes the main focus of attention for the reader (Emmott 1997: 123). As any sentence of narrative normally follows only one event in one context, that frame is the reader's main context and is therefore primed.

The question arises, then, as to what we do with the other narrative strands that have been bound into the story but which have been temporarily left alone by the narrator. Emmott points out that characters remain in a fictional place until there is an indication that they need to be 'bound out'. So for example in the hospital drama referred to above, a number of characters are bound into a variety of fictional places as each episode begins. We develop a mental frame to track these fictional characters and locations even when they are not primed, and indeed, we assume that the characters remain in place until we receive an explicit signal that they should be bound out. Unit C10 provides an opportunity to develop through textual analysis the concepts of binding and priming in more detail.

Summary

Like all models in stylistics, cognitive models are designed to facilitate the process of interpretation by helping us understand how we read texts. What distinguishes cognitive from other sorts of stylistic models is that the main emphasis is on mental representation rather than on textual representation. Finding the right balance on the cognitive–textual continuum is important, because a stylistic analysis can go too far in either direction. To be overly text-based risks losing sight of what readers do when they read, and this makes our stylistic analysis look as if it holds good for all readers in all reading contexts. To be overly cognitive risks losing sight of the way a text is made, and this tends to mask stylistic subtlety and creativity in textual composition.

The cognitive stylistic theme is sustained in C10 where a selection of practical activities are provided which probe the concepts developed here and in A10. The unit below takes the cognitive model in a different direction by focussing on the interconnections between style and conceptual metaphor.

B11 STYLES OF METAPHOR

This unit looks at some of the ways in which the study of metaphor has developed within cognitive stylistics. In unit A11, brief reference was made to the idea of *novelty* as a feature of metaphor in literature, and the following sub-unit will explore this issue in greater depth. Later in the unit, attention turns to a short poem by Roger McGough which, amongst other things, serves as a good illustration of some of the connections that can be drawn between metaphor and style.

Metaphors in everyday discourse and in literary discourse

The idea that a particular metaphor is 'novel' can be understood in a number of ways. It can be understood as referring for example to the newness or uniqueness of a conceptual mapping between a source and target domain, or alternatively, to a striking method of expression which a writer uses to relay a metaphor. However, taking the idea further requires that we work from the background assumption that most metaphorical mappings are transmitted through familiar, commonly occurring linguistic expressions. For instance, the metaphor IDEAS ARE FOOD is relayed through a variety of everyday constructions like 'I can't stomach that idea', 'Your theory's half-baked' or 'His story is pretty hard to swallow' and so on. It is interesting that the pattern in such metaphors involves the mapping between an abstract target domain (IDEAS) and a more physical source domain (FOOD). This pattern of 'concretisation', where we try to capture the essence of an abstraction by recasting it in the terms of something more palpable, is replicated in a great many metaphorical constructions and it offers an important insight into the way the human mind works.

The process of concretisation underscores the fact that metaphorical mapping is a conventional way of thinking and is not something remote to human thought. Not surprisingly then, many metaphors have become embedded over time into fixed expressions like *idioms*. Idioms are conventionally defined as clusters of words whose meaning cannot be read off their constituent parts, although it is important not to lose sight of the often metaphorical origin of a particular idiom. A good illustration of this principle of 'metaphoricity' is provided in the following slip of the tongue, said by a journalist of an overworked sports personality:

(1) He's burning the midnight oil at both ends.
(from Simpson 1992b)

In this example, two expressions embodying one conceptual metaphor have been unwittingly merged. The metaphor which is evoked is ENERGY IS A BURNING FUEL and it is commonly transmitted through idioms like 'burn the midnight oil' and 'burning the candle at both ends'. The popular term for this sort of slip, a 'mixed metaphor', is something of a misnomer because, as observed, this is really a blend of two idioms which draw on the same metaphor. But most importantly, the example explains well the cognitive basis of idioms by showing how the same conceptual storage system can contain related sets of fixed expressions.

To return to the issue of novelty, it is against this background of everyday metaphorical mapping that writers of literature seek not only to establish new connections, and new types of connection, between target and source domains, but also to extend and elaborate upon existing metaphors in various ways. Consider for instance the following fragment from Craig Raine's poem 'An Enquiry into Two Inches of Ivory':

(2) . . . the vacuum cleaner grazes
over the carpet, lowing, . . .

Here the target domain is an everyday domestic appliance and the source domain a familiar bovine animal. The source domain, as with many metaphorical expressions, is evoked by verbs which specify some action of the target ('grazes' and 'lowing'), so the overall metaphorical formula can be captured as: A HOUSEHOLD APPLIANCE IS A FARMED ANIMAL. As far as the novelty of the metaphor is concerned, it is the mental coalescence, or 'conceptual blending', of the familiar entities that offers a fresh perspective on an otherwise prosaic object like the humble vacuum cleaner. It is noticeable also that the two concepts in (1) are physical (one animate, the other not) so the transition between target and source is not like the process of concretisation seen above in the examples of everyday metaphorical mapping.

As a footnote to this discussion, it is worth reemphasising that novelty in stylistic expression cannot remain novel indefinitely, and what is foregrounded in an original context of use will become part of the background as time goes by (see B1).

Indeed, many of our common sayings and figures of speech originated from creative metaphors in literature. The expressions 'cold comfort', 'a tower of strength', 'play fast and loose', 'in my mind's eye' and 'to the manner born' may have little impact nowadays, but all of them saw their first use in the plays of William Shakespeare.

Metaphor and style

The following poem is by the Liverpudlian poet Roger McGough:

40 – LOVE

middle aged
couple playing
ten nis
when the
game ends
and they
go home
the net
will still
be be
tween them

(McGough 1971)

In this poem, McGough employs a range of linguistic-stylistic devices to relay a single underlying conceptual metaphor. Whereas the target domain is our understanding of a human relationship, the source domain for the metaphor comes from games and sport, yielding the formula: A HUMAN RELATIONSHIP IS A GAME OF SPORT. Regarding the source domain, we often apply concepts drawn from games and sports to a whole host of target domains – the game of chess alone services a great many metaphors in many different cultures. However, what is particularly marked about the McGough poem is the way this conceptual metaphor is sustained by patterns of graphology and other levels of language (see A2). Using this variety of devices, McGough develops the basic metaphor through two processes known as *extending* and *elaboration* (Kövecses 2002: 48). Extending a metaphor means expressing it through linguistic resources which introduce new conceptual elements from the source domain. In the poem, McGough extends the source domain from the more general concept of sport to one specific type of sport, and this enables yet further stylistic-expressive possibilities in the way the target domain is subsequently developed. The particular spatial organisation of tennis, with its back and forth movement between ball and players, is captured stylistically by the break up of the text into two columns, and this forces the reading of the text into a similar to and fro movement. Put another way, both sides of the game of love, as it were, are embodied in a textual layout which serves as an *orientational metaphor.* Conventional orientational metaphors use the idea of space as a vehicle for tracking human emotion, where GOOD IS UP ('I feel on top of the world') and BAD IS DOWN ('He's pretty low these days'). Unlike these vertical metaphors, McGough's orientation is horizontal, and this directionality embodies not only the emotional to and fro but the sense of implicit conflict that exists between the couple.

A range of levels of language are also exploited in order to *elaborate* the underlying conceptual metaphor in the poem. Elaboration involves capturing an existing component of the source domain in an unusual or unconventional way. For example, once the source domain has been extended to tennis, special features of this domain, such as its *props* (see A10 and B10), can acquire extra signification in the metaphorical mapping. The net which serves as the physical barrier in a tennis court symbolises a spiritual and emotional barrier between the estranged couple. Similarly, the numerical scoring system used in tennis allows for further elaboration, where the reference to '40' in the title parallels the age of the couple and, even more fortuitously, the reference to 'love' allows a metaphorical projection from the sport domain to the more abstract target domain of human relationships. Derived from the French *l'oeuf* on account of the resemblance of an egg to the zero symbol, the tennis-domain 'love' facilities a pun (A12) because it allows more than one sense to be projected. The score in the game of love for the middle aged couple is, it seems, at zero.

Throughout the poem, a variety of devices enable a conceptual projection to be made from the physical body of the poem into the more abstract world of human relationships. In sum, McGough's text illustrates well the idea of novelty in metaphor because it offers both a new type of conceptual mapping between a source and target domain as well as a striking method of expression to relay the metaphor.

The broad themes raised in this unit are translated into a set of practical activities across in C11, where some of the ideas developed in A11, including those on metonymy, are also reintroduced. The reading that concludes this strand, by Peter Stockwell, examines an important issue in the theory of metaphor which relates to how the two concepts involved in a metaphorical mapping are affected by the mapping process.

SECTION C

EXPLORATION

INVESTIGATING STYLE

C1

IS THERE A 'LITERARY LANGUAGE'?

As far as most stylisticians are concerned, the short answer to the question which heads this unit is 'no'. That is to say, there exists no feature or pattern of language which is inherently or exclusively 'literary' in all contexts. This may seem a curious stance to adopt given stylistics' close association with literary discourse. After all, literature offers the chance to explore language that is out of the ordinary, language which is often the preeminent embodiment of the creative spirit. It is also the case that there have been, over the centuries, certain conventions in writing styles that mark certain literary epochs, such as the alliterative style of the Anglo-Saxon poem, the sonnet form of later periods in literary history, or, later again, forms like the novel and the novella. However, these forms of writing are more representative of specific codes or conventions of use which may change over time, rather than confirmation of the existence of a special language which in its very essence is immutably, and for all time, 'literary'.

The question now begged is why, if there is such widespread rejection of the concept within stylistics, does the issue of 'literary language' need to be discussed or even mentioned? The answer to this question is the main focus of this unit. In the following sub-unit, some of the broader theoretical consequences of the 'literary language' debate are framed, while the sub-unit after that makes use of a short poem to extend and explore this problematic concept in a more practical and directed way.

The 'literary language' issue

Contemporary stylistics' resistance to a distinct form of 'literary language' might on the face of it seem like a rather cynical snipe at the many literary critics who believe the opposite; at those who believe not only that there exists a literary language, but that literature can be defined by its use of this special language. Let me address this issue this by making three basic points.

One of the most important concerns in the practice of stylistics is that the language used in literary texts should not be cut adrift from its reflexes in the common resources of everyday discourse. Stylistics is interested in what writers do *with* and *through* language, and in the raw materials out of which literary discourse is crafted. As noted across the strand in A1, the tools of modern linguistics are drawn from the full system of language and discourse, so it makes sense that those same tools be used to see what writers do against this broader context. The aim is not to sequester off into a special category significant aspects of literary style, but rather to look for the origins of this style in the overall totality of discourse.

Following directly from this is a second point. If we describe this or that piece of discourse as 'literary language', we immediately place a linguistic boundary around it. In fact, to set down stylistic parameters around a form of discourse is in some respect to codify it as a *register*, thereby making it a language variety that regularly co-occurs with a particular situation (see C2). But it is the very freedom of linguistic possibility which is an index of creativity in language, not the presence of a fixed set of linguistic guidelines within which a writer must work. To argue for the existence of a distinct literary register is effectively to argue for a kind of cliché, because it would involve reining stylistic expression into a restricted set of formulaic prescriptions.

A third issue raised by the literary language debate is somewhat more ideological than methodological in its general bearing. To claim that literary language is special, that it can somehow be bracketed off from the mundane or commonplace in discourse, is ultimately to wrest it away from the practice of stylistics. Followed through, such a move assumes that whereas language scholars might be better equipped to investigate forms of discourse like journalism or everyday conversation, it should fall to the literary critic alone to deal with the special language of literature. As the critic F. W. Bateson notes (see unit D1), the rather mechanical procedure of the stylistician is no match for the sensitivity of the critic.

I am reminded here of a curious episode which is germane to the present discussion. Some years ago, I approached a publisher who held copyright on the work of a well-known British poet. My request indicated the few lines of text required and included a sample of the proposed stylistic exercise, part of which involved a cloze test of the sort developed in B1. Not only was my request for permission refused point blank, it was accompanied by the following rather sniffy rejoinder: 'we cannot possibly countenance such a travesty of lines as magical and special as these'. At the risk of seeming to work out a personal angst in public, the relevance of the story is that it shows precisely what can happen when the language which writers use is hived off into a separate and indeed hallowed category. The 'travesty' (the stylistic analysis, in other words!) was considered irreverent because it tried to lay bare the very subtleties in expression the poet was conveying in language, yet to this self-appointed guardian of literary probity, my methods had clearly violated something that was deeply sacrosanct. It is worth noting that the injunction did not come from the poet himself – ironically, it is my experience that poets are often intrigued by what stylisticians have to say about their style.

Probing 'literary language'

Activity 

This short sub-unit explores further the problematic issue of 'literary language'. To start us off, you will find below two-thirds of a poem. The name of its author, and the reason why you have been given only two of its three stanzas will emerge later, but as you read it through try to identify any features of textual construction, words or phrases, that you feel are 'literary' or that you would normally associate with literature. Below the poem are some more detailed tasks which you can work through.

One Perfect Rose

A single flow'r he sent me, since we met.
  All tenderly his messenger he chose;
Deep-hearted, pure, with scented dew still wet –
  One perfect rose.

I knew the language of the floweret;
  'My fragile leaves,' it said, 'his heart enclose.'
Love long has taken for his amulet
  One perfect rose.

Activity With respect to the poem, consider the following questions:

- How many speakers are there in the poem and how can we work this out from the text?
- When is the poem set, and how do we know?
- What sort of vocabulary is used by the poet? That is, is it modern or archaic, formal or conversational?
- Can you identify a rhyme scheme in the poem? If so, what sort of scheme is it?
- Can you spot any marked or unusual features of grammar (see A3) in the poem?

My own response to these questions are that the text as it stands satisfies many of the generic conventions of a lyric love poem (see A2). A single speaker expresses an emotional state, and mediates this through the popular symbol of the rose. Other devices work to sustain this reading and to suggest that this is the written style of a bygone era. Some of the vocabulary is clearly archaic, as in the obsolete diminutive form 'floweret' or the contracted form 'flow'r'. The rhyme scheme is tightly configured into an *abab* pattern, and is maintained even on the trisyllables 'floweret' and 'amulet'. In terms of its grammatical organisation, many of the poem's clauses are structured in such a way as to bring to the front elements other than the grammatical Subject. In fact, the clause 'All tenderly his messenger he chose' is particularly marked in this respect because it is fronted by two elements, an Adjunct and then a Complement, with the Subject occurring in sentence-final position (cf. 'He chose his messenger all tenderly'). No doubt many more features could be identified which, in the conventional sense of the term, make this text feel like 'literary' writing.

With its third stanza now reinstated, read the poem again. Think particularly about how the addition of the final verse impacts on your initial reaction to and interpretation of the first two verses. Once you have read it, go back and reconsider your answers to the set of questions listed above.

One Perfect Rose

A single flow'r he sent me, since we met.
  All tenderly his messenger he chose;
Deep-hearted, pure, with scented dew still wet –
  One perfect rose.

I knew the language of the floweret;
  'My fragile leaves,' it said, 'his heart enclose.'
Love long has taken for his amulet
  One perfect rose.

Why is it no one ever sent me yet
  One perfect limousine, do you suppose?
Ah no, it's always just my luck to get
  One perfect rose.

The general tenor of the third stanza is a long way indeed from the discourse of the seventeenth- or eighteenth-century love poem, although it does create a humorous play on that discourse frame. In fact, the poem was written in 1926 by the American wit and socialite Dorothy Parker. What Parker does is to use a kind of style-shift for comic effect where the echoes of the lyric genre in stanzas one and two give way in the third stanza to an altogether more prosaic style of language. Constructions like 'Ah no', 'just my luck' and 'do you suppose' signal an informal register of discourse while in grammar the Subject is brought back to its more common first position in the clause ('. . . no one ever sent me yet . . .').

But the heart of the issue, as far as present discussion is concerned, is that it is simply not feasible to say that, in comparison with the third, the first two stanzas are 'literary language'. It is more the case that a convention of writing is echoed, and then is ultimately brought into collision with, the more contemporary idiom projected in the third verse. If asked outside this context which of the words 'floweret' or 'limousine' you considered to be 'literary', you would have probably opted for the first one, but as we have just seen both words are perfectly capable of being pressed into service in a poem. It is a question therefore of how these words function in context, not of how this or that word sounds in isolation, which is important. By exploiting a formal convention of writing of the sort mentioned earlier, Parker sets up a twist in expectation that works for comic effect. Echoing other discourses in new contexts is an important way of generating irony, but here the echo only becomes clear when the shift in style is delivered in the third stanza. Parker's poem is a good illustration, then, of how discourse is open to constant reinvigoration and transformation over time. Highlighting this principle, the theoretician Michel Foucault develops the term *transdiscursivity* to describe how the rules of discourse formation in one era become detached from its 'ulterior transformations' in later developments (Foucault 1986: 145–6).

Summary

A position which regards literary discourse as impervious to or resistant to linguistic analysis is utterly at odds with the rationale of modern stylistics. Stylistics is about interrogating texts, about seeing a text in the context of its other stylistic possibilities. One of the most effective ways of understanding how a text works, as Pope notes (1995: 1–2), is to challenge it, to play around with it or to intervene in its stylistic make-up in some way. Upholding the view that 'literary language' is somehow outside the boundaries of the overall language system does little to enable or facilitate this sort of textual intervention.

It makes sense therefore to treat the concept of 'literary language' with a healthy degree of scepticism. Indeed, a somewhat more useful way of approaching the issue of stylistic creativity, whether it be found in literature or in other types of discourse, is through the concept of *literariness*, a term first coined by Roman Jakobson. Literariness is a property of texts and contexts and it inheres in patterns of language in use as opposed to patterns of language in isolation. Crucially, in keeping with Jakobson's other important term, the poetic function (B1), literariness is not exclusive to literature. It is instead a principle of expressiveness that transcends literature into many types of discourse contexts of which journalism and advertising discourse are just two preeminent examples. Literariness also accommodates a text's capacity to absorb other voices and styles, the sorts of textual techniques witnessed in the example from Dorothy Parker. This particular theme, the 'multivoicedness' of literary discourse, is the main focus in the following unit.

C2 STYLE, REGISTER AND DIALECT

This unit explores a passage from Irvine Welsh's controversial novel *Trainspotting* and develops a sociolinguistically orientated activity based around variations in dialect, register and style. In order to help focus that analysis, the following sub-unit introduces some general categories of language variation.

Varieties of language

One of the six components of the model of narrative introduced in A5, *sociolinguistic code* is a term referring to the pool of linguistic varieties that both derive from and shape the social and cultural backdrop to a text. Sociolinguistic code is a key organising resource not just for narrative but for all types of literary discourse. In the case of monolingual writing in English, that code will remain largely within the parameters of a single language and its subvarieties, although in bilingual writing it is common for any number of indigenous language varieties to intermix, and often alongside a 'superstrate' language like English. Chicano literature, from the border regions of Mexico and the USA, draws on a sociolinguistic code which combines Spanish, English and localised American-Indian forms, while in the Nigerian literary context (embodied in the work of Wole Soyinka, for example), Standard English is mixed with West African Pidgin English and the indigenous African language, Yoruba. The term *code-switching* is normally used to explain transitions between distinct languages in a text, and literary code-switching is a sophisticated technique which signals movement between different spheres of reference and has important consequences for a range of thematic intentions (see further Hess 1996: 6 and Pratt 1993: 177).

Literary works which remain within the compass of a single language may still exhibit marked variation in terms of their use of sociolinguistic code. What follows is a summary of a number of key dimensions of such intra-lingual variation.

Idiolect

It a truism of modern linguistics that no two speakers use language in exactly the same way. We all have our own linguistic mannerisms and stylistic idiosyncrasies, and the term reserved for an individual's special unique style is *idiolect.*

Accents and dialects

Influenced and shaped by the regional origins and socioeconomic background of their speakers, dialects are distinguished by patterns in grammar and vocabulary while accents are distinguished through patterns of pronunciation. The Standard English dialect and the Received Pronunciation accent (see Table C2.1) represent jointly the high-prestige varieties of British English, although these are far outnumbered (in terms of numbers of speakers) by many non-standard regional varieties. Two further points of special relevance to stylistic analysis are worth making here:

(i) It is popularly yet wrongly assumed that Standard English is not really a dialect at all, but that this variety along with its high-prestige counterpart accent, RP, simply constitute 'real' English. A consequence of this is that when critics discuss the representation of 'dialect' in literature – as in, say, the novels of Thomas Hardy – they tend to be talking rather more narrowly about the regional, non-standard dialects, often of a rural and particularly conservative type, which are used by particular fictional characters. But *all* speech and writing is framed in a dialect of some sort, whether it be standard or non-standard, high-prestige or low-status.

(ii) Given that accent is a variety of language defined through *pronunciation*, it might seem that the study of accent has no place in the stylistic analysis of written literary discourse. However, writers make use of any number of often ingenious techniques for representing features of spoken discourse in print. For example, in the Irvine Welsh novel from which the passage used below is taken, the nuances of spoken Edinburgh vernacular are captured through a variety of orthographic techniques:

   a Vowel lengthening, which is a characteristic of all varieties of Scots English, is relayed by doubling the vowels in spelling, so that *got* becomes 'goat', *off* becomes 'oaff' and so on.

   b A feature widespread in Scots English is an older style vowel pronunciation which dates back to the time of Chaucer. Whereas most contemporary British accents now have diphthongs in words like *about* and *down*, their realisation in Scots is as long monophthongs, represented in spellings like 'doon' and 'aboot'.

   c A particular feature of the low-status variety of Scots English targeted by Welsh (a feature it shares, curiously, with London's Cockney English) is 'L-vocalisation'. This involves the realisation of the /l/ sound as a vowel rather than a liquid consonant, such that *ball* becomes 'baw', *always* 'eywis', *football* 'fitba' and so on.

Table C2.1 Standard and non-standard accents and dialects

	Accent (varieties of pronunciation)	**Dialect (varieties of grammar and vocabulary)**
Standard:	Received pronunciation (RP)	Standard English
Non-standard:	Regional Accents ('Scouse', 'Cockney'; 'Belfast'; 'Glaswegian' and so on)	Regional Dialects ('Scouse'; 'Cockney'; 'Belfast'; 'Glaswegian' and so on)

Register

Whereas a dialect is a linguistic variety that is defined according to the user of language – it tells you things about their social and regional background – a *register*, on the other hand, is defined according to the *use* to which language is being put. In other words, a register shows, through a regular, fixed pattern of vocabulary and grammar, what a speaker or writer is doing with language at a given moment. Registers are often discussed in terms of three features of context known as *field*, *tenor* and *mode*. Field of discourse refers to the setting and purpose of the interaction, tenor to the relationship between the participants in interaction and mode to the medium of communication (that is, whether it is spoken or written). For example, if we take a particular field of discourse like *chemistry*, and specify that the language event take the form of written interaction between a student and lecturer, then these parameters will strongly constrain the sort of text-type that is anticipated. Only the first of the following two sequences is appropriate to the demands of this discourse context:

(1) A quantity of copper sulphate crystals was dissolved in a beaker containing 200ml of H_2O. The aqueous solution was then heated.

(2) I was just sayin', Jimmy, that me and my mate Will were putting some copper sulphate stuff into a jug of water the other day. It was bloody great fun.

The vocabulary and grammar of (1) confirm its field of discourse as science and its mode as written discourse. Moreover, the use of the *passive voice* (see A6) without any explicit interpersonal markers and terms of address, suggests a relatively formal tenor of discourse. By contrast, it is the very presence of first person pronouns, along with evaluative adjective phrases ('bloody great'), that makes the second example inappropriate to the context of formal scientific prose but appropriate to the context of a spoken narrative of personal experience. Notice also how tenor of discourse is made more informal in (2) through both the *vocative* (the term of direct address, 'Jimmy') and the swear word ('bloody'). In that they can occur in all social and regional dialects, swear words and taboo language generally are important features of register, and not, as is commonly assumed, of dialect.

Antilanguage

Antilanguages are the semi-secretive languages born out of subcultures and alternative societies. These societies, 'antisocieties', are consciously established as alternatives to mainstream society such that their relationship to the dominant social order is one of resistance, even active hostility. Antilanguages are therefore typically characterised by references to proscribed drugs, to alternative sexual behaviours or more generally to the various activities of a criminal underworld (Halliday 1978). Antilanguages play an important part in, and often dominate completely, the style of literary works which are thematically concerned with such subcultures and antisocieties. Notable examples of such fiction are William Burroughs's *The Naked Lunch*

(1959), Hubert Selby Jnr's *Last Exit to Brooklyn* (1966), and Anthony Burgess's anti-language novel *sine qua non, A Clockwork Orange* (1962). The most important process in the formation of an antilanguage is *relexicalisation* which involves recycling established words in the language into new structures and meanings. For example, in Welsh's novel, there are numerous coded antilanguage references to proscribed drugs, to types of criminal activity and to the police and other figures of authority. Relexicalisation in the 'drugs' field of discourse alone is heavily foregrounded, with a single page of text likely to produce items such as the following and more: *skag, works, smack, gear, speedball, shootin gallery, cookin up* and *shootin home.*

Levels of style in Irvine Welsh's *Trainspotting*

If we accept the argument made both along this thread and in unit C1, that literary discourse has the capacity to stack up or absorb other varieties of language, the difficulty that then presents itself is how to separate out in a rigorous way these various elements in stylistic analysis. In the stylistic analysis of sociolinguistic code, for example, we need to identify and explore the connections between features like accent, register or antilanguage in a text. The following exercise is designed as one method for helping to tease out these stylistically significant varieties of language.

Activity 

Below you will find a passage from Irvine Welsh's novel *Trainspotting.* This episodically written novel is set in Edinburgh, and follows the interconnected lives of a group of drug addicts and that of their violent and psychotic friend, Frank Begbie. The novel's 'hero' is its first person narrator, Mark Renton. More intelligent and articulate than his peers, Renton manages ultimately to break free from the strictures of this drug-ridden, repressed existence. In this particular episode, Renton and Spud Murphy, having stolen books to sustain their heroin habit, find themselves in a Magistrate's court defending a charge of shoplifting. They are watched from the public gallery by their friends Sick Boy and Begbie. Although Spud is sent to Saughton prison, Renton is released subject to his participation in a drugs rehabilitation programme. Read the passage through a couple of times. You could even try to read it aloud!

Courting Disaster

The magistrate's expression seems tae oscillate between pity n loathing, as he looks doon at me n Spud in the dock.

– You stole the books from Waterstone's bookshop, with the intention of selling them, he states. Sell fuckin books. Ma fuckin erse.

– No, ah sais.

– Aye, Spud sais, at the same time. We turn aroond n look at each other. Aw the time we spent gittin oor story straight n it takes the doss cunt two minutes tae blow it.

The magistrate lets oot a sharp exhalation. It isnae a brilliant job the cunt's goat, whin ye think aboot it. It must git pretty tiresome dealin wi radges aw day. Still, ah bet the poppy's fuckin good, n naebody's asking the cunt tae dae it. He should try tae be a wee bit mair professional, a bit mair pragmatic, rather than showin his annoyance so much.

– Mr Renton, you did not intend to sell the books?

– Naw. Eh, no, your honour. They were for reading.

– So you read Kierkegaard. Tell us about him, Mr Renton, the patronising cunt sais.

– I'm interested in his concepts of subjectivity and truth, and particularly his ideas concerning choice; the notion that genuine choice is made out of doubt and uncertainty, and without recourse to the experience and advice of others. It could be argued, with some justification, that's it's primarily a bourgeois, existential philosophy and would therefore seek to undermine collective societal wisdom. However, it's also a liberating philosophy, because when such societal wisdom is negated, the basis for social control over the individual becomes weakened and . . . but I'm rabbiting a bit here. Ah cut myself short. They hate a smart cunt. It's easy to talk yourself into a bigger fine, or fuck sake, a higher sentence. Think deference Renton, think deference.

The magistrate snorts derisively. As an educated man, ah'm sure he kens far mair aboot great philosophers than a pleb like me. Yiv goat tae huv fuckin brains tae be a fuckin judge. S no iviry cunt thit kin dae that fuckin joab. Ah can almost hear Begbie sayin that tae Sick Boy in the public gallery.

– And you, Mr Murphy, you intended to sell the books, like you sell everything else that you steal, in order to finance your heroin habit?

– That's spot on man . . . eh . . . ye goat it likesay, Spud nodded [. . .]

The magistrate looks closely at us tae see if thirs any sign ay mockery oan ma face. No chance it'll show [. . .] Convinced it's no bullshit, the doss cunt dismisses the session. Ah walk tae freedom; perr auld Spud gits taken doon.

A polisman gestures tae him tae move.

– Sorry mate, ah sais, feelin cuntish.

– Nae hassle man . . . I'll git oaf the skag, and Saughton's barry fir hash. It'll be a piece ay pish likesay . . . he sais, as he's escorted away by a po-faced labdick.

(Welsh 1993: 165–8)

Now work through the passage paying particular attention to its various levels of stylistic organisation. Drawing on the topics covered in the previous sub-unit, try to identify specifically the different strands of language variation, such as *accent*, *dialect*, *register* and so on, that occur in the passage. Consider the stylistic impact of these strands, especially in the way they serve to advance the plot and the way characters (especially that of the first person narrator) are developed. The grid in Table C2.2 may help you organise your analysis. The left hand side of the grid lists the categories introduced above. Try to find an *exponent* (a textual example) for each category and, if this is your book, write it in the space provided and make comments on its stylistic impact. For the analysis of register, the space for *mode* can be used to track, amongst other things, those features of the *written* medium that are used to capture the particular nuances of *spoken* vernacular. Given the formal legal setting of the passage, there are spaces in the grid to accommodate this 'main' field of discourse as well as other fields of discourse which may supplement or even stand in conflict to the forensic theme. The same principle is extended to tenor of discourse, where in addition to the exchanges between defendants and judge, there are a number of other interactive levels involving different participants in discourse. And remember, swear words and taboo language are register variables, not dialect variables.

Table C2.2 Register and dialect in narrative: grid for *Trainspotting* activity

Feature of sociolinguistic code		Examples in text	Comments
Accent	prestige/standard?		
	non-standard?		
Dialect	standard?		
	non-standard?		
Field	main field of discourse?		
	other field(s) of discourse?		
Tenor	main tenor of discourse?		
	other tenor(s) of discourse?		
Mode			
Antilanguage vocabulary?			
Idiolect (features of 'individual' speech)?			

To help direct your analysis further, consider the following issues:

(i) Much is made in the literary critical commentary on this novel of Welsh's 'vibrant' and 'energetic' language, his 'spectacular' use of Edinburgh vernacular and his ability to blend and balance different voices within a narrative (and see further the reading in D5). Can your analysis of this passage help explain why critics often react to Welsh's work in this way?

(ii) In the study of dialect variation in literary discourse, the 'default' position is that the standard variety of the language is used for core narrative description while regional, non-standard varieties are allocated to various individual characters in the story. Thus, the standard dialect forms the matrix variety, the non-standard dialects the satellite varieties. On the basis of your reading of the passage, is this true of Welsh's narrative technique? What is *his* matrix dialect? And what are the satellite varieties?

(iii) Whereas Renton escapes serious punishment, his accomplice, and less than articulate foil, Spud, is punished more severely. In terms of discourse representation, how are these two characters differentiated in the passage?

(iv) Related to (iii), if you found certain aspects of the passage amusing or humorous, try to work out why. What for example is the impact of Renton's disquisition on Kierkegaard? Shifts in style often form the basis for humour. To what extent is style shift of this sort a feature of the passage?

Summary

The purpose of this exercise has been to try to develop some systematic methods for exploring how multiple and higher-order levels of style can work in a text. The grid devised to help itemise the main categories of the analysis can of course be modified to accommodate different types of sociolinguistic code in other contexts of writing. Whereas Welsh's novel is principally 'monolingual' in the sense that it exploits sociolinguistic variation in and around a single language, the grid can be extended to account for literary code-switching which straddles different languages. And it can also work for both poetry and drama, as well as for works of prose fiction.

There are a number of advantages to being rigorous in the identification of the various styles employed in a literary text. The procedure serves well to illustrate in practice the concept of *polyphony*. Coined by the Russian theoretician Mikhail Bakhtin, polyphony refers to a quality of 'multi-voiced-ness' which is displayed by certain genres of discourse. These genres, known as 'complex speech genres', arise in the artistic discourses of 'more complex and comparatively highly developed and organised cultural communication' (Bakhtin 1986: 62). Bakhtin adds that during the process of their formation, complex speech genres 'absorb and digest various primary (simple) genres that have taken form in unmediated speech communion' (62). Literary discourse is a preeminent example of a complex speech genre and the principle of polyphony is situated at its core. Irrespective of how the academic literary institution views Irvine Welsh's work, the stylistic activity suggested here does indeed highlight this writer's capacity to build a text through multiple and varied aspects of language and style.

C3 GRAMMAR AND GENRE: A SHORT STUDY IN IMAGISM

This unit experiments with grammatical patterns in poetry in order to help us think about the processes involved in translating experiences and thoughts into the type of text that is a poem. The activity proposed here draws principally on the concepts introduced and developed across units A3 and B3, and it will also feed into unit D3, an article by Ronald Carter which offers a detailed stylistic analysis of grammatical patterns in modern poetry.

From experience to language

Below you will find part of a letter that was penned in 1911 by a well-known American writer to his friend. It tells of an experience that befell the writer while he was resident in Europe. Read the letter through carefully:

> For well over a year I have been trying to make a poem of a very beautiful thing that befell me in the Paris Underground. I got out of a train at, I think, La Concorde, and in the jostle I saw a beautiful face, and then, turning suddenly, another and another, and then a beautiful child's face, and then another beautiful face. All that day I tried to find words for what this made me feel. That night, as I went home along the Rue Raynouard I was still trying. I could get nothing but spots of colour. I remember thinking that if I had been a painter I might have started a wholly new school of painting.

Activity

This is the inspiration, the 'felt experience', that prompted the writer eventually to construct a poem. Before we move on to look at this poem, think of the sort of poem that *you* might produce if you had had such an experience in the Underground. If you were asked specifically to produce a short poem of only a few lines, what sort of imaginative impulse would you draw upon? Here are some further questions that might shape and influence your creative thinking:

(i) Would you, as the writer does in his letter, position yourself as a 'voice' in the poem? (Notice the 'I' pronouns in the letter which locate the writer as the authorial source for the text.)
(ii) Would you situate your poem in a specific time and place (as, again, the writer does)?
(iii) What type of evaluative vocabulary would you use to capture the impact of this experience on you?
(iv) Would you address your poem to an imagined reader, through markers of direct address such as 'you'? Or would you instead prefer to depersonalise it, making it stand as a more generalised statement for all readers?
(v) What sort of sound and rhythm structure (if any) would you use? Would you try to adopt a formal metrical scheme or instead prefer to render it in 'free verse'? (See unit A4.)

Jot your poem into the box below (if this is your book, of course). Don't feel you have to shape a complete and rounded piece of poetry – you may simply have some ideas for fragments or particular constructions of language that might begin to capture the experience. We shall return to this exercise shortly.

Probing grammatical patterns, back to front

Activity 

Your next task is to look at the following text, which is the complete text of a very short poem (including its title). The poem has been grammatically 'scrambled' in that the *noun phrases* and *prepositional phrases* (see A3) which comprise it have been jumbled up. Orthography (the capitals, punctuation and so on which normally signal line endings and sentence boundaries) has been stripped away, so that all that you are left with is a collection of unordered phrases.

Referring where possible to the grammatical information provided in units A3 and B3, now try to reassemble the poem into some form of coherent unit. What kind of grammatical steps are necessary for such a reconstruction? What aspects of language are responsible for the difficulties (if any) that you encounter? Before proceeding to the next sub-unit, write your reconstruction in the box below the text.

in the crowd
the apparition
in a station
petals
of these faces
of the metro
on a wet black bough

Grammar and literary genre

On the basis of some give-away lexical items like 'station' and 'metro' in the scrambled poem, you may indeed have begun to suspect some connection between this text and the letter writer from earlier. But before we explore that connection, let us reflect for a moment on your reconstruction work. There are indeed many ways of bolting together the phrases that comprise this poem, resulting in a number of possible permutations. This comes about largely because of the absence in the original of one crucial grammatical feature, which we shall consider shortly. Here first of all is the unadulterated text. And in the commentary that follows, consider how it compares to both your own poem and your rearrangement.

In a Station of the Metro

The apparition of these faces in the crowd;
Petals on a wet, black bough.
(Pound 1969 [1912])

One important aspect of the grammar of this short couplet, which is based loosely on the seventeen syllable Japanese *haiku* poem, is that it contains no verbs. With that go many contingent structures such as finiteness, tense (and time reference) and propositional value (which means that you cannot 'argue' with the ideas expressed here) (see units A3 and B3). From this, other aspects of clause structure collapse: a grammatical Subject cannot be formed, nor can Complement elements be positioned relative to a verb. What remains is pared down to its stylistic 'bare bones', so to speak, encoding a sequence of phrases to do with things and their locations. Gone, for instance, are the self-referential pronouns ('I') which so characterised the letter; gone also are the explicit references to time which were signalled through finite verb forms (eg. 'I *have been trying*'; 'I *think*'; 'I *got out*') and temporal Adjuncts ('over a year'; 'that night'; 'all that day'). Notice also how the repetitions ('a beautiful face') and parallel formations ('another and another') of the letter give way to the most minimal and sparsest of lexis in the poem. Yet this is not to say, in terms of the ideas discussed in unit A6, that the absence of verbs means that there are no *processes* in the poem. There is one clear example of *nominalisation*, where a noun embodies a process of action. As in unit A6, you can test a text for nominalisation by asking the question 'what happened?' and seeing if, in the reply, any nouns slot into the frame 'there was a(n) ________'. Here, that question would be answered by the word 'apparition', so it is not the case that nothing happens, it is just that the happening has been made a 'thing' and has been cut adrift from any agency and from any locus in time. It is interesting also that even the deictic word 'these' (unit A2) suggests proximity to a speaking source even though explicit reference to that speaker has been erased.

What remains, in the light of these grammatical operations, is the sparest juxtaposition of a statement of experience and a statement of interpretation. The relationship between the two is a metaphorical one (see unit A11) in that it involves a conceptual mapping between two domains: the perceived experience encoded in the first line, and its mapping in the second onto a metaphorical plane. The result is a frozen crystallised moment, cut adrift from time but very much an instantiation of things and place. An 'image', rather than a proposition.

In stylistic terms, this short poem does indeed appear to embrace the credentials of the Imagist movement in poetry, which flourished for a few years from 1910 and of which Ezra Pound was a preeminent figure. Pound described an image as 'an intellectual and emotional complex in an instant of time' and characterised Imagist poetry by its exactitude of vocabulary, its hard and clear images presented 'instantaneously', and its direct treatment of the 'thing'. To what extent did your own poem, based on the experience in the Metro, embody (if at all) any of these features? Did you put a personal subject into your poem, and was that subject a speaking or narrating voice?

Was your own poem more contemplative and meditative, more 'lyrical' in the sense of a single speaker reflecting on thoughts and emotions? And finally, if your own poem had none of the stylistic markers of of Imagism, what literary genre *did* it embody?

In this unit, our principal aim has been to examine the connection between stylistic technique, as it translates to grammatical experimentation, and literary genre. That is one of the themes that will be resumed across the book in the reading in D3. In the next unit, C4, the focus will shift to exploring patterns of sound and metre in poetry.

C4

STYLES IN A SINGLE POEM: AN EXPLORATION

This unit offers a set of framing questions designed to help organise the exploration of a single literary text from multiple stylistic perspectives. The text selected for analysis is Michael Longley's short poem 'The Comber', which appears in his collection *The Weather in Japan* (2000). The questions asked of the text cover a range of stylistic models, which include, but are not restricted to, the material on sound and rhythm which was developed along this strand. They also bring in grammar (thread 3) and other levels of language (thread 2), although later threads in the book will no doubt offer yet further models of analysis. The set of questions posed in the following sub-unit are picked up in the web material which accompanies this book, where some advice and commentary is offered on the various activities suggested.

Going to work on a poem

Activity

First of all, read the poem closely:

The Comber

A moment before the comber turns into
A breaker – sea-spray, raggedy rainbows –
Water and sunlight contain all the colours
And suspend between Inishbofin and me,
The otter, and thus we meet, without my scent
In her nostrils, the uproar of my presence,
My unforgivable shadow on the sand –
Even if this is the only sound I make.

(Longley 2000)

Now work through the questions, and if you have to, double-check their terms of reference by looking again at the other units to which they relate. For the most part, you can deal with the questions in any order, although it is important to recognise that a particular feature of language targeted in one activity will always intersect with features of language covered in the other activities.

Question 1: what can we say about general patterns of grammar in the poem?

(Refer to units A3, B3 and C3 when undertaking these activities)

Identify the main clauses in the poem, and any subordinate clauses that are placed around them. (Remember, there can only be one S element and one P element in any main clause). What pattern emerges as the overall grammatical system of the poem? For example, where are units like Adjuncts and subordinate clauses positioned? Do they function as anticipatory, trailing or equivalent constituents?

Question 2: what can we say about foregrounded patterns of grammar in the poem?

(Refer to units B1 and A3 when undertaking these activities.)

Identify any sequences which break from the basic grammatical pattern you have identified for the poem as a whole. For example, are there any places in the poem where clause structure gives way to sequences of phrases which are *not* connected to a Subject and Predicator element?

Question 3: what can we say about sound and rhythm in the poem?

(Refer to units A4 and B4 when undertaking these activities)

Identify any significant aspects of sound patterning in the poem. Does the poem display a dominant metrical pattern? Or is its versification based more on the rhythm of natural speech than on a formal metrical scheme? In other words, is the poem written in *free verse*?

Does the poem contain any significant features of sound symbolism like onomatopoeia? If so what, what is the function of these devices in the poem?

The term *grammetrics* describes the convergence between grammatical structure and rhythmical structure. Can you identity any significant coalescence(s) of grammar and metre in the poem?

Question 4: what can we say about the graphology of the poem?

(Refer to units A2 and B2 when undertaking these activities)

How is the poem as language 'on the page' formally organised? What impact does its visual arrangement have on other levels of language? In particular, how does the graphology of the poem complement (or interfere with) its grammatical organisation?

Question 5: what can we say about vocabulary and word-structure in the poem?

(Refer to this thread and to units A2 and B2 when undertaking these activities)

Are there any individual words or word-structures that are foregrounded? Does anything deviate from the ordinary, and if so, how does it intersect with other levels of language like sound and rhythm?

Question 6: in what other ways might the poem have been written?

(Refer to unit B3 and to any other units of the book which contain rewrites and transposition exercises)

How might the poem read if its basic stylistic organisation (at any level of language) were altered? In particular, what would happen if its grammatical structure were rearranged into a more linear representation?

Summary

This unit has interrogated a single text using a set of questions which draw on material from a number of units in the book. Other questions could of course be asked of the same text. The poem's organisation as *narrative* represents one such line of inquiry. It is noticeable, for instance, that the conjunction 'before' near the start of the poem signals a so-called 'previous to given time' relationship. This means that the later event (the comber turning into a breaker) is relayed first and, in an inversion of natural narrative ordering, the earlier event ('water and sunlight contain . . .') is relayed second. However, developing further this sort of angle requires a fuller account of the organisation of narrative. Providing such an account is the remit of the next unit.

C5 A SOCIOLINGUISTIC MODEL OF NARRATIVE

This unit makes some practical suggestions for exploring further the structure of narrative. It draws upon one particular model of narrative: the framework of *natural narrative* developed by the sociolinguist William Labov. Labov's concept of narrative structure, which has already featured in this strand (A5), has proved a productive model of analysis in stylistics. After a brief sketch of the model, some narrative texts will be introduced and some practical activities developed around them.

Labov's narrative model

The enduring appeal of Labov's model of natural narrative is largely because its origins are situated in the everyday discourse practices of real speakers in real social contexts. Working from a corpus of hundreds of stories told in the course of casual conversation by informants from many different backgrounds, Labov isolates the core, recurrent features that underpin a fully formed natural narrative. Six key categories are rendered down from this body of data (Labov 1972: 359–60). Each of these categories serves to address a hypothetical question about narrative structure ('What is this story about?', 'Where did it take place?' and so on) so each category fulfils a different function in a story. Table C5.1 lists the six categories, the hypothetical questions they address and their respective narrative functions. The table also provides information on the sort of linguistic forms that each component typically takes. With the exception of Evaluation, the categories listed on the Table are arranged

Table C5.1 Labov's model of natural narrative

Narrative category	Narrative question	Narrative function	Linguistic form
ABSTRACT	What was this about?	Signals that the story is about to begin and draws attention from the listener.	A short summarising statement, provided before the narrative commences.
ORIENTATION	Who or what are involved in the story, and when and where did it take place?	Helps the listener to identify the time, place, persons, activity and situation of the story.	Characterised by past continuous verbs; and Adjuncts (see A3) of time, manner and place.
COMPLICATING ACTION	Then what happened?	The core narrative category providing the 'what happened' element of the story.	Temporally ordered narrative clauses with a verb in the simple past or present
RESOLUTION	What finally happened?	Recapitulates the final key event of a story.	Expressed as the last of the narrative clauses that began the Complicating Action.
EVALUATION	So what?	Functions to make the point of the story clear.	Includes: intensifiers; modal verbs; negatives; repetition; evaluative commentary; embedded speech; comparisons with unrealised events.
CODA	How does it all end?	Signals that a story has ended and brings listener back to the point at which s/he entered the narrative.	Often a generalised statement which is 'timeless' in feel.

in the sequence in which they would occur in a typical oral narrative. Evaluation tends to sit outside the central pattern because it can be inserted at virtually any stage during a narrative. Evaluation is also the most fluid of the narrative categories stylistically: it may take a variety of linguistic forms depending on what particular evaluative job it is doing. However, the insertion of evaluative devices is generally very important as it helps explain the relevance of the central, reportable events of a story. A fully formed narrative will realise all six categories, although many narratives may lack one or more components.

Putting the model to work: a natural narrative

Activity

Below you will find a transcription of a story recorded during linguistic fieldwork in Northern Ireland. Although narrative analysis was not the primary aim of the fieldwork, the resulting interviews often involved informants telling of amusing episodes that had happened to them. This story, which took well under a minute to tell, is a fairly compact example of a natural narrative – even if the storyteller has a somewhat sniffy attitude to the events described. In the transcription, pauses are indicated by three dots while other relevant glosses are placed in square brackets. Beside each chunk of the story are five boxes, corresponding to five of Labov's categories. Evaluation has not been included because, as noted above, this component tends to permeate the other categories and can occur throughout a narrative. Read the story through now and identify which category is which by writing (if this is your book) the name of the component in the box to the right of the relevant piece of text:

. . . well erm a weird one [i.e. episode] happened to me a couple of years back . . .	
y'know when I was working in Belfast at the time . . . I was out for erm out for a drive in the car the weekend y'know of the May Bank holiday I think it was . . .	
erm . . . I picked up a hitchhiker thumbing a lift to Derry, rounabout Toome [a village] . . . I wouldn't often do that, mind you , but well I didn't mind the company that day. Rounabout Magherafelt [another village], yer man puts a cigarette in his mouth and looks at me, like sort of inquring y'know . . . so I pushed in the dashboard lighter in the . . . [inaudible] When it popped out, I handed it to him but, b'Jesus, after him lighting the fag he sorta glanced around like puzzled and ye wouldn't believe it, he opened the window on his side and . . .	
chucked the bloody lighter out into the field!	
There's not much you can say about a thing like that, is there?	

Now go through the story again, this time underlining the Evaluation devices the narrator uses. How much variety is there in the linguistic forms that are used for narrative Evaluation? And what would be lost from this story if Evaluation was not there?

Stylistics and natural narrative

Stylisticians have made much of the Labovian model, not least because it enables rigorous comparisons to be drawn between literary narrative on the one hand and the social stories told in everyday interaction on the other. However, the model's simple six-part structure tends to make it best suited to literary narratives that are (literally) short, which is why stylistic applications have tended to concentrate either on narrative texts of only a hundred words or so (eg. Simpson 1992a) or on 'narratives within narratives' such as the sorts of stories told by individual characters within a longer novel or play (eg. Toolan 2001: 150–9). Although the general application of the Labovian model to a full-length novel is theoretically viable (see Pratt 1977: 38–78), the replication of its six basic components, sometimes over many hundreds of pages of text, means that the results of a direct analysis can be less than exhilarating. However, the seeking out of shorter literary texts for natural narrative analysis is, it has to be said, rather like the drunk man who loses his keys on the way home one evening and who, on retracing his steps, looks for them only under lamplight. So with a theoretical disclaimer duly delivered, what follows is a practical narrative exercise based around a short 'narrative within a narrative'.

Activity 

The passage below is from Eugene Ionesco's absurdist play *The Bald Prima Donna*, a play which satirises, after a fashion, its author's perception of the social and intellectual sterility of the English middle classes (see Burton 1980: 24). In this episode, two couples, Mr and Mrs Smith and Mr and Mrs Martin, engage in a bizarre story telling round in which Mrs Martin is encouraged to recount a narrative of personal experience about something 'interesting' that befell her. Read the passage through, concentrating particularly on the story told, across several speaker turns, by Mrs Martin:

MR MARTIN: [*to his wife*] Tell them, darling, what you saw today.

MRS MARTIN: Oh no, I couldn't. They'd never believe me.

MR SMITH: You don't think we'd doubt your word! [. . .]

MRS MARTIN: [*graciously*] Well, then! Today I witnessed the most extraordinary incident. It was absolutely incredible [. . .] As I was going to the market to buy some vegetables, which are still going up and up in price . . .

MRS SMITH: Yes, where on earth's it going to end!

MR SMITH: You mustn't interrupt, my dear. Naughty girl!

MRS MARTIN: In the street, outside a restaurant, was a gentleman, respectably dressed and about fifty years old, perhaps less, who was . . . Well, I know you'll say that I'm making it up: he was kneeling on the ground and leaning forward.

MR MARTIN:
MRS SMITH: } Oh!
MR SMITH:

MRS MARTIN: Yes! Leaning forward!
MR MARTIN:
MRS SMITH: } It can't be true!
MR SMITH:
MRS MARTIN: Yes! Leaning forward he was! I went right up to him to see what he was doing . . .
MR MARTIN:
MRS SMITH: } What ? What?
MR SMITH:
MRS MARTIN: His shoelaces had come undone and he was tying them up!
MR MARTIN:
MRS SMITH: } Fantastic!
MR SMITH:
MR SMITH: If I'd heard that from anyone else, I'd never have believed it.

(Ionesco 1963 [1958]: 98–9)

Now work through the following tasks which relate to the delivery, content and reception of Mrs Martin's 'shoelaces' story.

- ❑ What elements of the six-part Labovian model can you identify in Mrs Martin's story?
- ❑ Labov notes that it is understood among interactants that a narrative of personal experience must have a central reportable event. What is the central reportable event of Mrs Martin's story?
- ❑ To what extent does the category of Evaluation feature in Mrs Martin's story? In other words, what tactics does she use to ward off the 'so what' question? How many (and what sort of) Evaluation devices can you identify?
- ❑ With reference to the reaction her story draws from her interlocutors, is Mrs Martin's story successful *within* the interactive world of the play? That is, does it work at the *diegetic* (see A7) level?
- ❑ Going on your own reactions to it, to what extent is Mrs Martin's story successful *outside* the world of the play? In other words, does it work at the *extradiegetic* level?
- ❑ Following from the previous point, would you expect an audience (or readers of the play) to react in the same way as Mrs Martin's co-conversationalists to the story? How have the requirements for successful story-telling in the real world been transformed in the world of the absurd? Accepting that you may not have found it especially funny, can this piece of dialogue's potential for humour be explained by reference to this transformation?
- ❑ Ionesco's professed aim in this play is to break down the cliché-ridden and formulaic 'social language' that typifies polite bourgeois society (Ionesco 1964). How successful is this sort of dialogue in accomplishing this aim?

Drama dialogue is explored in depth across thread 9, where a range of stylistic issues and interests are covered. In the next three units the attention shifts away from the more structural aspects of narrative to consider models for the analysis of narrative as discourse. *Transitivity* is the first of those models.

TRANSITIVITY, CHARACTERISATION AND LITERARY GENRE

This unit offers some practical activities based around the model of transitivity developed in A6 and B6. It details first of all a stylistic experiment where transitivity can be used to highlight techniques of characterisation in narrative. It then widens the scope of the analysis to illustrate the ways in which transitivity can work as an important marker of literary genre.

Transitivity profiles

Some years ago, I co-authored an article with Martin Montgomery which examined a range of narrative devices, including patterns of transitivity, in Bernard MacLaverty's novel *Cal* (Simpson and Montgomery 1995). The implications of the article for the present unit will be clear soon. As far as our analysis of transitivity was concerned, we noted how certain types of process functioned to cast the novel's central character, Cal, as a rather ineffectual and passive observer on the events around him. Specifically, Cal is often represented as the Sensor in mental processes of perception or as the Actor in material processes which are not Goal-directed. Here is a flavour of the transitivity framework through which Cal the character is portrayed. Using the material provided in units A6 and B6, you should be able to identify the process types by yourself:

> A. Several times Cal saw the yellow Anglia pass in the opposite direction and followed it with his eyes. During the day he occasionally saw Marcella's child playing in the back garden or heard her prattling from another room when he was standing having a cup of tea in the kitchen. He also heard again the stomach-churning bubble of coughing from somewhere in the house.
>
> (MacLaverty 1984: 69)

In essence, Cal's actions are portrayed through a regular pattern of transitivity choices, a *transitivity profile* in other words. The transitivity profile embodied by a text is a generally useful indicator of character in prose fiction.

Part of the impetus for the Simpson and Montgomery paper referred to above came, like many publications in stylistics, from experience of teaching a text to students. In this particular case, our work on the MacLaverty novel took the form of a workshop on stylistics with thirty or so fluent speakers of English as an additional language. With respect to the idea of the transitivity profile, we were struck by how quickly the participants, while reading a novel, came to intuit a kind of stylistic template for the delineation of character. Evidence for this template came in the shape of an experiment involving pairs of related sentences, with one member of the pair a real sentence in the novel and the other a fake. On the basis of the short passage above, you may already be able to make reasonably strong predictions about which of these sentences 'fit' the novel and which do not:

(1a) The big one grabbed Cal.
(1b) Cal grabbed the big one.

(2a) She noticed that Cal was crying.
(2b) Cal noticed that she was crying.

(3a) Crilly handed two photographs to Cal.
(3b) Cal handed two photographs to Crilly.

(4a) He [Cal] moved his mouth to smile and the muscles of his face responded properly.
(4b) He [Cal] moved his mouth to smile but the muscles of his face would not respond properly.

The actual *Cal* sentences are 1a, 2b, 3a and 4b. Remarkably, the workshop participants, who had read the novel only once and without any accompanying stylistic explication, were *all* able to identify the correct sentences. (How did *you* fare?). It is not that the remaining sentences are 'impossible' or 'wrong' as such; it is more that they come across as stylistically anomalous, as incongruent with the overall tenor of characterisation in the novel. As suggested in A5, the relationship between transitivity and characterisation is a close one, and the usefulness of a simple exercise like this, where a set of actual patterns are paralleled by a set of variant patterns, is that it can bring this relationship to the forefront of the analysis. The exercise can also be replicated on any narrative text, and even on some non-narrative texts. What happens is that over the course of a narrative, which may span many hundred of pages of prose, certain elements are experientially foregrounded while others are suppressed. While we cannot expect to remember every sentence in a story, we do seem to develop a sense of a transitivity profile, a profile based on broad process and participant types as they relate to individual characters.

Genre

We can develop further the idea of the transitivity profile by moving up from the narrower features of characterisation to the broader area of literary *genre*. This move works on the premise that the styles of individual genres of literature, such as the popular romance, the Gothic horror tale, the fairy tale, the 'hard boiled' detective novel and so on, are in part defined by special and recurrent configurations of transitivity. Focussing on the first two of the literary genres just cited, you will find below two passages for analysis. The first is from a 'Mills and Boon' popular romance and the second from Bram Stoker's classic horror story *Dracula*:

B. Suzie closed her eyes, knowing that she should make the effort to go upstairs and go to bed, but reluctant to move. When she heard Carlos' deep voice, it was obvious he was standing very near to her. Her eyes flickered open to see him leaning over her, his face close to hers [. . .]

And then his mouth was on hers, taking her by surprise and stopping her breath. His arms locked around her, pulling her close. Like a knife, a sudden panic cut through Suzie's body as her brain screamed out the message that this was wrong – wrong! She struggled futilely against him, trying desperately to push him away, knowing full well that if she succumbed she would be lost and knowing also that she was fighting against herself. Even as her common sense told her this was pointless and wrong, her lips parted under his as if by a will of their own . . .

(*Escape to Love* by Claudia Jameson; cited in Nash 1990: 141)

C. There lay the Count, but looking as if his youth had been half-renewed, for the whole hair and moustache were changed to dark iron-grey; the cheeks were fuller, and the white skin seemed ruby-red underneath; the mouth was redder than ever, for on the lips were gouts of fresh blood, which trickled from the corners of the mouth and ran over the chin and neck. Even the deep, burning eyes seemed set amongst swollen flesh, for the lids and pouches underneath were bloated. It seemed as if the whole, awful creature were simply gorged with blood; he lay like a filthy leech, exhausted with his repletion.

(Stoker 1998 [1897]: 51)

Activity 

First of all, work through the two passages following this set of general exercises:

(a) Analyse the transitivity patterns in the two extracts, looking closely at:
  (i) The types of *processes* that are present.
  (Specify whether they are material, mental, behavioural and so on (see A6))
  (ii) The types of *participants* associated with each of the processes.
  (Identify participant roles like Actor, Goal, Sensor and so on (A6))
  (iii) Any special *types* of participant role.
  (See for example if you can distinguish *meronymic* agency from *holonymic* agency (see B6))
(b) What does your analysis of transitivity reveal about the key stylistic characteristics of each of the two genres of writing?

Having undertaken an analysis of the broader patterns, consider now the following issues and sub-activities which are directed more specifically to each of the passages:

Passage B:

(a) A generally useful framing question for the analysis of transitivity is to ask: *who or what does what to whom or what?* (and see further D6). The question provides useful orientation for the Mills and Boon passage, where it can help distinguish the two characters through the sorts of actions they perform. In a sense, the question helps differentiate who *does* from who *thinks.*

(b) A related issue in transitivity analysis concerns the success or failure of a semantic process. It is common for narrative description to indicate that a character *attempts* to carry out a process, but that the process either fails, or ends up being self-directed. In a self-directed material process, for example, the Actor and Goal become the same entity. Notice how in example (4b) from *Cal*, the process attributed to Cal as Actor is not only self-directed ('He moved his mouth to smile') but it fails as well ('the muscles of his face would not respond . . .').

(c) Look again at the Mills and Boon passage exploring the issues raised in (a) and (b). Is it true to say that its romantic heroine is portrayed as 'helpless'? And if so, is the portrayal of a female central character in this way sexist?

Passage C:

(a) The framing question set out for passage B obviously works better for material processes which express action than it does for relational processes which represent states of being. Not much seems to happen by way of physical action in the passage from *Dracula* and you may have found this passage more difficult to analyse for this reason. However, transitivity still has an important part to play even in heavily descriptive passages like text C. Furthermore, relational processes, of which there are many in C, are very much tied up with the sense of stasis in the scene and with the image of inertia and repletion which is attributed to the vampire.

(b) In the light of the observations in (a), look again at the relational processes in C. Remember, this process type is not just coded through the verb 'to be' but through a variety of intensive verbs like 'seem', 'appear', 'become' and so on. The participant roles for these processes include the elements Carrier and Attribute. What sort of entities make up the Carrier element and what sort of descriptions (Attributes) are attributed to them? Does the pattern you uncover give the impression of the Count as a whole being, or is his portrayal delivered in a more corporeally fragmented way?

(c) While transitivity is undoubtedly an important feature of style, it forms only part of the overall organisation of narrative discourse. Passage C offers a good illustration of how the experiential function is supplemented by other aspects of language, most notably markers of the *interpersonal* function (and see further C7). Notice for example how the narrator modulates his description of the vampire's post-prandial torpor. This is a narrator who seemingly struggles to make sense of the awful events in front of him, and this stamp of uncertainty and bewilderment is, in true Gothic horror style, manifested in heavily foregrounded references to visual appearance and to the interpretation of visual appearance. Look again at the passage and see how many of these archetypal markers of horror writing you can identify.

This unit has illustrated some of the ways in which the model of transitivity can usefully be employed in the study both of characterisation and of literary genre. Of course, the practical activities offered here are no more than a snapshot of a type of analysis that can be extended to many other styles of writing; nor are they intended to suggest that the experiential function is the only component of narrative that can offer insights into characterisation and genre. The interpersonal function of language, as signalled in the activities based around text C, plays an important role in the organisation of narrative discourse. This theme is developed further in the next unit.

EXPLORING POINT OF VIEW IN NARRATIVE FICTION

C7

This unit is designed to explore further the concept of point of view by building on the observation, made towards the end of C6, that the *interpersonal* function of language works in parallel with the experiential function in the overall stylistic make-up of a narrative text. The synthesis of the two functions is an important marker of style in its own terms, and the regular co-occurence of certain functional patterns often serves to distinguish different genres of writing. Unit B7 introduced and reviewed four principal types of point of view. The conclusion to that review was that, of the four types surveyed, *psychological* point of view is the pivotal term of reference for this dimension of narrative organisation. This unit offers the opportunity to develop some practical work around the key interpersonal features which serve to mark out psychological point of view in narrative.

Modality and style

The *interpersonal* function, as the term itself suggests, is about how we orientate, shape and measure our utterances as discourse. This function is expressed principally by the grammatical system of *modality* which is that part of language which allows us to attach expressions of belief, attitude and obligation to what we say and write. Modality is therefore the grammar of explicit comment, and it includes signals of the varying degrees of certainty we have about the propositions we express, and of the sorts of commitment or obligation that we attach to our utterances.

A useful way of fleshing out this rather abstract definition of modality, and in a way that helps align it with the concept of psychological point of view, is to consider some alternative types of modal patterning in a short sample narrative. The three invented 'mini-stories' that follow were scrawled on the back of a napkin in a British airport late one November evening some years ago. No more than the slightly deranged ramblings of a stylistician at a loss for something to do, these narratives make no claim whatsoever to any kind of literary accomplishment, although they do serve a useful purpose in sketching some basic concepts in modality and style. With all disclaimers delivered, consider the first version:

(1) *In the Heathrow cafeteria*
What a nuisance! The bally London to Tunis flight had been delayed, *quelle surprise.* The tannoy sheepishly attributed this to the late arrival of an incoming flight. Fog is normally the problem at this time of year.

I needed a robust coffee, so I felt I had to confront the busy cafeteria. A lone waitress patrolled the tables.

'What'll it be?' she asked, harassed.

'Strong coffee please,' I replied.

Her face tightened in a way that registered the request as unreasonable. She eventually brought to me, in a flowery mug, a pale grey liquid which I understood was to pass for filter coffee.

This is a homodiegetic narrative where actions and events are relayed through a first person 'participating' narrator. So much is obvious, but it is the manner by which these actions and events are relayed that is rather more significant here. The narrator of (1) tells you not only what happens but also what he thinks. Throughout, interpretations and interpolations are offered as to why events unfold in the way they do, with the narrator cooperatively orientating what they say towards an implied reader. Text (1) thus embodies a particular type of modal framework which in narrative discourse is marked by certain key expressions. The narrator, for example, expresses clearly their own desires, duties, obligations and opinions in relation to events and other characters: 'I *needed* a coffee'; 'I *felt I had to* confront the busy cafeteria' and so on. Modality which expresses desire and obligation is known as *deontic* modality. Notice also that the narrator of (1) – and this self-analysis is not to suggest any craft in its creation – employs a generic sentence in the sequence 'Fog is normally the problem at this time of year'. This key marker of narratorial modality, which is always expressed through the timeless simple present tense, allows the narrator confidently to represent what they say as a universal truth. The text is also rich in what Uspensky (1973) calls *verba sentiendi.* These are words denoting thoughts, feelings and perceptions, as embodied in mental processes like 'I felt . . .' or 'I understood . . .'. Overall, the text is dominated by clearly articulated personal interpretations of felt experience where the narrator makes sense of the experience before relaying it. Let us adopt the term *positive shading* for this type of modal pattern.

Consider now another version, another embodiment in discourse as it were, of the same basic narrative *plot.* Here the first person narrator appears to have a little more trouble in making sense of and relaying experience:

(2) *In the Heathrow cafeteria*
The London to Tunis flight must have been delayed because the tannoy said something about the late arrival of another flight. Perhaps it was fog?

I must have been hungry, or maybe thirsty, because I found myself in a large busy room whose appearance suggested it was a cafeteria. A woman, in the attire of a waitress, patrolled the tables.

'What'll it be?' she asked, as if harassed by my presence.

'Strong coffee please,' I seem to recall saying.

Her face tightened as though she found my request unreasonable. She eventually brought to me, in a flowery mug, a pale grey liquid which must have been filter coffee.

The overall interpersonal dynamic of this (admittedly bizarre) piece of narrative is very different from (1). This is a narrator who *tries* to make sense of the world around him, but does so with only limited success. His account is marked by *epistemic* modality which refers to the system of modal markers used for signalling judgments of belief, certainty or truth. Epistemic modality works principally in (2) to foreground the narrator's efforts to interpret and make sense of what he sees and hears: '[the] flight *must have been* delayed . . .'; '*Perhaps* it was fog . . .' and so on. The passage is also rich in 'words of estrangement' (Fowler 1996) which reinforce the narrator's seeming uncertainty about what is going on around him. A consequence of this is that description tends to rely on the narrator's interpretation of external appearance; notice how it is the appearance of the room which suggests it was a cafeteria, and the woman's attire that suggests she was a waitress. To accommodate this sort of modal framework, where the epistemic system is heightened as the narrator struggles to make sense of the world, let us reserve the term *negative shading.*

Finally, consider a third variant:

(3) *In the Heathrow cafeteria*

The London to Tunis flight had been delayed. The tannoy referred to the late arrival of an incoming flight. I went into a cafeteria. A woman patrolled the tables.

'What'll it be?' she said.

'Strong coffee please,' I said.

Her face tightened. She eventually brought me a mug of coffee.

This version is characterised by, if anything, a marked absence of narratorial modality. It is constructed entirely from *categorical assertions*; that is to say, from raw propositions which have no trace of explicit modal comment. Because they are stripped of modality, categorical assertions are in a certain respect non-negotiable, and the removal of interpersonal markers in (3) explains in part why it is much shorter than the first two versions. In this type of modal framework (or, better, 'demodalised' framework), the narrator withholds subjective evaluation in favour of an ostensibly more 'neutral' description of events. Straightforward physical description dominates, while there is little or no attempt at any psychological development or interpretation. Even the reporting clauses which are used to relay sequences of Direct Speech (see thread 8) have been stripped of their adverbial embellishments, so that nothing other than the most basic of reporting verbs remain. Let us refer to this type of modal framework as *neutral shading.*

Before we move to consider the significance of this exercise and of the three narrative modalities identified, it is worth noting that transpositions to third person variants are possible with all three texts. In other words, the same basic modal framework can be transferred across into corresponding heterodiegetic modes. For example, version 2 might be rewritten thus:

(2a) *In the Heathrow cafeteria*
The London to Tunis flight must have been delayed because the tannoy said something about the late arrival of another flight. Perhaps it was fog?
Simpson must have been hungry, or maybe thirsty, because he found himself in a large busy room whose appearance suggested it was a cafeteria. A woman, in the attire of a waitress, patrolled the tables.
'What'll it be?' she asked, as if harassed by his presence.
'Strong coffee please,' he replied.
Her face tightened as if she found his request unreasonable. She eventually brought to him, in a flowery mug, a pale grey liquid which must have been filter coffee.

In this version, the original narrator of (2) becomes a character within the story, a character who in fact occupies the role of reflector of fiction (see A7), while the new narrator is 'heterodiegetic' in the sense of being different from and external to the story. Although the negatively shaded modality follows the transposition, the source of the epistemic warrant for what is narrated is now less clear. Is it the reflector of fiction who is the 'bewildered' focaliser here? Or is it the external, non-participating narrator? Or is it even some combination of both? Both of the other original versions can be similarly transposed, so that the same modality (of lack of it) carries over into the third person framework. Again, the same questions are raised about where the source for the modal comment should be situated. Basically, the third person framework offers two options: either align the modality with the external narrator or locate it in the viewpoint of the character-reflector. This means that the point of view model becomes a little more complex when applied specifically to the third person mode because it offers two variants for each of the three modal possibilities. It also means that there is considerable scope for ambiguity, and sometimes for irony, in this mode, because we are often less certain about whose point of view exactly is being relayed in third person narratives.

Modality and psychological point of view

This sub-unit outlines some practical activities that follow from the point of view rewrite exercise undertaken above. Before going on to consider some of the implications of the exercise for passages of 'real' fiction, it will be worth recapping upon and tightening up the three basic types of modal patterning identified thus far in our survey:

Positive shading: this is a narrative modality where the narrator's desires, duties, obligations and opinions of events are foregrounded. The *deontic* modal system is prominent and the narrative is rich in generic sentences and in *verba sentiendi* (words denoting thoughts, feelings and perceptions). Positive shading is perhaps the most common point of view modality, underpinning a great many first and third person fictional works.

Negative shading: this is a narrative modality where an often 'bewildered' narrator (or character) relies on external signals and appearances to sustain a description. The *epistemic* modal system is foregrounded and the narrative is rich in 'words of estrangement'. The narrator's uncertainty about events and about other characters' motivations is often expressed through structures based on human perception (*as if*; *it seemed*; *it appeared to be*, etc.). Negative shading often characterises 'existentialist' or 'Gothic' styles of narrative fiction.

Neutral shading: this style is characterised by a complete absence of narratorial modality and is typified by *categorical assertions* where the narrator withholds subjective evaluation and interpretation. This type of shading often comprises 'neutral' physical description at the expense of psychological development. Neutral shading embodies the principle of 'objective realism' in fiction and it corresponds to what the narratologists Genette (1980) and Rimmon-Kenan (1983) have called 'external' focalisation. Given the often sparse feel this mode engenders, narratives written entirely in a neutrally shaded modality are rare.

It is, of course, possible for a literary text to shift from one pattern to another, even while a particular pattern dominates overall.

Activity 

You will find below seven passages of prose fiction. The passages are not ordered in any particular or significant sequence, and the only thing to bear in mind is that there are present at least two representatives of each of the three categories of modal shading. As you work through each passage, follow the guidelines below:

(i) Identify (as far as you can tell) the narrative *mode* in which the passage is written. That is, say whether it is first person or third person.
(ii) Identify the *dominant* type of modal shading in each passage. Do not try to analyse the passage on a sentence by sentence basis, but rather pick out the modal framework which best describes the passage as a whole. Highlight any of the tell-tale devices that help confirm your interpretation.
(iii) If you identify a passage as third person, try to work out whether its modality (ie. the attitudes, opinions and beliefs it expresses) comes from (a) an external heterodiegetic narrator who is situated *outside* the story or (b) from an individual character, a reflector of fiction (A7), who is situated *inside* the story.
(iv) Wherever feasible, think of the stylistic impact of both the narrative mode and the point of view framework that each writer has chosen. What would happen if either the narrative mode or the particular modal shading were altered?

Seven passages

a) Shaking off from my spirit what *must* have been a dream, I scanned more narrowly the real aspect of the building. Its principal features seemed to be that of an excessive antiquity. The discolouration of ages had been great. No portion of the masonry had fallen; and there appeared to be a wild inconsistency between its still perfect adaptation of parts, and the crumbling of the individual stones. Beyond this indication of extensive decay, however, the fabric gave little token of instability. Perhaps the eye of a scrutinising observer might have discovered a barely perceptible fissure [. . .]

(*The Fall of the House of Usher*, Edgar Allan Poe 1986 [1839])

b) In my younger and more vulnerable years my father gave me some advice that I've been turning over in my mind ever since.

'Whenever you feel like criticising any one,' he told me, 'just remember that all the people in this world haven't had the advantages that you've had.'

He didn't say any more, but we've always been unusually communicative in a reserved way, and I understood that he meant a great deal more than that. In consequence, I'm inclined to reserve all judgments, a habit that has opened up many curious natures to me and also made me the victim of not a few veteran bores. The abnormal mind is quick to detect and attach itself to this quality when it appears in a normal person [. . .]

(*The Great Gatsby*, F. Scott Fitzgerald 1994 [1925])

c) The fat white circles of dough lined the pan in rows. Once more Sethe touched a wet forefinger to the stove. She opened the oven door and slid a pan of biscuits in. As she raised up from the heat she felt Paul D behind her and his hands under her breasts. She straightened up [. . .]

(*Beloved*, Toni Morrison 1987)

d) Someone must have been telling lies about Joseph K., for without having done anything wrong he was arrested one fine morning. His landlady's cook, who always brought him his breakfast at eight o'clock, failed to appear on this occasion. That had never happened before. K. waited for a little while longer, watching from his pillow the old lady opposite, who seemed to be peering at him with a curiosity unusual even for her, but then, feeling both put out and hungry, he rang the bell. At once there was a knock at the door and a man entered whom he had never seen before in the house. He was slim and yet well knit, he wore a closely fitting black suit, which was furnished with all sorts of pleats, pockets, buckles, and buttons, as well as a belt, like a tourist's outfit, and in consequence looked eminently practical, though one could not quite tell what actual purpose it served.

'Who are you?' asked K., half raising himself in bed. But the man ignored the question, as though his appearance needed no explanation.

(*The Trial*, Franz Kafka 1985 [1925])

e) He [Strether] was to to delay no longer to reestablish communication with Chad, and [. . .] he had spoken to Miss Gostrey of this intention on hearing from her of the young man's absence. It was not, moreover, only the assurance so given that prompted him; it was the need of causing his conduct to square with another profession still – the motive he had described to her as his sharpest for now getting away [. . .] He must do both things; he must see Chad, but he must go. The more he thought of the former of these duties the more he felt himself make a subject of insistence of the latter.

(*The Ambassadors*, Henry James 2001 [1903])

f) We were in a garden in Mons. Young Buckley came in with his patrol from across the river. The first German I saw climbed over up the garden wall. We waited till he got one leg over and then potted him [. . .] Then three more came over further down the wall. We shot them. They all came just like that.

(from a story in *In Our Time*, Ernest Hemingway 1925)

g) Different though the sexes are, they intermix. In every human being a vacillation from one sex to the other takes place, and it is only the clothes that keep the male or female likeness, while underneath the sex is the very opposite of what it is above.

(*Orlando*, Virginia Woolf 1998 [1928])

Summary

I hope your analysis of the sample passages above will have underscored the stylistic significance of modal shading as a marker not only of point of view but of narrative style more generally. As with all the units in this Exploration section, I do not propose to provide a circumscribed set of 'answers', and in any case my own interpretation counts as just one of many possible interpretations that can be systematically reached on the basis of a stylistic analysis. I will however footnote briefly one of the passages, the Toni Morrison excerpt c), because of the particularly interesting issues it raises.

On the grounds that it is devoid of any modality at all, my analysis suggests that this passage embodies neutral shading. Whereas its narrative mode is third person, its point of view is aligned, significantly, with the reflector of fiction. That is to say, in spite of the third-person framework, the narrative camera angle assumes the vantage point of a particular character, here Sethe, and it is her experience of events which is recorded and relayed. (Notice how this is established by the word 'felt', the one verb of perception in the passage.) Interestingly, this generally 'flat' modal framework tends in this discourse context to make the central character seem numb, and very much acquiescent to the advances of Paul D. We are given no information as to whether she welcomes or is offended by his advances, the sort of information that would be communicated precisely by a positively shaded modality. Prior to this point in the novel, we have learned of Sethe's experience of having to have sex with a stonemason simply to get an engraving on a dead child's headstone, and this and other traumatic events may have rendered her emotionally dead, and unable or unwilling to react to the events around her. This is not to argue, though, that the modality of the novel as a whole is neutrally shaded nor indeed that this character's perceptions of the world are always relayed in this way. It is very much in the idiom of the 'post-modern' novel, of which *Beloved* is a preeminent example, that it tangles up different domains of discourse and allows its characters to migrate between different text worlds (McHale 1987). To my mind, variable narrative focalisation is just one of the reflexes of the post-modernist 'style', such as it is, where the oscillations in point of view give rise to many alternating viewing positions and modalities.

Looking at how patterns in point of view mark out not just the postmodern novel but other genres of narrative fiction would make for a useful future study. Another would be to see if additional modal frameworks could be developed, beyond the three proposed in this unit, which could more subtly delineate types of writing style. Some more general issues to do with narrative viewpoint are raised in Mick Short's reading, D5, which 'doubles up' as a useful reading for this thread.

C8

A WORKSHOP ON SPEECH AND THOUGHT PRESENTATION

This workshop programme is designed to encourage you to use your stylistic analyses in tandem with your affective responses to literary texts and to enable you to challenge and (re)evaluate some of the literary critical commentaries that have been written on the texts you are studying. Before moving onto the more practical aspects of the programme, it is worth introducing here the short passage that will form the nucleus of the workshop activity. It is taken from American writer Ernest Hemingway's short novel (or novella) *The Old Man and the Sea* (see also unit B1). The intention will ultimately be to place this passage against a series of literary-critical comments about the novella and then to use an analysis of speech and thought presentation as a way of reappraising these critical comments and of reaching more systematic interpretations about Hemingway's narrative technique.

Activity

The passage itself is taken from the lengthy central section of the story which covers the time the old man spends at sea during his struggle with the huge marlin that he has hooked. This particular episode occurs early in the morning of the second day of his battle with the fish (thus explaining the references in the text to 'the line' slanting into the water). He is confronted with two practical problems: eating the small tuna that he caught the day before and solving the problem of his cramped left hand. The passage is quite neatly rounded in that it stretches from the preparatory stages to the completion of the old man's meal. To facilitate subsequent referencing to the passage, lines have been numbered and paragraph boundaries have been double-spaced. Read the passage now. Don't worry about locating any stylistic features in the passage at this stage and don't feel you that are being asked to make any kind of interpretative judgment about the text.

The Text

He knelt down and found the tuna under the stern with the gaff and drew it toward him keeping it clear of the coiled lines. Holding the line with his left shoulder again, and bracing on his left hand and arm, he took the tuna off the gaff hook and put the gaff back in place. He put one knee on the fish and cut strips of dark red meat longitudinally from the back of the head to the tail. They were wedge-shaped strips and he cut them from next to the back bone down to the edge of the belly. When he had cut six strips he spread them out on the wood of the bow, wiped his knife on his trousers, and lifted the carcass of the bonito by the tail and dropped it overboard.

'I don't think I can eat an entire one,' he said and drew his knife across one of the strips. He could feel the steady hard pull of the line and his left hand was cramped. It drew up tight on the heavy cord and he looked at it in disgust.

'What kind of a hand is that,' he said. 'Cramp then if you want. Make yourself into a claw. It will do you no good.'

Come on, he thought and looked down into the dark water at the slant of the line. Eat it now and it will strengthen the hand. It is not the hand's fault and you have been many hours with the fish. But you can stay with him for ever. Eat the bonito now.

He picked up a piece and put it in his mouth and chewed it slowly. It was not unpleasant.

Chew it well, he thought, and get all the juices. It would not be bad to eat with a little lime or with lemon or with salt.

'How do you feel, hand?' he asked the cramped hand that was almost as still as rigor mortis. 'I'll eat some more for you.'

He ate the other part of the piece that he had cut in two. He chewed it carefully and then spat out the skin.

'How does it go, hand? Or is it too early to know?'

He took another full piece and chewed it.

'It is a strong full-blooded fish,' he thought. 'I was lucky to get him instead of dolphin. Dolphin is too sweet. This is hardly sweet at all and all the strength is still in it.'

There is no sense in being anything but practical though, he thought. I wish I had some salt. And I do not know whether the sun will rot or dry what is left, so I had better eat it all although I am not hungry. The fish is calm and steady. I will eat it all and then I will be ready.

'Be patient, hand,' he said. 'I do this for you.'

I wish I could feed the fish, he thought. He is my brother. But I must kill him and keep strong to do it. Slowly and conscientiously he ate all of the wedge-shaped strips of fish.

He straightened up, wiping his hand on his trousers.

Hemingway (1976 [1952]: 47–9)

A workshop on stylistics and literary evaluation

The following five statements, written by different literary critics, are concerned with aspects of language and style in Hemingway's *The Old Man and the Sea.* Now that you have read a section of this novella and perhaps formed your own impressions of Hemingway's style of writing, try to rank the five statements in order of accuracy and appropriateness. Try to say why you consider a particular remark to be more or less effective than another:

A As a matter of fact, Hemingway takes pains to avoid the *mot juste*, probably because it sounds too 'literary' to him, preferring the general, unspecific word like 'and' . . .

B . . . there is a really heroic piece of narrative in *The Old Man and the Sea*, told with a simplicity which shows that Mr. Hemingway has forgotten that he is a tough writer . . . the first few pages are almost strangely sentimental with relapses into the 'ands' of children's storybooks.

C The reader who expects a psychological novel will feel disappointed, despite the superb handling of the material and the style which is classical in its simplicity and force, pure as poetry, sonorous as music, flowing on the rhythms of the sea it describes.

D The plain, dry, restrained and documentary style succeeds in lending an extraordinary glow and depth to its simple subject matter.

E Granted, then, that Hemingway's diction is thin; that in the technical sense, his syntax is weak; and that he would be rather be caught dead than seeking the *mot juste* or the balanced phrase. Granted that his adjectives are not colourful and his verbs not particularly energetic.

What my students said

On the basis of their earlier reading of the passage, a group of thirty of my students were asked to rank these statements in the manner detailed above. It has to be said that the students whose comments are reported here found very little of value in any of the critical statements. Statement A was felt to be 'not particularly informative', though it was 'reasonable enough' as far as it went. Statement B was 'too personalised about the writer' but otherwise seemed 'OK'. Statement C fared very badly, and the comment about style 'flowing on the rhythms of the sea' was singled out for particular criticism ('naff'; 'too airy-fairy'; 'completely daft'). Statement D was responded to more positively, although students found it hard to see how a 'documentary style' could make subject matter 'glow'. Opinion was divided on statement E, largely because students felt that it was 'too out of context' to know what the critic was getting at, although 'what he [*sic*] did say might be interesting'. The tutor was rebuked for this oversight and urged to replace statement E with something more accessible in future. Overall, though, there was some measure of agreement across the group of students about the usefulness or otherwise of the five statements. The overall ranking, beginning with the most favoured statement, runs as follows: D, A,

E, B, C. How did your own ranking compare with this sequence? We will return to these rankings later.

The analysis of speech and thought presentation

The next stage of the programme involves an analysis of speech and thought presentation in the passage using the criteria outlined in units A8 and B8. You should refamiliarise yourself with the broad categories introduced in these units before progressing any further. As there are many types of speech and thought modes in evidence, a good idea is to mark up on the text the modes you spot. Try to see how many modes you can identify and how they are used to signal and accommodate different aspects of the story. (A full analysis of the passage in terms of its patterns of speech and thought presentation is provided in the web material which accompanies this book.)

The bigger picture: seeing transitions between speech and thought

Now that you have identified in the passage the many and varied modes of speech and thought presentation, and the patterns of oscillation between these modes, it might be worth trying to see if we can develop a visual representation for the stylistic fabric of the text. Figure C8.1 works as a template for charting the two main directions of narrative organisation in the passage. The horizontal axis on the figure represents the simple forward development of the passage, moving from line 1 through to line 42. The vertical axis marks the transitions between one strand

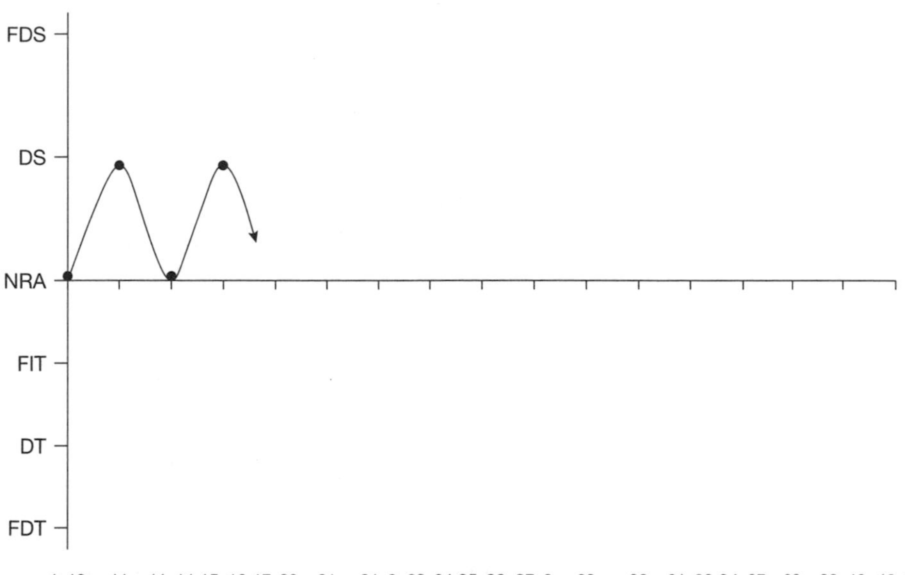

Figure C8.1 Template for charting narrative organisation in *Old Man and the Sea* extract

of speech and thought presentation and another, such that every one of the modes realised in the passage can be assigned a position on the vertical axis. Speech modes are plotted above the NRA line on the vertical axis; thought modes below. I have marked up, with dots in the relevant places, the four modes in evidence up to line 16. Using dots to chart subsequent modes, complete the figure. Then, once you are satisfied that all the modes have been plotted on the figure, join up (with a single line moving from left to right) all the modes. Each of the transitions in the passage will now be represented by a through-line connecting each node on the axis. You should end up with a wavy line which intersects with the straight line in the middle.

Stylistic analysis and critical (re)evaluation

The implications of this figure will be the main issue developed in this part of the workshop programme. First of all, you should reevaluate the five literary-critical comments provided earlier in the light of your analysis of the text and in the light of the visual representation of the narrative texture provided by the figure. Are any of the critical comments, in your opinion, a true reflection of Hemingway's prose style? Do any of the critics come close to giving a genuine insight into the language of this text? Is it true, as most of the critics seem to suggest, that the style of the passage is 'simple'? And, importantly, have you been tempted, since doing your analysis, to modify your initial rankings in any way?

The figure, with its double axis showing narrative development, suggests perhaps a degree of subtlety in narrative organisation that had not hitherto been identified by the critics. The group of students who produced the initial ranking offered some illuminating feedback on the basis of their analysis of speech and thought. For the most part, their analysis only served to consolidate the impression that the critical statements offered little in the way of concrete information about Hemingway's use of language in the passage. Having said that, there was one particular statement that caught the attention of the group when it was set against the figure. This was statement C, which had been resolutely and unequivocally consigned to the bottom of the original ranking list.

The points of intersection between the layout of the figure and critic C's remarks are interesting. The critic suggests that narrative technique is foregrounded at the expense of psychological interpretation, and to the extent that the style of the novella echoes the very physicality of what it sets out to depict. This culminates in the reference to the style 'flowing on the rhythms of the sea it describes'. Although scoffed at initially, this remark, when placed in the context of the completed figure, no longer reads like the critical excess it first seemed. Indeed, it prompts a hypothesis that is both tendentious and fanciful but is nonetheless worth mooting as a point for debate. Consider the following argument. Our figure essentially captures a dual movement in the passage: the linear progression of the text as narrative on one level, and the movement created by oscillations between speech and thought modes on another. There is a curious analogy between this dual movement at the level of narrative structure and the implied movements of the old man and his boat. On the one hand, the boat moves on the sea horizontally – the effect of being dragged by the huge marlin; on the other, it moves up and down vertically as a consequence of the swell of the Gulf Stream. Both types of movement are referred to frequently by the narrator in the novella's central section. Moreover, the particular wave-like pattern of speech and thought presentation identified in our analysis is *only* initiated once the old man sets sail in his boat. Thereafter, it is sustained with almost mathematical consistency during his time at sea. Is it the case, then, that the 'narrative waves' created as stylistic texture are an analogue of the fictional environment portrayed in the story? Has critic C – whose remarks seemed so outlandish at first glance – perhaps stumbled intuitively upon one of the novella's central motifs?

We cannot really answer this question with any degree of certainty. Stylistic categories and affective responses are simply not homologous spheres of reference, and the interpretative pathway that connects them is abstract, indirect and multidimensional. That said, my students were noticeably divided in their opinion about the 'narrative wave' argument when it was put to them. Some simply were not convinced by my suggested connection between the stylistic analysis and the physical elements of the fictional world. However, they were hard put to explain *why* they found the theory unconvincing. Around two-thirds of the group, by contrast, found the theory appealing. There was a general sense that the rhythmical texture displayed by the narrative analysis echoed the very movements of the old man on the sea and, as a consequence, these students wanted to elevate comment C to the top of their ranking. They felt that the critic had had an 'insight' into the style of the story, though they added the proviso that no evidence was offered in support of this insight. As far as the 'narrative waves' idea is concerned, you can decide which side you want to come down on: is the idea a fanciful conceit based on a mere stylistic coincidence, or is it the perception of a deftly crafted *leitmotif* embodying the very essence of the novella? There is no right or wrong answer to this. What is important is that we think of the reasons why we might adopt one position or the other. In other words, we need to ground what we say about the language of a text in a model that does precisely that; we need a language for talking about language, a *metalanguage*, as was argued in unit A1. In this workshop we looked at five rather speculative critical comments which all stressed the supposed 'simplicity' of the story's style. What little stylistic evidence there was on offer tended to be drawn from perceived patterns in vocabulary. Yet parts of speech such as nouns, verbs and adjectives are not necessarily the principal indices of narrative style; nor is the specific connective 'and' about which, frankly, some preposterous comments were made in the critical statements. Indeed, the evidence provided by our analysis and figure suggests a level of complexity and depth in narrative organisation that appears to have eluded the critics completely. That said, the present workshop is not about the validity or otherwise of the 'narrative wave' hypothesis. It is about the way we link analysis and interpretation, the way we present our case to others, and the way we seek to explain how a stylistic analysis can impact on the literary evaluation of a text.

C9

C9 EXPLORING DIALOGUE

An important organising principle across this thread has been the working assumption that dialogue occurs in a discourse context and that the structures and strategies of dialogue need to be investigated with reference to this context. Awareness of context, in its physical, personal and cognitive dimensions, and the forms of communication that are appropriate to it, is what constitutes part of a speaker's communicative competence (see A9). This unit develops a practical activity around this intersection between dialogue, context and communicative competence. In keeping with work in this branch of discourse stylistics (B9), the activity is designed to provide an analytic method for exploring fictional dialogue. By looking at *unusual* dialogue, it also seeks to highlight the underlying patterns of non-fictional interaction through the analysis of fictional communication. It has not escaped discourse stylisticians that the analysis of unusual dialogue is both an important critical tool in its own terms and a useful way of bringing into sharper focus the commonplace routines of discourse that often pass us by in everyday social interaction.

Discourse and context

Not exactly drama dialogue, the passage selected for analysis is part of a well-known comedy sketch from the television series *Monty Python's Flying Circus.* Before the text is introduced, it will be worth undertaking a short contextualising exercise as a preliminary to the analysis. To a certain extent, this is an exercise in communicative competence because it requires the matching up of appropriate forms of discourse to a specific set of contextual variables (see A9). Consider the following set of instructions:

> Think about the sort of verbal interaction that would typically take place in the following contextual circumstances:
>
> A. The participants in dialogue are two white middle-class, middle-aged English males. They have never met before. Both are dressed reasonably formally and they both speak with relatively high-prestige southern English accents. These are the only obvious features that they have in common.
>
> B. The physical context of interaction is a plush English public house. The pub is busy, and most seats are taken. Having just brought drinks from the bar, the two strangers end up sitting side-by-side at the same table.
>
> Working from this contextualisation and drawing on the ideas developed in A9 and B9, try to predict:
>
> (i) what sort of dialogue would be likely to ensue between the two men should they decide to talk to one another.
>
> (ii) what sorts of discourse strategies are likely to be used by the respective parties in interaction.

(iii) what sorts of terms of address or politeness tactics would characterise this sort of interaction.

(iv) what sorts of topics of discourse would be considered suitable in this interactive context.

On the basis of your responses to (i-iv) write down a short piece of dialogue that would be typical in this sort of interactive context.

The fragment of dialogue below is the opening of Monty Python's famous 'Nudge Nudge' sketch, first broadcast on BBC2 in 1971. For ease of reference in the transcript, the anonymous characters have been named metonymically through slight differences in their dress, the first man as CRAVAT and the second as TIE. Throughout the interaction, CRAVAT embellishes each of his utterances with highly exaggerated nonverbal gestures that include nudging his interlocutor with his elbow at appropriate cues in his speech. CRAVAT also uses an exclusively sexual nonverbal gesture brought about by crossing his forearms and rapidly raising and lowering one fist. As you read the extract, think about the extent to which your predictions about dialogue and context are fulfilled:

CRAVAT: Is your wife a . . . goer . . . eh? Know what I mean? Know what I mean? Nudge nudge. Nudge nudge. Know what I mean? Say no more . . . know what I mean?
TIE: I beg your pardon?
CRAVAT: Your wife . . . does she, er, does she 'go' – eh? eh? eh? Know what I mean, know what I mean? Nudge nudge. Say no more.
TIE: She sometimes goes, yes.
CRAVAT: I bet she does. I bet she does. I bet she does. Know what I mean. Nudge nudge.
TIE: I'm sorry, I don't quite follow you.
CRAVAT: Follow me! *Follow* me! I like that. That's good. A nod's as good as a wink to a blind bat, eh?
TIE: Are you trying to sell something?

(*Monty Python's Flying Circus* 1971)

Commentary: incongruity in discourse

In its day, the Monty Python series marked a radically new comic genre, although their sometimes surreal and dark humour was not to everyone's taste. The 'Nudge Nudge' sketch is archetypally Pythonesque in its design, although, like much of the team's output, its sexism can make it feel uncomfortable by today's standards. That said, it does offer an illuminating example of how to create humour through a simple mismatch between context and utterance. Your own analysis, which was effectively based on the exploration of your communicative competence, may have already gone some way towards explaining the oddity of TIE and CRAVAT's interaction. There are for example very strong interactive constraints on what can be said at the beginning of a conversation between two people who don't know each other, and I imagine that your responses to questions (i) to (iv) above would have predicted a fairly narrowly circumscribed set of utterance types. The sorts of utterances used for conversational openings – what linguists refer to as *phatic communion* – are expected to be neutral and uncontroversial. Thus, interactively 'safe' gambits in the context established in the sketch would include references to the weather ('Nice day') or comments on the shared physical context ('About time someone cleared these glasses'). What is manifestly *not* cued by the context is the interrogation of the interlocutor about his private life. While the marital status of a stranger is obviously a delicate subject, topics concerning sexual behaviour are even more taboo. CRAVAT's thinly veiled insinuations about the sexual behaviour of his interlocutor's wife (about which TIE is perversely slow on the uptake) are thoroughly incongruous in this sort of discourse context.

Of many other discoursal features of stylistic interest, it is worth noting how TIE's apparent bewilderment at CRAVAT's questions impacts on the development of the structure of *exchanges* (see A9 and B9). CRAVAT's initiations tend to be followed by requests for restarts from TIE. TIE's seeming inability to take up CRAVAT's sexual references creates an impasse which leads to repeated loops in discourse structure, and this is further compacted by CRAVAT's single-minded pursuit of the same basic innuendo even beyond those phrases conventionally used as sexual double-entendres ('*Follow* me! I like that'). And it is only after thirty more lines of the same cyclical pattern of discourse that TIE eventually begins to grasp the point when finally, in a comment that summarises the sketch's entire topical drift, he says 'Look, are you insinuating something?'

Summary

Although not drama dialogue *per se*, the Python sketch can be placed, as can many other types of non-dramatic dialogue, in Short's layered interactive schema (see A9). This is particularly useful for interpreting the comic effect of the dialogue. The viewer/reader positioned at the higher interactive level occupies the position of a kind of discoursal 'on-looker'. The communicative competence that organises everyday interaction for the on-looker acts as a frame for interpreting the incongruity of the displayed interaction down at the character level. The greater part of the humour of this Python sketch arguably stems from the mismatch between character speech and the discourse context in which it is embedded within the text. As noted earlier, analysing unusual talk implicitly draws attention to the canonical and the everyday in interaction. Indeed, it may be possible to read this text as, amongst other things, a skit on the repressively mundane trivia that often passes for conversation between non-familiar interactants.

The intersection between style and humour is further addressed in two units, A12 and D12, where additional types of comic language are explored. In the following unit, a variety of practical activities are developed, some of which involve the analysis of play dialogue with some attention to humour. However, the methods developed there mark a new perspective, which is altogether more cognitive than discoursal in orientation.

COGNITIVE STYLISTICS AT WORK

This unit offers an opportunity to apply a number of the constructs developed across this strand to different types of literary text. Although no more than a snapshot of the range of methods currently available in cognitive poetics, it should nonetheless signal the type of direction such an analysis might take. A more comprehensive analysis is provided in the reading that accompanies this unit (D10), where Margaret Freeman explores from a cognitive stylistic perspective a special kind of grammatical pattern in the poems of Emily Dickinson.

Schemas in literary discourse: that restaurant again

Schank and Abelson's 'restaurant script' was touched upon in B10, and given the fame, not to say notoriety, their illustration has acquired over the years, we should probably undertake a stylistic activity that explores this very scenario. As noted, Schank and Abelson build the idea of temporal progression into a script by defining it as a *stereotyped sequence of actions* that define a well-known situation. This ties in well with models of discourse (see C9) which take account of our assumptions about how certain routines of discourse should progress.

Activity 

Read through the following two extracts from Steven Berkoff's play *Greek* (the extracts are separated by around forty lines of dialogue, which includes interaction between characters other than the two featured here):

(1) *Cafe. Chorus of kitchen cafe menu sounds and phrases.*
EDDY: One coffee please and croissant and butter.
WAITRESS: Right. Cream?
EDDY: Please.
(. . .)

(2) EDDY: Where's my fucking coffee? I've nearly finished this cheesecake and then my whole purpose in life at this particular moment will be lost. I'll be drinking hot coffee with nothing to wash it down with.
WAITRESS: Here you are, sorry I forgot you!
EDDY: About fucking time!
WAITRESS: Oh shut your mouth, you complaining heap of rat's shit.

(Berkoff 1983: 35f)

With respect to the obvious transition in discourse strategies that occur in (2), try to highlight any features of discourse that challenge your understanding of the natural progression of this familiar service encounter. To what extent is Berkoff's dialogue an example of *schema disruption* as described in B10? And to what extent can our predictions about the development of a script (in this case the progression of the restaurant script) be aligned with our predictions about discourse and dialogue (especially politeness strategies)?

Text worlds and sub-worlds: stream of consciousness writing

The second activity suggested in this unit is likely to prove the more difficult. Its purpose is to try to balance the ideas about text worlds and narrative comprehension that were outlined in B10 and to apply them to a short piece of 'stream of consciousness' writing from Joyce's *Ulysses.* Here first of all is the passage in question which, when delivered 'cold' like this, is alarmingly dense:

> (3) You might pick up a young widow here. Men like that. Love among the tombstones. Romeo. Spice of pleasure. In the midst of death we are in life. Both ends meet. Tantalizing for the poor dead. Smell of frilled beefsteaks to the starving gnawing their vitals. Desire to grig people. Molly wanted to do it at the window. Eight children he has anyway.
>
> (Joyce 1980 [1922]: 110)

Even though undoubtedly complex as a narrative style, it is still possible to unpack this text stylistically and also to use cognitive models to explain how we might 'make sense' of it. First of all, let me provide the context to (3). Taken from the 'Hades' chapter of the novel, this fragment details Leopold Bloom's visit to Glasnevin Cemetery to attend a funeral. Just prior to this piece of text, Bloom has been in conversation with the cemetery caretaker, John O'Connell. From this verbal encounter, Bloom begins to muse on the implications of O'Connell's job and on how, particularly, such employment might affect one's chances of forming romantic attachments. This is in effect the main *text world* which Joyce has established for Bloom.

Bloom's musings at the level of the text-world translate into projections, which as noted in B10, mark out different sub-worlds. Some of these projections are intertextual, which is to say that they evoke other texts and especially other literary works. Others are more of the order of reactions to elements at the text world level, to aspects of Bloom's immediate environment. As a first stage in a cognitive unpacking of the multiple sub-worlds of (3), here is the text again, now in a list format for easier annotation:

(3′)
(1) You might pick up a young widow here.
(2) Men like that.
(3) Love among the tombstones.
(4) Romeo.
(5) Spice of pleasure.
(6) In the midst of death we are in life.
(7) Both ends meet.
(8) Tantalizing for the poor dead.
(9) Smell of frilled beefsteaks to the starving gnawing their vitals.
(10) Desire to grig people.
(11) Molly wanted to do it at the window.
(12) Eight children he has anyway.

Activity ✪

Now go through the text and try to identify the elements which mark out the different sub-worlds which are projected through Bloom's consciousness. Look out for what Werth calls *deictic signatures* (1999: 186) because these alert the reader to the particular narrative world they are currently in. For example, what sort of anchoring function is achieved by the deictic marker 'here' in the first sentence? The next strand to the analysis involves tracking the techniques of *binding* and *priming* as it applies to various characters in the sub-worlds. For example, to whom does the pronoun 'he' refer in the last sentence? Is it to Romeo? If not, what previously 'bound in' character needs to be (re)primed for this reference to make sense?

Bloom's thoughts are not only fixed on ideas about romantic-sexual attachment. He also reflects on death (unsurprisingly given his location) and food (it is after all approaching lunch time – and see reading D4). These preoccupations are ever-present in Bloom's mind (as they are no doubt for many of us) but one of the subtleties of Joyce's narrative technique is that these three domains of experience are often carried over in a kind of radial structure from one sub-world to another. You can check the extent of this by going the down the text again and marking up any words that refer, either implicitly or explicitly, to either sex, death or food. You may find that the same word cross-refers to more than one experience. If so, to what extent does Joyce establish a *web* of connections in Bloom's consciousness between the three experiential domains on the one hand and the various sub-worlds on the other?

I do not propose to follow through in detail these guidelines for analysis, only to offer some short comments by way of conclusion to this unit. One of the most striking transitions in the passage, to my mind, occurs in the progression from 11 to 12, where one sub-world shifts to another. Throughout the morning, Bloom's thoughts have constantly returned to his wife, Molly, as the reflection on past experience in sentence 11 shows. However, these thoughts are reined in rather abruptly when sentence 12 jolts us into another sub-world space. As well as the change in tense, the pronoun in this final sentence is a good indicator of how the minutiae of textual detail can often have significant implications on the development of text worlds and sub-worlds. The question asked above looked for a referent for the pronoun 'he'. Although the most 'recent' male subject in the text is 'Romeo', we need to look much further back, and this is where the concepts of binding and priming come to the fore. Remember, the concept of binding serves to establish a particular character in a particular place until we receive a signal that that character is to be bound out. Even though many lines of prose have passed since his last mention, we have so far had no indication that John O'Connell is to be bound out of the location of Glasnevin Cemetery. This type of stylistic technique is very much the essence of 'stream of consciousness' as embodied by Joyce's novel. The process of binding involves locating different characters in *different* sub-worlds, such that we need not only to retain and juggle these various planes of textual representation but we need to be able to recall each character's location in each sub-world at a moment's notice.

Finally, in his commentary on this very passage in Joyce's novel, the literary critic Harry Blamires remarks that after the conversation with O'Connell, Bloom's thoughts 'run out *centrifugally* from the figure of O'Connell' (Blamires 1988 [1966]: 37; my emphasis). This is an intriguing comment, but it is also the sort of critical intuition

that cries out for support from stylistics, and especially from cognitive stylistics, because it touches on the essence of compositional technique and understanding. I hope that the analytic activities suggested here will have begun to probe the way Bloom's mind style is developed by Joyce, and I will therefore leave it to you to explain how it might be said that Bloom thinks 'centrifugally'.

C11

EXPLORING METAPHORS IN DIFFERENT KINDS OF TEXTS

Continuing the cognitive-stylistic theme established in C10, this unit offers a selection of practically orientated activities for exploring in texts both metaphor and the related trope, metonymy. The activities suggested make use of a variety of texts because, as observed across the strand, these tropes are endemic to human thought processes. So while literary texts feature in the unit, the activities themselves tend to emphasise the commonality of metaphor and metonymy as important types of figurative thought.

Metaphor and metonymy in different kinds of texts

Activity

The exercises developed in this sub-unit are more an appetiser than a main course. What follows is a set of ten attested examples of language use which have been taken from a variety of sources. Mixing the 'literary' with the manifestly 'non-literary', the set, which features both metaphor and metonymy, draws in material from journalism, song lyrics, spoken discourse and, of course, literary texts. Instructions about how to organise your analysis follows below the examples.

Examples

1 Downing Street is thought to be furious over the International Development Secretary's radio interview.

(from British newspaper, *The Guardian* 2003)

2 I have other irons in the fire but I am keeping them close to my chest.

(British football manager discussing his plans for the forthcoming season)

3 My luve is like a red, red rose
That's newly sprung in June:
My luve is like the melodie
That's sweetly played in tune.

(from a song by Robbie Burns)

4 Top rod for the day was visiting angler Mr. Simpson who had eight trout

(*Angling Reports Wales*; Tallylyn)

5 When the evening is spread out against the sky
Like a patient etherised upon a table

(from 'The Long Song of J. Alfred Prufrock' by T. S. Eliot)

6 *Houllier targets £13m Cissé.* Gérard Houllier has reacted to Liverpool's costly failure to qualify for the Champions' League by pledging to lure the France International striker Djibril Cissé. The Liverpool manager is also preparing to swoop on Blackburn Rovers' Damien Duff . . .

(from British newspaper, *The Guardian* 2003)

7 When the still sea conspires an armor
And her sullen and aborted
Currents breed tiny monsters . . .

(from 'Horse Latitudes' by Jim Morrison of rock band *The Doors*)

8 Of course, with the Soviets' launch of Sputnik, the Americans had been Pearl Harbored in space.

(Arthur C. Clarke, interviewed in 2001)

9 Whether 'tis nobler in the mind to suffer
The slings and arrows of outrageous fortune,
Or to take arms against a sea of troubles,
And by opposing end them?

(from *Hamlet* by William Shakespeare)

10 The exercises developed in this sub-unit are more an appetiser than a main course.

(the first sentence of this sub-unit)

Instructions

A For each of 1–10, decide whether the example represents metonymy or metaphor. If you are in doubt, you should apply the 'simile test' which was set out in A11. If you decide an example is metonymy, follow instruction B below; if metaphor, then follow instruction C. Some examples may well exhibit both tropes, in which case you will need to follow both A and B in your analysis.

B Specify which type of associated concept is the vehicle of the metonymy. For example, is the metonymy based on a part-for-whole relationship, a location-for-institution relationship, or on a more contingent 'one-off' connection between the associated concepts?

C Specify the source domain and the target domain for the metaphor. Follow this procedure even if there is more than one metaphor in the example. (Remember, the same target domain may be mapped through different source domains.) Referring to material in B11 if necessary, try to say if the metaphor has been extended or elaborated in any way.

Metaphor in prose fiction: an example

Now, to the main course. This sub-unit narrows the focus by developing some practical work around a single passage from prose fiction. The passage is from Jeanette

Winterson's novel *Written on the Body* (1993). To say that metaphor features in this text is somewhat of an understatement (as you will soon see), but the passage offers an excellent opportunity for a more detailed analysis of metaphorical composition. Analysis of the passage will also help to consolidate many of the concepts introduced across this strand, including those relating to novelty, concretisation, and extending and elaboration in metaphor.

Before you proceed to the Winterson text, read through the following guidelines which will help give shape to your analysis and interpretation of the passage:

(i) When thinking about metaphor, it is important not to lose sight of the distinction between source and target domains. It is not uncommon to come across a target (that is, the concept you are describing through the metaphor) which has been mapped onto several distinct source domains. The concept of LOVE, for instance, can form the target domain for a range of source domains, and conventional metaphors with this pattern include LOVE IS A BATTLE ('They've been at each other's throats for months'), LOVE IS A JOURNEY ('Our relationship is going nowhere') or LOVE IS A NUTRIENT ('He's sustained by her love') and so on. In the analysis of text, it is important to differentiate sets of metaphors which develop the same target domain from other, unrelated metaphors which develop different target and source domains.

(ii) Related to (i), a key stylistic question that needs to be addressed concerns the extent to which the mapping between source and target is novel. That is, is the mapping conventional (as in the examples provided for LOVE above) or are the mappings striking or unusual in comparison to what we encounter in day to day language? Another important question concerns the degree of concretisation, or otherwise, embodied by a metaphor. Does the mapping go, for example, from an abstract target to a concrete source domain, or is some other permutation involved?

(iii) Elaboration and extending are two of a number of techniques for embellishing metaphors by making new concepts available for mapping. This is especially common in metaphors containing a broad source domain (involving say, buildings, food or economic exchange) because part of the mental representation for that domain includes entries for various *props* and *roles* (see A10 and B10). This enables certain individuated concepts within these domains (such as rooms or corridors within a building) to be brought into play to further elaborate the metaphor.

(iv) Metaphors can be *chained*, by which I mean that a source domain from one metaphor may itself be opened up to form the target domain for possibly a whole series of sub-metaphors. For example, a chain for the LOVE IS A NUTRIENT metaphor would mean taking the source domain (the nutrient concept) and making it the target domain for a new metaphorical mapping. (It is worth paying particular attention to the idea of chaining when examining the Winterson passage.)

Working from these four guidelines, now look closely at the passage from *Written on the Body*:

> Misery is a vacuum. A space without air, a suffocated dead place, the abode of the miserable. Misery is a tenement block, rooms like battery cages, sit over your own droppings, lie in your own filth. Misery is a no U-turns, no stopping road. Travel down it pushed by those behind, tripped by those in front. Travel down it at furious speed though the days are mummified in lead. It happens so fast that once you get started, there's no anchor from the real world to slow you down, nothing to hold on to. Misery pulls away the brackets of life leaving you free to fall. Whatever your private hell, you'll find millions like it in Misery. This is the town where everyone's nightmares come true.
>
> (Winterson 1993: 183)

Overall, this 'C' section has largely resisted the temptation to try to provide 'answers' to the practical activities it has put forward, and this particular unit is no different in this regard. It is however worth tying up the unit with a few informal comments on Winterson's technique. Almost theatrical in its style of delivery, the passage develops a single target domain (which you will have identified by now) by mapping it onto an almost bewildering array of source domains, and the sheer exuberance of this style of metaphorisation suggests perhaps some sense of irony (A12). Not only do the metaphors come thick and fast, but they begin to trip over one another as metaphorical chains develop. Without giving too much away, notice how the reference to the 'tenement block' is developed through the reference to 'rooms', a good example of a source domain being elaborated through one of the concepts it embraces. However, the individuated concept itself plays a role in the development of a new metaphor, where it becomes the target domain of a mapping where 'battery cages' forms the source domain. Thus the passage develops, with a range of stylistic devices being brought into play for the creation of a series of novel metaphors.

The passage raises another, more theoretical issue to do with the stylistic analysis of metaphor. One of the functions of metaphor is to alter or transform our perception of the target domain, while leaving unaltered our perception of the vehicle for the metaphor. With respect to the Winterson text, is it really the case that our perception of the many source domains on display is left unaltered during the mapping? Or is it more the case that our understanding of *both* target and source domains is affected? This very issue is taken up in D11, in a reading by Peter Stockwell, which completes this strand on metaphor and style.

SECTION D

EXTENSION

READINGS IN STYLISTICS

HOW TO USE THESE READINGS

Throughout this book, and in the Further Reading section in particular, emphasis is put on the importance of supplementing your work in stylistics by reference to original scholarly sources. While this principle applies to all academic study, it sometimes happens that some advanced scholarship is not particularly accessible and its relevance to the task in hand not immediately apparent. Bearing that in mind, what has been assembled here is a broad selection of generally relevant work that has been carried out by well-known stylisticians from around the world. The readings cover an extremely wide array of texts, topics and issues. Some of the readings may be more challenging than others, but not to the extent that they are opaque and inaccessible. Close and extensive reading will always be rewarded because:

- it provides you with the necessary background to the history of the discipline;
- it familiarises you with the key research areas;
- it allows you to see the sorts of methods and approaches that are used by different stylisticians;
- it gives you a model for how to express yourself in appropriate academic and scholarly language.

Wherever necessary, contextualisation to individual readings is offered in the form of brief prefatory notes. Additionally, follow-up comments and suggestions for further work are offered under the banner heading 'Issues to consider'.

D1 LANGUAGE AND LITERATURE

The following reading tracks two sides of a debate between Roger Fowler and F. W. Bateson about the usefulness of stylistics as an academic activity. The debate was played out during the 1960s in the academic journal *Essays in Criticism* and its individual contributions were later gathered together in Roger Fowler's collection of essays (Fowler 1971). It was stimulated by an unfavourable review by the literary critic Helen Vendler of another of Fowler's books, *Essays on Style and Language* (Fowler 1966). F. W. Bateson entered the fray by adding an editorial postscript to that review, whereupon the battle commenced with two polemical instalments each from Fowler and Bateson. Now somewhat immortalised in stylistic folklore as the 'Fowler–Bateson controversy', the confrontation between these two scholars is important because it represents the first head-on collision between stylistics, then a fledgling discipline, and traditional literary criticism, then a well-established discipline. Although the debate, genteel and vitriolic by turns, may seem antiquated by contemporary standards, it nonetheless marks an important historical watershed in the way it establishes some basic principles of stylistics by direct engagement with literary criticism. The Fowler–Bateson controversy arguably produced the first blueprint for stylistics, the first manifesto for, to adopt Roger Fowler's term, 'the practice of linguistic criticism'.

The languages of literature

Roger Fowler and F. W. Bateson (reprinted from Fowler, R. (1971) *The Languages of Literature* London: Routledge and Kegan Paul)

Roger Fowler and F. W. Bateson

Literature and linguistics: Roger Fowler

Mrs Vendler, in her review (Vendler 1966) of my *Essays on Style and Language* (Fowler 1966), is apparently optimistic that 'descriptive linguistics will in the end be of immense use to literary criticism'. If, however, we were to accept her generalisations about the critical attempts of linguists, we would have to doubt whether this prediction can come true; certainly it is doubtful that she wishes it. The hostility of Mrs Vendler's voice is depressingly familiar to those of us who have suffered from an unnecessary schism between 'language' and 'literature' which has so long marred English studies. Her tone betrays the fear, common among teachers of literature although perhaps less so among the great critics, that linguists may invade and ravage precious literary territory. I shall reserve my remarks on this opposition of linguists and critics until the end of this paper, commenting at the moment only that Mrs Vendler's open invitation of confrontation in her first paragraph is a damaging strategy. [. . .]

I hope that in these unsettled days linguists will be slow to claim too much, and literary critics for their part [will be] more patient than Mrs Vendler. One can agree on one level with some of her comments: 'that is what most linguists are – beginning students' (1966: 458), 'linguists . . ., who are simply under-educated in the reading of poetry, tend to take on, without realising it, documents whose primary sense and value they are not equipped to absorb' (460). In so far as this means that linguistics has only just started to attempt literary analysis, and that linguistics has thus not yet finalised its methods, this is a just observation. But to turn it into an unkind accusation, as Mrs Vendler does (as if 'linguists as a species are incapable of treating literature'), is only harmful to the progress she pretends to welcome. True, sometimes linguists have approached literature with non-critical motives (e.g. Thorne 1965) and some work will probably be cited more often by linguists than by critics (Levin 1962). I personally see no objection to a linguist deliberately advancing his linguistic research by the study of literary uses of language which really put his assumptions to the test. Critics and linguists [. . .] should welcome the fact that we have at last turned to material which inevitably forces us out of our assurance. Although the 'use' of literature is really not the issue here, it needs comment because critics seem to consider that linguists doing such kinds of linguistic work with literature think it is critical work. The real allegation is that, perhaps because of their 'scientific' education, linguists are not equipped to know the difference between linguistic analysis and criticism, nor indeed sensitive enough to be critics. This is nonsense. Many mathematicians and physical scientists are fine musicians and poets. There is no reason why a linguist should not be a humane, literate, sensitive person. He may write on literature (1) purely as a linguist for linguistic ends; (2) for critical motives, using only a selection from his linguistic apparatus; or (3) no differently from the non-linguist, without appeal to linguistics at all. The three separate approaches are all valuable, and I would urge non-linguists to stay their conviction that a knowledge of linguistics must make only the first approach possible.

The primary justification for the use of the methods of linguistics in literary study is that noted by Mrs Vendler (1966: 458): any information about language is useful in studying an art-form whose stuff is language. If linguistics is defined as 'the study of language' *tout court*, then its contribution is unchallengeable. But this bleak logic does not allow that all specific brands of linguistics are admissible. Briefly, this means that, in the first case (1), although literature is language and therefore open to ordinary formal linguistic investigation, it has, like other formally distinctive texts, essentially distinctive contexts which the linguist no less than the critic must study. That is, the investigator must be curious about the extra-linguistic features which condition the distinctive style of a literary work. As for the applicability of different linguistic models (2), this is obviously variable. The appropriateness of the model is a concern for the individual analyst; just as important for this general discussion is that all those who engage in it realise that bland undefined accounts of 'linguistics' lead nowhere. There is no one linguistics except in community of certain basic and general ideals held since Saussure's time. We cannot switch on a standardised linguistic analysis machine and stand by while it puts out a definitive breakdown of a text. Doubtless the lack of such a device has its advantages.

My third prescription for a successful linguistic criticism is that it should proceed not merely from a theory of language but also from a respectful consideration of the demands and peculiarities of the many kinds of literary study. Now, the substance of this remark is addressed not only to linguists. There is no single thing 'criticism' any more than there is 'linguistics', although literary people, faced with the imagined threat of linguistics, tend to talk as if there is. (This impression is gained partly from the tendency to use 'criticism' and 'critical' as treasured value terms.) [. . .] In the real world, we are dealing with, above all, teachers of literature whose pedagogic relations with their subject-matter and with their students are much more vital than the role of the public critic. Most often literature teachers are involved in nothing more mystical than, at various degrees of sophistication, showing the ways to efficient reading of literature. Many a time literary study comprises historical, stylistic or openly technical investigation: genre description, stylistic tests of authorship, metrical analysis, for example. For some reason, 'interpretation' (an exceedingly difficult term) and 'evaluation' have come to be regarded as the only activities which are worth doing and which are actually done. Just as we need to be wary in our use of 'linguistics' as a term describing all procedures involving the study of language, so we should give careful scrutiny to terms like 'criticism', 'interpretation', 'evaluation', 'explication', 'stylistics', ensuring that we do not think that there is just one objective (of whatever kind) in studying literature, with 'linguistics' straightforwardly an alternative 'technique' for reaching that goal.

Literature and linguistics: a reply by F. W. Bateson

Roger Fowler is in effect proposing – both here and in the collection of essays he edited (Fowler 1966) which was reviewed by Mrs Vendler – an academic alliance between post-Saussure linguistics and post-I. A. Richards criticism. And why on earth shouldn't he? *A priori*, as it were, it sounds a good idea. After all, even if a literary masterpiece is more than the sum of its words, still when the words are taken away what is left? Blank pages! To invite the reader to look hard, really hard, at the words on the page is indeed what the modern critical doctrine of close reading amounts to, when it is reduced to its simplest terms. And, since a similar concentration is the initial premise of modern descriptive linguistics, some degree of amicable co-operation between the two approaches should not be impossible.

Unfortunately it doesn't work. Or rather, when it does work, it is only at the most elementary level. In this reply to Mr Fowler I shall try to indicate rather more fully than was possible in my short postscript to Mrs Vendler's review why the sort of co-operation that Mr Fowler and his colleagues are pleading for is a vain hope.

[. . .]

Descriptive linguistics is always at least headed towards total description – a detached, objective, universally available discipline (whatever the user's age, sex, nationality, or culture). Literature, on the other hand, has its ineradicable subjective core, which tends to define the range and effectiveness of its uses. The point of departure between the two specialisations from the vulgar tongue can also be put in strictly linguistic terms. It is a matter either of breaking down the sentence into its separable parts – or else of taking the sentence as the unit and building up larger units as the sentences accumulate. The close reader conscientiously intent on the words in front of him, can opt either way. If he is a natural grammarian he will divide and subdivide the verbal material; if he has been born a literary critic he will synthesise and amalgamate it. What is it, then, in the words of literature that encourages the literary reader to amalgamate and not to subdivide? The answer to this question is a crucial one in my argument with Mr Fowler, though to prove it as a case is proved in a court of law would require a book instead of a short article. But I can at least summarise the theoretical objections to the mating of the language of description and the language of evaluation. Grammar, for one thing, is essentially logical in its linguistic presuppositions, and as such it is governed by the principle of non-contradiction; literary criticism, on the other hand, assumes in the verbal material criticised the presence of opposite and discordant qualities whose provisional balance and reconciliation the common reader will agree under certain circumstances to accept. Those circumstances, considered linguistically, can be summed up in the word 'style' – a term that includes the whole armoury of rhetorical devices, phonetic and semantic, with their larger structural extensions such as tragedy and comedy. The function of style is to unify – or at least encourage the reader to attempt to unify – literature's disparate linguistic parts. As such it is the exact opposite of grammar, whose function is not primarily to unite but to divide. (A sentence is grammatical when its separate parts have been found subject to classification, the 'parsing' process, and then shown to cohere.) Although some grammaticalness certainly survives in literature, it is as it were accidentally and incidentally, a left-over of logic from the common speech of which the language of literature is one derivative. The reader is scarcely aware of it. What he is aware of – especially in poetry but also in prose with any literary pretensions – is the style (in the wider sense already indicated). If my attention is drawn to breaches of grammar in a work of literature, I can always invoke the magic word 'ellipsis' – a term apparently invented to save grammar's face when we really ignore it.

May I offer Mr Fowler a definition of literature? A work of literature is successful linguistically, the best words in the best order, when appropriate stylistic devices co-operate to unify humane value judgments, implicit or explicit, on some aspect of life as it is lived in the writer's own society. As for the reader of such a work, he will only be successful if he registers, consciously or at least semiconsciously, the unifying stylistic devices that enable him to respond to the human situation available to him in it. In a word, the role played by grammar in description is comparable to that of style in evaluation. But if comparable they are also mutually incompatible, because grammar is primarily analytic in its methods and premises, whereas style is essentially synthetic.

To Mr Fowler's optimistic escape-clause that, because 'some mathematicians and physical scientists are fine musicians and poets', therefore a linguistic training will sometimes be useful for the literary critic, the answer is simple and obvious: musical physicists do not improve as physicists by learning to play the piano. I am not sure who Mr Fowler's mathematicians and physicists are who are also fine poets, but these ambidextrous geniuses certainly don't grow on blackberry bushes. I can't think of one. On the other hand, it is common knowledge that most structural linguists don't write particularly good English prose. Why indeed should they as long as they are intelligible? The temperamental predisposition that results in Smith becoming an eminent grammarian is normally very different from that which turns Brown into a good critic. Let us agree to be different. [. . .]

Stylistic discrimination is the one indispensable prerequisite for the aesthetic appreciation of great literature. That some knowledge of linguistics, historical and descriptive, has certain minor uses in literary studies is not to be denied, but for the native speaker of English this additional knowledge is, as it were, supplementary either in eking out one's birthright by the help available in the OED for an unusual word or idiom, or in saving one from incidental errors outside one's immediate range of linguistic experience. Such information may be compared to the odds and ends of social and political history with which the scholar-critic will also have to equip himself. A little learning of this kind will go a long way, though with none at all the reader's fingers can sometimes be badly burnt. But for the literary beginner the best way to acquire such information – including the sign-posts to the topic's more sophisticated levels – is *ad hoc*; in other words, by consulting a glossary or an editor's notes only when he needs them. What he naturally resents is the traditional compulsory spoon-feeding with grammar or history most of which he will never need. Of course, if he is interested in either descriptive linguistics or the history of the language or social history for its own sake, that is another matter. My real quarrel with Mr Fowler – or rather with the cause for which he is pleading – is that he is presenting the study of language as a necessary concomitant to the study of literature. For the native speaker, except occasionally and superficially, this is simply not true. It is not true even for the reading of Chaucer.

This has been a fighting retort and I hope the words I have used will not seem unnecessarily offensive. But *pace* Mr Fowler, the things I have said do need to be said.

Language and literature: Roger Fowler

Mr Bateson's attempt to disqualify linguistics as a discipline of relevance to literature comprises a very cunning and apparently substantial argument inter-woven with a misleading line of polemic. In his usual masterly fashion, he has constructed a case against which it is very difficult to argue in an organised way. I will try to show that his argument (1) rests on premises which cannot provide an adequate aesthetic for literature, (2) is ineffective as a disqualification of linguistics because of misconceptions about the nature of linguistics, (3) is motivated by a set of prejudices which inhibit constructive discussion of the present issue. [. . .]

(1) Mr Bateson's case is basically a somewhat complicated version of ideas he has offered linguists and medievalists for at least the last ten years. He compounds (a) Coleridge's 'homely definition' of poetry as 'the best words in the best order'; (b) I. A. Richards' distinction between scientific and emotive language; and (c) de Saussure's distinction between *langue* and *parole*. These formulae are jumbled together to support an assertion of a unique and exclusive aesthetic so constructed as apparently to make literature inaccessible to objective study [. . .]

- (a) 'The best words in the best order' is, except in Mr Bateson's first book, an empty catch-phrase. Coleridge used it to distinguish verse from prose, and his requirement that 'the words, the media, must be beautiful, and ought to attract your notice' becomes impertinent when the phrase is employed to mark off literature from nonliterature, as Mr Bateson uses it currently. It is obviously at best incomplete when applied to most kinds of poetry, and quite wrong for narrative verse and for drama and the novel. [. . .]
- (b) I. A. Richards' distinction between emotive and scientific language is generally agreed to be without reasonable foundation: it is much too simple to serve as a linguistic theory or to provide an isolation of the characteristics of 'literary language'. [. . .]
- (c) I do not think the reference to de Saussure is merely a sop to the linguists. Unfortunately, taken as a serious proposal it doesn't make sense. *Langue* and *parole* together, according to de Saussure, make up the *faculté du langage*. *Langue* is the abstract system of rules which enables a speaker to communicate with others. *Parole* is a particular concrete act of speech, or a corpus collected from many such acts. Chomsky has recently revived and adapted the distinction using the terms *competence* and *performance*. Mr Bateson, like de Saussure and Chomsky, says that linguists study *langue*, which is true in so far as linguists write grammars of languages and enquire into the linguistic mental capabilities of speakers. But, Mr Bateson says, [. . .] the study of literature is the study of *parole* – or rather, the study of

a special kind of *parole* of which the *langue* is not *langue* but 'style' [. . .] This is an illegitimate and meaningless adaptation of de Saussure. It is illegitimate because the original scheme works only if it applies in the same way for all uses of language; it is meaningless because of the poverty of Mr Bateson's definition of the linguistic components of style and because of his misunderstanding of the interests and procedures of grammatical study in relation to *langue* and *parole*.

(2) [. . .] we should not regard the linguistic description of a text as the discovery of structure. A linguist ought only to claim to make articulate what a native speaker tacitly knows about a text he understands. In this way, linguistic description is a representation of (part of) the process of understanding: it shows how a native speaker encounters and interprets sentences generated by the grammar (*langue*) that he knows. The 'linguistic analysis' of literature is an attempt to make explicit part of the process of reading by the use of terms and concepts which have psychological reality (are humane even if they are scientific) through being appropriate to the reader's individually internalised yet culturally shared grammar of the language. Some such description is necessary because speakers do not *know about* their language anything like as efficiently as they *know* it. I see no reason derived from either the supposed opposition of science and literature, or the theoretical potential of linguistics (as distinct from the claims of many linguists and some linguist critics), why such a linguistics should be intrinsically alien to certain parts of literary study.

(3) The 'misleading line of polemic' derives from Mr Bateson's feelings about the old and disgraceful 'language-literature controversy'. There are still large numbers of people in English departments who, for reasons of academic politics, feel obliged to parcel the world into two intractably opposed groups. This is not the proper place to make a fuss about that issue, since only by association does it affect the dispute between Mr Bateson and me. Modern linguistics is only accidentally the 'successor' of the old philological medievalism. Linguistics lays fair claim to be an autonomous discipline in its central concern, the theory of *langue*; it provides a theoretical status for *parole*, but needs augmenting by other disciplines in the study of *parole*. In places where *parole* is studied (e.g. English departments) linguistics has obvious uses. But its value cannot be appreciated while people's words and votes are governed by oversimplified and historically irrelevant 'sets' towards imagined opponents. Reciprocal ignorance about literary criticism and linguistics is also, as I have several times argued, deeply inhibiting.

We can now attempt to rebuild the theory of style. I will argue that linguistic theory provides a definition for a level of language which we may call 'style'. Since no workable theory has ever been constructed which uniquely isolates a category of language 'literature', there seems no good reason why the concept of style should be exclusively literary. (Whether or not a particular text is regarded by its readers as being literature is an important cultural fact, but an irrelevant fact from our point of view.) The linguistic theory which provides a definition of style by the same definition establishes the contribution, and the limitation of contribution, of grammar to the study of style. [. . .]

I hope the general strategy of my reorientation is clear. The distinction between competence and performance provides the only fruitful way of understanding the special formal qualities (style among them) of texts. Wellek and Warren speak of 'the contrast of the language system of a literary work of art with the general usage of the time' (1949: 177). The contrast attempted is evident from the mention in the next line of 'common speech, even unliterary speech': the false norm of non-literary language is being invoked to provide background for a spurious category 'literary language'. But in reality the sense in which there is a gap between the 'normal language' and any distinctive text is the same for all texts: there is the grammar (langue, competence) and what you do with the grammar (parole, performance, e.g. texts identified stylistically). In the light of this fundamental tenet of linguistic theory there is no formal category 'literature'. In my opinion no study of texts which recognises the critical importance of 'style' can afford to define 'style' against any background other than that provided by a linguistic theory of this kind.

Language and literature: a reply by F. W. Bateson

Would I allow my sister to marry a linguist? It is a good question. And I suppose, if I am honest, I must admit that I would much prefer not to have a linguist in the family. But at least I would not forbid the banns – as Lincoln Barnett, for example, would certainly do. Here is a specimen passage from Barnett's informative if unprofessional *The Treasure of Our Tongue*:

> To almost everyone who cherishes the English language for its grace and beauty, its combination of precision and flexibility, the social philosophy of the Structural Linguist seems past comprehension – epitomising indeed the 'anti-intellectualism of the intellectual'. Among all the forces of cultural vandalism at work in the country, their influence has been, perhaps, the most insidious. The vulgarities of advertising and mudflows of jargon can be shovelled aside. But the impact of the Structural Linguists is like that of slow atomic fallout: through their influence on teachers' colleges and teachers, hence on the schools and the pupils within them they are incapacitating the coming generation.
>
> (Barnett 1964: 85–6)

Mr Barnett is, of course, an American and the linguists who supply him with the monstrosities of prose style that he has collected in his book are also Americans. But one knows what he means, and the vandalism has, I am afraid, begun to infect some English linguists too.

Mr Fowler is not a vandal and I have no faults to find with his English. What I do find disturbing in his attempt to woo the literary critic and student is his inability to provide actual, concrete examples of the usefulness of the linguistic approach to a proper understanding and appreciation of particular poems, plays, or novels – or even particular parts or aspects of such works. Instead all that we get is theorising – often of much interest simply as theory – and some skilful linguistic propaganda.

[. . .] our two disciplines do not overlap. Under the condition that I have been assuming – *viz.* that the literary student is a sensible native speaker of the language whose literature he is studying – the linguistic assistance he will need is surely minimal. Occasionally, in the case of the long historical continuum that we think of as English literature (which gets spatially more extensive each year as well as temporally older), a glossary, dictionary or grammar will have to be consulted, but *linguistically* English literature remains essentially homogeneous. Once you have got used to Chaucer's spelling and pronouns, or the oddities of vocabulary employed by some Scotch, American or Australasian writers, there are really next to no language problems for an English reader that the context of the passage will not solve. Style, however, is different; its complexities and implications *are* almost infinite. Language, as we say, is 'picked up'; style, on the other hand, has to be learnt – and taught. It should not be forgotten that 'rhetoric' was the intellectual core of Greek and Roman education, and that the only languages the school-boy acquires by a conscious and deliberate process, then and now, are foreign languages. In an English-speaking country English is breathed in as part of the cultural atmosphere. [. . .]

The student of literature cannot be content with a description of the external mechanics or mere structure of langue. As he reads a work of literature he will have to almost identify himself with the author he is reading or with his various *dramatis personae.* Now the critical controls to be applied to prevent any misreading of this or that particular passage or work are the *inter-subjective phenomena of style.* Whatever Coleridge may or may not have meant by his 'homely definition', the study of literature written in one's native language reduces itself to a recognition that the words with which the reader is confronted are (or are not) *really,* in their context, approximately the best words in the best order. In the case of the author a style precedes the words. He knows more or less what he wants to say and how he proposes to say it *before* the final verbal formulation on paper. The reader, on the other hand, finds the process reversed, beginning with the specific individual words and working his way through them, as it were, to reach the style. And it is only via the style that he becomes capable of a proper literary response to what he is reading.

[. . .] Mr Fowler finds it difficult to pass from the linguistic to the stylistic phase, as I have described them. And as a consequence the full aesthetic response is apparently denied to him. Other linguists, of course, remain solidly stuck at the level of *langue.* Ultimately it is, I suggest, because of this verbal immobility, this failure to recognise that in literature language is for the reader a mere preliminary to style – as style itself is a preliminary to the literary response in its fullest sense – that the critic finds so little nourishment in modern linguistics in any of its forms. *Not here, O Apollo, are haunts meet for thee.*

ISSUES TO CONSIDER

Roger Fowler's contributions articulate much that has theoretical currency in contemporary stylistics. He raises the 'literary language' issue (see C1), making the point that '. . . no workable theory has ever been constructed which uniquely isolates a category of language "literature"'. Nor, according to Fowler, is there any good reason why 'the concept of style should be exclusively literary'. For Fowler, the 'false norm of non-literary language' is being invoked by Bateson 'to provide background for a spurious category 'literary language''. Whereas this position might appear to reflect the side with which stylisticians would naturally concur, it is worth observing as you develop your own reading the extent to which Fowler's approach is embodied in more contemporary stylistic work. Do *all* stylisticians agree with Fowler's position? Or is the current situation rather more complicated?

F. W. Bateson's contributions are interesting on a number of levels. For a start, his position is archetypally that of the 'liberal humanist' tradition in literary study. This tradition is defined on the understanding that the critic as social subject is untrammelled by political or cultural constraints, and that critical response, by imputation, arises out of the free interplay of individuals in society. This 'liberal' conception of the critic's position is also supplemented by a 'humanist' doctrine which treats literature as a valid index of the human experience; a doctrine which even suggests that the sensitive reading of *good* literature can make you a better person. Notice how Bateson frames this perspective in certain key remarks. Dismissing social and political history, he suggests that good literature is measured by 'humane value judgments'. Following from this, Bateson argues that one is either a 'natural grammarian' or one is 'born a literary critic'. This position has implications for the stylistician, not least because it assumes that there is a 'natural' distinction between the two disciplines which no amount of sensitive stylistic analysis can bridge. In this respect, think about which of these two skills is *your* natural predisposition.

More suggestions follow:

Activity 

- ❑ In the course of his first reply to Fowler, Bateson offers an interesting definition of literature. He claims that 'a work of literature is successful linguistically'. How might we measure linguistic success? Do you know of any works of literature that are *not* successful linguistically? Is the idea of linguistic success (such as it is) a prerequisite for literary success?
- ❑ What prospect does Bateson's programme afford the non-native speaker of English? If English is not your first language, how do/would you approach the critical study of English literature? Does your approach correspond to Bateson's model for literary study or is Fowler's model more appealing? Or are more suitable approaches to be found elsewhere?
- ❑ Fowler's contributions place constant emphasis on the importance of *grammar* in stylistic analysis. To what extent is this weighting towards 'the culturally shared grammar of the language' a true reflection, as far as you can tell, of current methods of stylistics? Is it really all about grammar?
- ❑ Bateson's comment that 'our two disciplines do not overlap' suggests that there is little hope of agreement or compromise between the literary critics and the stylisticians. Going by your own experience (eg. of the academic institution where you study), is this still the case today? Has there been a meeting of minds? Or is the literary–linguistic divide as marked as it ever was?

D2

STYLE AND VERBAL PLAY

In this light-hearted article from 1992, Katie Wales explores the stylistic strategies pop and rock musicians use when they name their bands. Wales uncovers an array of naming practices, which, even in this relatively narrow sphere of discourse activity, illustrates again how stylistic creativity can work simultaneously on a number of levels of language.

Zodiac mindwarp meets the horseflies

Katie Wales

Katie Wales (reprinted from *English Today*, 29, January 1992, 50–1)

The world of popular music is all too easily branded as bland by those who dislike it: 'a sameness' that results from its blend of technological reproduction and appeal to mass consumption. However, the *Music Master* database of 1990 lists over 69,000 singles released since the 1950s, and is fascinating reading. What impresses is not only the sheer variety of the recordings, but also the linguistic creativity of the performers: in the names they give themselves. Any readers of *English Today* thinking of launching out on a career in the pop industry will find naming their groups a daunting task, unless they follow certain trends.

The safest line is to choose a popular modifier, like *Big, Beat, Bad, Hot, New, Red, Blue, Little* and *Sweet.* But is this enough to grab the attention of the DJs and your audience? For those who think pop music is a meaningless, repetitive noise, then clearly names like *A-ha, Buppi Buppi K, Blam Blam, Kajagoogoo, Oingo Boingo, Slam Slam, Ya Ya* and *Zaga Zaga* might appeal. Actually, such sound-play forms are quite rare. You might do better by punning: at least you will raise a smile: *Acid Reign, Terry Dactyl, Idol Rich, Split Enz, Well Red, Hear 'N' Aid*, for example. For those who think pop music sounds like the cries and noise of wild animals, it will be no surprise to learn that animal names are much more popular: *Animals, Balham Alligators, Bats, Big Pig, Boomtown Rats, Budgie, Cheetahs, Crickets, Dalmations, Elephant Talk, Frogs, Horseflies, Lions, Monkees, Piranhas, Reptiles, Sharks in Italy, Stingrays, Vipers, Wolfhounds, Zebras*, etc. But perhaps because pop music is to a lot of people's taste, quite a number of names are quite tasty and mouth-watering: *Applejacks, Bananarama, Bread, Blancmange, Bucks Fizz, Candy, Coconuts, Famous Potatoes, Finest Ingredients, Golden Syrup, Hot Chocolate, Scrambled Eggs, Sugar Cubes, Tangerine, Vanilla Ice, Wobbly Jellies, Whiskey & Soda.*

If pop group names are indicative, then the performers have come from a wide range of occupations that they wish to be reminded of: there are *Administrators, Ambitious Beggars, Captains of Industry, Chefs, Dead Milkmen, Diplomats, Engineers, Fire Brigade, Hunters & Collectors, Janitors*, a *Lecturer, Law Lords, Men at Work, Monks, Police, Scientists, Shop Assistants, TV Personalities, Undertakers, Vets*, and *Waitresses.* The V.I.Ps include *The Royal Family*, and especially the *Queen* and *Prince Charles.* Many would appear to have been artists (*Deep Green, Deep Purple, Frigid Pink, King Crimson, Pink and Black, Simply Red, Vicious Pink, Snowy White, Yello*), scientists (*Air Supply, Antenna, Einstein, Flying Saucers, H2O, Silicon Chip*), and botanists (*Blue

Orchids, Chrysanthemums, Edelweiss, Holly & The Ivys, Little Acorns, Poppies, Persian Flowers, March Violets). More depressing, however, is to discover just how many are hypochondriacs (*Anorexia, Antidote, Anthrax, Cramps, The Cure, Double Visions, Fatal Microbes, Fear of Flying, Hypertension, Malaria, Mental As Anything, Scars, Sore Throat, Social Illness, Suicidal Tendencies, Talking to Walls, Varukers, Vapors*).

Just from the names alone, there is a truly revealing image presented of late twentieth century society, its social symbols and flotsam and jetsam. Mobility and technology are reflected in transport (*Blue Mercedes, Cars, Fifty-Three Bus, Freight Train, Heathrow Flyers, London Underground, Metro, Taxi*), and all its social ramifications (*Car Crash, Crawling Chaos, Jet Set, Love Train, Taking the Trains Out*). The media of journalism and television are captured in the names that reproduce the catch-words, buzz-words, idioms and collocations that many up-to-date dictionaries try hard to record also: *Alternative TV, Colour Supplement, Local Boy Makes Good, Mystery Guests, Personal Column, Send No Flowers, Small Ads, Tabloids.* Images of other aspects of contemporary society are captured in names like *Neighbourhood Watch, Overdraft, Photofit, Kissing the Pink, State of Play* and the abbreviations *UB 40, UFO and VDUs.*

More general in distribution are the names which repeat the cliches, similes and proverbs of everyday spoken language: *Curiosity Killed the Cat, Hear No Evil, Humble Pie, If All Else Fails, If It Moves, Keep it Dark, Lip Service, Look Before You Leap, Midas Touch, The Name Escapes Me, Scotch Mist, Soft Touch, Tongue in Cheek.* Perhaps some performers are actually ex-linguists, so sharp is their ear for contemporary idiom. Indeed, how else are we to explain names like *ABC, Accent, Bad English, Broken English, Coptic Roots, English Subtitles, Esperanto, Learning Process, Stylistics, Talk Talk, Talking Heads* and *Word of Mouth.* Not to mention: *He She Him; It; Me and You; Thee People; Them; The Who; Who Me;* and *Which is Which.*

Another creative source of naming practice comes from the register we normally associate with linguistic creativity: literary language. *The Bards* and *Poets* join with the *Romantics* and *The Bloomsbury Set, Dante* with *Virginia Wolf* (sic), *Keats* and *Milton* with *Shakespear's Sister*, to give us many *Books, Characters* and *Chapter and Verse*, much *Culture* and *Drama, Pulp* and *Poesie Noire, Science Fiction* and *Symbols.* Here we find (*The*) *Dubliners, Stephen Hero* and *Finnegans Wake, Catch 22, Erewhon, Eyeless in Gaza, Fra Lippo Lippi, Godot, Dorian Gray, Hard Times, Look Back in Anger*, the *Bible* and *Genesis*, the *Odyssey, Romeo and Juliet, Uriah Heep* and *Twelfth Night.* And here we can identify many quotations: *Fiat Lux, Have No Fury, Midnight Oil, Hollow Men, This Mortal Coil.*

From the *Fiction Factory* comes the 'archetypal' story immortalised in pop lyrics themselves: *Boys Meets Girl* on a *Blind Date* after a *Lonely Hearts* advert, *Perfect Strangers* hoping to be *Loveless* and *Lonesome No More.* After a *Long Pursuit* followed by the first *Kiss*, a few *Seconds of Pleasure, Lover Boy* and his *Platinum Blonde* are bitten by the *Love Bug*, full of *Passion* and *Naughty Thoughts.* With *Terms of Endearment* and *Promises, Promises, Super Lover* the *Seducer* with his *Fatal Charm* makes his *Valentine*, his *Venus in Furs*, fall into the *Tender Trap.* And *So to Bed. Tempting Fate*, he agrees to a *White Wedding*, with *Silk* and *Velvets*, and a *Long Honeymoon, Any Day Now.* But *Believe It or Not* soon *Something Happens*: it's a *Love*

Gone Wrong, no *Paradise* ahead. *Big Trouble*: he doesn't like the *Company She Keeps*; he's been *Caught in the Act* with someone else. They become *Passive Friends*. '*Admit You're Shit*', the *Iron Maiden* says with *Dirty Looks*. The *Lover Speaks*: '*Oh Well*' he concludes.

However, by far the most inventive and colourful naming, and the most productive, evokes the surrealism of science fiction, of fantasy and modernist poetry. The roots of inspiration may well lie in the psychedelic visions of the hippy drug culture of the 1960s, but the witty deviation of the incongruous collocations is eye-catching and mind-bending, like the concepts of Metaphysical poetry. Undoubtedly there is the same kind of 'poor man's poetry' that Eric Partridge and others have associated with slang, in names like the following: *Angels in Aspic, Aztec Camera, Ballistic Kisses, Bone Orchard, Dead Pan Tractor, Digital Dinosaurs, Electric Prunes, Exploding Seagulls, Flaming Mussolinis, Fourteen Iced Bears, Green Telescope, Groovy Chainsaw, Immaculate Fools, Laughing Apples, Lemon Kittens, Lovin Spoonful, Liquid Gold, Magnolia Siege, Leather Nun, Mind Over Muesli, Pink Noise, Glass Ties, Prefab Sprout, Reverend Sunshine, Sad Cafe, Singing Sheep, Soup Dragons, Spandau Ballet, Stone Roses, Suede Crocodiles, Velvet Underground, Voice of the Beehive* and *Wishbone Ash* – a real *Zodiac Mindwarp!*

ISSUES TO CONSIDER

As a follow-up to Wales's entertaining paper, readers interested in general issues connected with the language of popular music might wish to consult Trudgill (1983) and Simpson (1999). Both of these articles explore, from a sociolinguistic perspective, the singing styles adopted by pop and rock musicians. Keeping within the same field of discourse, Steen (2002a) is an insightful anlaysis of metaphor in the lyrics of Bob Dylan's song 'Hurricane'.

More suggestions follow:

- Wales's article concentrates on a field of discourse that is transient by nature, where fashions change almost overnight and where an artist's popularity is measured by weeks and not years. What then is the current 'state of play' as far as naming techniques used in rock and pop go? Are the practices identified by Wales still in evidence or are other techniques now used in the names of contemporary pop and rock groups? Do different decades have different characteristic naming practices, for example?
- The array of stylistic strategies which Wales uncovers relates exclusively to pop and rock bands, but how widespread are these naming strategies in other musical sub-genres? Are the same tendencies found in the names of, for example, jazz or folk groups? And if not, why not?
- Do the names of albums and singles receive similar stylistic treatment to those of bands? Is there, for example, a correlation between having a 'wacky' band name and giving an album a comparably wacky title? Or can there be too much stylistic wackiness in pop music naming practices?

- ❑ What other areas of discourse (outside 'literary' writing) do you know of which make use of similar techniques in linguistic creativity?

TEACHING GRAMMAR AND STYLE

D3

In this reading, comprising an article written by Ronald Carter, two important issues in stylistics are raised. The first is to do with the development of a stylistics of poetry, which Carter addresses by offering a detailed lexico-grammatical analysis of a 'concrete' poem written by Edwin Morgan. The second issue concerns pedagogical stylistics, in respect of which Carter elaborates a programme for teaching about grammar in the narrower context and for teaching about language and style in the wider context. Carter's article makes a number of useful proposals for language teaching, emphasising further the importance of pedagogical issues and methods in contemporary stylistics.

A more localised point to note as you read through Carter's article is that he draws on the term *nominal group* in his study. This structure, which is heavily foregrounded in the poem he analyses, is a cluster of words that has a noun has its main element. To all intents and purposes, then, it means the same thing as *noun phrase*, which is the term that we have been using across the strand to refer to this grammatical feature.

What is stylistics and why can we teach it in different ways?

Ronald Carter (reprinted from Mick Short (ed.) *Reading, Analysing and Teaching Literature* Harlow: Longman, 1989: 161–77).

Ronald Carter

The nature of stylistics

Given that stylistics is essentially a bridge discipline between linguistics and literature it is inevitable that there will be arguments about the design of the bridge, its purpose, the nature of the materials and about the side it should be built from. Some would even claim it is unnecessary to build the bridge at all. In such a situation there is always a danger that stylistics can become blinkered by too close an affiliation to a single mode of operation or to any one ideological position. There is already a considerable division in the subject between literary stylistics (which is in many respects an extension of practical criticism) and linguistic stylistics (which seeks the creation of linguistic models for the analysis of texts – including those conventionally thought 'literary' and 'non-literary'). Such divisions can be valuable in the process of clarifying objectives as well as related analytical and pedagogic strategies, but one result can be the narrowing of classroom options and/or the consequent reduction in the number and kinds of academic levels at which stylistics to literature students can operate. For example, literary stylistics can be more accessible to literature students because it models itself on critical assumptions and procedures already fairly well established in the literature classes of upper forms in schools, whereas the practice of linguistic stylistics tends to require a more thorough acquaintance with linguistic methodology and argumentation. [. . .]

Off Course

the golden flood the weightless seat
the cabin song the pitch black
the growing beard the floating crumb
the shining rendezvous the orbit wisecrack
the hot spacesuit the smuggled mouth-organ
the imaginary somersault the visionary sunrise
the turning continents the space debris
the golden lifeline the space walk
the crawling deltas the camera moon
the pitch velvet the rough sleep
the crackling headphone the space silence
the turning earth the lifeline continents
the cabin sunrise the hot flood
the shining spacesuit the growing moon
the crackling somersault the smuggled orbit
the rough moon the visionary rendezvous
the weightless headphone the cabin debris
the floating lifeline the pitch sleep
the crawling camera the turning silence
the space crumb the crackling beard
the orbit mouth-organ the floating song

Edwin Morgan (1966)

I shall now work through this short text and point to some ways in which it might be explored in the classroom from within an expanded framework for stylistics. [. . .]

Approaches to study and teaching

TEACHING THE GRAMMAR

Most striking here is the consistent pattern of nominal groups across the whole text. In each case the structure is that of **d m h** where d = definite article, m = modifier and h = headword. The predominant modifier of the headwords in the nominal groups of this poem is an epithet. But they are not all of the same type. We distinguish in English (though by no means exhaustively) between three main types of epithet:

e^a = qualitative epithet; e. g. *marvellous, interesting, strong*

e^b = colours; e.g. *red, blue*

e^c = classifying epithet; e.g. *classical, wooden.*

The usual order for these is **a b c**; so that you cannot normally have 'a red, classical, wonderful vase' but you can have 'a wonderful, red, classical vase'. In addition to these epithets English allows numerals, past and present participles (e.g. 'shining' [14] and 'smuggled' [15]) and other nouns (e.g. 'the space walk' [8] – sometimes called nominators) to act as modifiers in the nominal group. What kind of exploitation of these features is made in the text?

Epithet ordering rules do not really surface since only one modifier occurs at any one time. Morgan employs a mixture of modifiers including colours ('the golden life-line' [8]), nominal modifiers ('the cabin debris' [17]) and participles (e.g. lines 3 & 5). In terms of classes of epithet, classifying epithets (e^c) seem to predominate: e.g. 'the weightless headphone' (line [17]); 'the floating lifeline' (line [18]); 'the imaginary somersault' (line [66]); even to the extent that the majority of participles are of a classifying kind. In fact, 'the golden lifeline' may be seen to describe a characteristic of the lifeline as much as it does its colour. Thus, one cumulative effect of the use of this structure is that a number of objects are classified and reclassified. Occasionally, a particular qualitative contour is imparted to the things seen but the predominantly defining procedure suggests something more in the nature of an inventory (the run of articles reinforces this) or, more specifically, a ship's log with only occasionally the kind of qualitative reaction allowed in line [6] 'the visionary sunrise'. [. . .]

Other key structural features which must be noted are the absence of a verb and the particular use to which the participles are put. One main result of the omission of a verb is that there are no clear relations between objects. Objects either do not seem to act upon each other or have no particular 'action' of their own. Verbs generally work to establish a clear differentiation between subject and object and to indicate the processes contracted between them; a resultant effect here is that processes between things become suspended. The poet's suspension of some of the normal rules of grammar can be seen in part, at least, to contribute to this effect. Yet this observation can be countered by a recognition that there are verbs in the poem; for example, the participles already observed (e.g. 'crawling', lines [9] & [19]; 'floating', lines [3] & [21]; 'growing', lines [3] & [14]) are formed from verbs. The difference between the two verbal items in the following sentences:

(i) the world turns (ii) the turning world

illustrates the point that in the participial form the 'verbs' work both with a more defining or classificatory function and to underline a sense of continuing, if suspended, action. The present participles convey a feeling of things continuing endlessly or, at least, without any clear end.

From a teaching or classroom viewpoint there is much that can be done with the above observations. They can be used in the service of fuller interpretation of the text; they can form the basis of discussion of the function of different parts of speech; and, more specifically, the text can be used to introduce and form the basis of teaching some key structural features of English syntax such as nominal group organisation, participles, verbal relations, etc. There is no reason why a literary text cannot be used to illustrate such features. In fact, one real advantage of such a framework is that grammatical forms are not learned in a rote or abstract way or in relation to made-up examples; instead, grammar is taught in action and in terms of its communicative features (cf. Widdowson 1975). We are made to ask both what is grammatical and, practically, what specific job a grammatical form can do in addition to what the semantic relations are which underlie noun-phrase sequences. This can be of direct value to both native English language students and foreign-language learners of English.

TEACHING THE LEXIS

One procedure here involves discussion and definition of what the individual words mean; it is a conventional and time honoured procedure and is clearly of most practicable use to foreign students. However, the introduction of the notion of lexical collocation can be rather more instructive. Here we are asking more direct questions about 'the company words keep' and exploring the different degrees of acceptability in the semantic fit between lexical items – in this case, between modifier and head-word. Such exploration can teach more to foreign students about the meaning of words than dictionary-type definitions; we are forced in relation to this text into explaining, precisely, why 'crackling headphone' (line [11]) contains items which sit more comfortably alongside each other than 'crackling beard' (line [20]) or why 'smuggled' has a greater degree of semantic compatibility with 'mouth-organ' (line [5]) than with 'orbit' (line [15]). Idioms are explained, e.g. 'pitch black' (line [2]), as well as the extent of convertibility of idioms, e.g. 'the pitch sleep' (line [18]) or 'the pitch velvet' (line [10]); the range of meanings or associations carried by particular words can be discussed in relation to collocations such as 'the rough sleep' (line [10]); 'the rough moon' (line [16]); and the possibilities of metaphoric extension can also be investigated through the uses to which items like 'crawling' or 'crackling' are put e.g. 'the crawling deltas' (line [9]); 'the crackling somersault' (line [15]); 'the crawling camera' (line [19]); 'the crackling beard' (line [20]).

One central insight into the structure of the poem which should emerge as a result of such lexico-semantic analysis concerns the concentration of metaphoric extensions, semantic incompatibilities and generally unusual collocational relations in the last six lines of the poem. It is almost as if the typographic inlay at line [15] signals a markedly changed set of relationships between objects and their classifications even though both object and attribute remain fixed and finite. There is thus a basis laid for further interpretative investigation and for conjunction with the syntactic analysis above. [. . .]

THE TEACHING OF TEXT AS DISCOURSE

[. . .] From a classroom viewpoint one of the most instructive and helpful means of distinguishing textual discourse is analysis through a juxtaposition of one discourse with another. In the case of 'Off Course' it may be useful to set it alongside texts containing instructions, or inventories, or lists of participants at a meeting, or even perhaps a recipe. In other words, texts which can be shown to contain linguistic conventions of a similar nature to the poem under consideration. One main aim here should be to focus attention on the nature of the textual organisation of 'Off Course'; as a result, the following features should be discerned:

(i) readers should be uncertain as to how they are to read it. Across? Or down? The typography is not a reliable guide in this respect.
(ii) the lineation is unusual. There is an unexplained indentation at line [15]. The second column lacks the order and patterning of the first column although there is an equal space between noun phrases in both columns.
(iii) repetition of words is a marked feature although there is never repetition with the same collocational partner. A crisscross patterning occurs across columns, with modifiers sometimes turning up elsewhere as headwords (e.g. 'camera', lines [9] & [19])
(iv) the relation of the title to the text is not a direct one. Compare this with: 'Chicken and Vegetable Broth'; 'How to Use the Pump'; 'Shopping List' etc.
(v) the poem has no punctuation.

Once again the discernment of features such as these can be used to augment an interpretation of the text. But it can also be stylistic analysis of the kind that aids recognition of different styles of discourse and their different functions. Such work can be of particular use to the foreign-language learner who in some cases may have to learn totally new sets of conventions for different discourses. How explicitly he or she needs to learn this depends on the teacher's assessment of the needs of the class and the overall aims and objectives of the group's learning, but it can also be valuably underlined how different kinds of literary discourse can create their own rules for their reading, or can set out deliberately to disorientate a reader and how all literary discourse – however unusual – requires reference to one or other set of norms in order to create effects at all. Learning about the nature of literature involves learning about some of its operations as discourse. Learning about its operation as discourse is one essential prerequisite for reading the sort of concrete poetry of which 'Off Course' is a notable representative text.

[. . .]

INTERPRETING THE TEXT

For some people this is where we should arrive as well as the whole object of arrival. I've taken a long time to get here in order to try to demonstrate how much linguistic awareness can be derived from an examination of the language of a text as language and to challenge a prevailing view that literary texts cannot 'merely' be used for purposes of developing language competence. For me a stylistic approach to textual or literary interpretation is no more or less than another approach and is valuable only in the sense that it is a valuable activity for some students (but not necessarily for all). It would be wrong for our teaching of stylistics to be dominated by interpretative strategies; otherwise stylistics can become a restricted academic activity – both ideologically and pedagogically.

Put in a crude way, stylistic interpretation involves a process of making equations between, or inferences about, linguistic forms and the meanings contracted by the function or operation of these forms in a literary context. The whole issue of what is precisely involved in this is very complex and stylisticians are as involved as others in debates over what goes on in the process and over how particular interpretative facts can be established in a verifiable way. These issues cannot be addressed directly here although one perspective is offered in the next section; the following comments therefore carry the danger that they are based on assumptions which have not been made particularly explicit.

One of the 'equations' that can be made in relation to 'Off Course' is between the omission of verbs and an impression of weightlessness and suspension in which objects appear to be located in a free-floating relationship with each other and with the space surrounding them. The absence of verbal groups in the poem equates with and produces a sensation of a weightless, suspended condition of outer space where objects float about according to laws different from those which normally pertain.

Another central point [. . .] is the way in which the text shifts 'off-course', so to speak, at line [15]. From about line [10] to the end of the text no new headwords or modifiers are introduced. The same features recur but in different combinations resulting initially in something of a loss of identity of the objects concerned. But from line [15] the collocations of modifier and headwords become increasingly random or even incompatible. So the connections in our 'inventory' between object and its attribute/classificatory label seemingly get more and more arbitrary and void.

The typographical 'arrangement' of the text means that at the end we are left in an unpunctuated, unending space of free floating connections where the mind perceiving these features in this 'stream-of-consciousness-like' progression is apparently as disconnected and 'off-course' as the objects themselves. What was previously an embodiment of a disorientation in gravity-free conditions has now become a more profound dislocation. Where for the most part the lines up to line [15] represent a clear and definite, even if constantly changing, categorisation of things, the remaining lines succeed only in embodying the sense of a world and/or mind shifting out of control.

COMPARATIVE TEXTOLOGY

Texts are usually compared on the basis of related or contrasting themes; and there is little doubt that particular features of a text are placed in sharper relief through a process of comparison. A further dimension can be added by comparing texts which are constructionally and formalistically related. A stylistic examination of a text can provide a systematic and principled basis for grading texts for comparison or for further analysis. These texts can then be progressively introduced to students on the basis of their linguistic accessibility.

Literary stylistic work can be enhanced by such comparison as can be seen from a comparison of 'Off Course' with texts which have finite verbs deleted and/or exist as strings of nominal groups. Among the most interesting 'juxtapositions' are: Louis MacNeice, 'Morning Song'; George Herbert, 'Prayer'; Theodore Roethke, 'Child on Top of a Greenhouse'; Ezra Pound, 'In a Station of the Metro' [see unit C3 – P.S.]. Prose passages organised in this way include the opening to Dickens's *Bleak House* [see unit B3 – P.S.] and the opening to Isherwood's *Goodbye to Berlin*. We should explore here the similar and different effects produced in different literary contexts by the same linguistic procedures. [. . .]

Comparative textology moves the focus more centrally on to the essentially literary nature of the text (though the underpinning is consistently by linguistic means) and allows questions concerning differences between prose and poetry, between writers from the same period writing in similar ways, about literary movements, etc., and allows these questions to be generated at an appropriate level of abstractness. One seminal insight students should derive is that the same linguistic forms can function in different ways to produce different meanings according to context and according to the nature of the overlay of effects at other levels of language organisation. As we shall see in the next section, interpreting such 'meanings' is no simple matter of one-for-one correlation between form and function.

STUDYING THE 'NATURE' OF LITERARINESS

[. . .]

Two basic questions are: what is it in the organisation of the language of a text which makes it a literary text? how and why does it differ from other discourse types? Comparative textological investigation is going to be primary here and in its relation to the poem 'Off Course' we should want to return here to such features of the text as the way punctuation is used, the nature and function of the repetitions and parallelisms, the role of the title and of typography, the way it displays its own language, the interpenetration or convergence of different linguistic levels in the creation or constitution of meanings. This may lead to further exploration of plurality of meaning in literary discourse (the hyperactivity of the signifier), of how different literary discourses and kinds of reading are socially constituted and of how different cultures can impose different kinds of 'reading'. [. . .]

ISSUES TO CONSIDER

Carter sets considerable store by the notion of 'literariness' as a concept in and for stylistic investigation. Although not attempting to distinguish literature from non-literature on purely linguistic grounds, Carter, like Jakobson (see B1 and C1), argues for the existence of a type of linguistic praxis which links and underpins various creative uses of language, of which literature is (uncontroversially) a preeminent example. This model of 'literariness', and the stylistic theory which informs it, is fleshed out in the second chapter of Carter and Nash (1990) and this makes for useful follow-up reading.

Carter flags up many other areas for further study throughout his article. In particular, or additionally, consider the following suggestions:

Activity 

- With respect to Carter's call for a 'comparative textology', the structures which make up the poem 'Off Course' are like a number of the 'verb-less' patterns observed across this unit which might be classed as *minor clauses* (A3). That is not to say that the stylistic effect of these patterns will always be the same, nor will they share the same interpretative outcomes. Think of other literary texts which display dominant minor clause patterns. Worth chasing up are some of the texts which Carter himself suggests: Louis MacNeice's 'Morning Song', George Herbert's 'Prayer', Theodore Roethke's 'Child on Top of a Greenhouse' and the opening of Christopher Isherwood's novel *Goodbye to Berlin.*

- ❑ Think of text-types other than literature where features like minor clauses tend to congregate. Then assess the stylistic impact of the same grammatical structure in these different discourse contexts. (Newspaper headings and subheadings would be a good place to start.)
- ❑ Related to the previous task, consider the following newspaper headline from the British tabloid *The Daily Mirror* (1/11/02):

Barcelona lining up Eriksson

In grammatical terms, what does this sequence have in common with the passage from Dickens examined in B3? Do grammatical similarities invite the same type of interpretation across different discourse contexts? In other words, can we say that the newspaper text is 'Dickensian' in feel? Or is it that the Dickens text is newspaper-like in feel?

D4 SOUND, STYLE AND ONOMATOPOEIA

The principal focus of attention across this strand has been on the stylistic significance of patterns of sound. The sound system of language offers numerous resources for linguistic creativity in style, with metrical and rhythmic structure on the one hand, and phonetic and phonological patterning on the other. In B4, a distinction was drawn, echoing Attridge (1988), between *lexical* and *nonlexical* onomatopoeia, and that unit went on to explore the way the former category can function in poetry. The reading that follows, which concentrates on the second type of onomatopoeia, is an extract from the same ground-breaking study by Attridge. Nonlexical onomatopoeia is perhaps the most direct form of verbal imitative art insofar as patterns of sound are crafted to represent the real world without the intercession of grammatical or lexical structures. Attridge's is a slightly irreverent yet hugely entertaining account of this principle at work in a passage from James Joyce's *Ulysses.*

'Fff! Oo!': nonlexical onomatopoeia

Derek Attridge

Derek Attridge (reprinted from: Derek Attridge, *Peculiar Language: Literature as Difference from the Renaissance to James Joyce* London: Methuen. 1988, p.136–47)

Joyce's dexterity in handling the sounds and patterns of English is evident on every page of his published work, but one episode of *Ulysses* is explicitly concerned with music and imitative sound, the chapter known from the Odyssean scheme as 'Sirens'. We can expect to find here not only Joyce's customary linguistic agility and ingenuity but also some consideration – if only by example – of the whole question of language's capacity to imitate directly the world of the senses. In the well-known closing passage of the chapter, we find a very rudimentary type of onomatopoeia: the use of the phonetic characteristics of the language to imitate a sound without attempting to produce recognisable verbal structures, even those of traditional 'onomatopoeic' words. I shall call this type *nonlexical onomatopoeia.* Indeed, the device is perhaps too simple to be called 'onomatopoeia,' which means in Greek 'word-making' and usually implies reliance on the imitative potential of the accepted lexicon. In its naked ambition to mimic the sounds of the real world, however, nonlexical onomatopoeia exposes sharply some important but easily overlooked features of more sophisticated imitative figures.

Leopold Bloom, having imbibed a glass of burgundy at lunch and a bottle of cider at four o'clock, is walking along the Liffey quay uncomfortably aware that the after-effects of this indulgence will be embarrassing for him should they be heard by any passer-by. In particular, he wants to avoid being noticed by an approaching prostitute, and he therefore gazes strategically into a shop window that happens to contain a print of Robert Emmet together with Emmet's famous last words on Irish nationhood. Just at that moment a tram passes, providing an acoustic cover under which he can achieve the desired release without fear of detection:

> Seabloom, greaseabloom viewed last words. Softly. *When my country takes her place among.*
>
> Prrprr.
>
> Must be the bur.
>
> Fff! Oo. Rrpr.
>
> *Nations of the earth.* No-one behind. She's passed. *Then and not till then.* Tram kran kran kran. Good oppor. Coming. Krandlkrankran. I'm sure it's the burgund. Yes. One, two. *Let my epitaph be.* Kraaaaaa. *Written. I have.*
>
> Pprrpffrrppffff.
>
> *Done.*
>
> (11.1284 [Numbers refer to the corrected text, ed. Hans Walter Gabler *et al.*, and indicate episode and line nos])

Several nonlexical onomatopoeic sequences occur here, proffering with a vivid and comic directness the sounds and sensations of tram and fart and contributing to the undoubted memorability of the writing:

> Prrprr.
> Fff! Oo. Rrpr
> . . . kran kran kran.
> Krandlkrankran.
> Kraaaaaa.
> Pprrpffrrppffff.

But how simple, obvious, or direct *is* the onomatopoeic imitation of sound here? Several factors complicate the picture, and I shall isolate eight of them. The first four are concerned with the assumption that onomatopoeia involves an unusually *direct* or *unmediated* link between language and its referent, the next four with the complementary assumption that onomatopoeia involves an unusually *precise* representation in language of the physical world.

(1) The most elementary question to be asked is how these black marks on the page represent sound at all, and the answer is, of course, that they rely as much on the reader's knowledge of the phonological system of spoken English and the graphological system of written English as does lexical onomatopoeia or, for that matter, any English text. Onomatopoeia does not lead us into a realm of direct and concrete significance, where many writers have dreamed of going; we remain firmly held within an already existing system of rules and conventions, and whatever mimetic capability the sequences have they owe entirely to this fact. Putting it another way, although these are not words and sentences, they mimic words and sentences – and it is this mimicry that permits us to pronounce them at all. In reading 'Fff! Oo. Rrpr,' for instance, we give a specific phonetic interpretation to the sequence exclamation mark (or full stop)/space/capital letter and treat it quite differently from the rhythmic repetitions of 'Tram kran kran kran,' with its absence of punctuation and its lower case, or the continuous 'Krandlkrankran,' which has the graphic form of a single word. Even if the normal phonological restrictions are breached, as in the climactic string of letters ('Pprrpffrrppffff'), the resulting articulatory awkwardness helps draw attention to the sounds themselves, an effect that is equally dependent on the reader's prior familiarity with rules of graphology and phonology. Elsewhere in *Ulysses* Joyce goes even further in the direction of unpronounceability within the conventions of English: the Blooms' cat goes 'Mkgnao!' 'Mrkgnao!', and 'Mrkrgnao!' (4.16, 25, 32), and in 'Circe' the 'dummymummy' produces the sound 'Bbbbblllllblblblblobschb!' as it falls into Dublin Bay (15.3381). The difficulty of pronunciation is obviously part of the comic point (when Bloom imitates the cat in reply he goes, conventionally, 'Miaow!' [4.462]).

(2) The sequences we are looking at do not constitute lexical items, but they do not function purely as phonetic chains either, without reference to the morphological system of the language and its semantic accompaniment. (It would be difficult to find a string of letters that had no semantic colouring, given a specific fictional setting and the eagerness of readers to find meanings in what they read.) The letter 'f' hints at the word 'fart,' and 'kran' is not very far from 'tram.' There are also links with words accepted in the lexicon as representations of sound: 'Prr-' suggests 'purr' (another long-drawn-out sound made by the expulsion of air through a restricted passage), and 'kran' has elements of two of the words used elsewhere in the novel to represent the sound of trams, 'clang' (7.10) and 'crack' (15. 190). 'Krandl-' evokes phonetically related verbs of movement and noise such as 'trundle,' 'rumble,' 'grumble,' 'shamble,' 'scramble' – what has been called a 'phonesthetic constellation'' (Bolinger 1965: 191–239; see also Graham 1981 for further discussion of the 'phonestheme'). Mechanical associations, moreover, are evoked by its closeness to 'handle' and by the presence of '-krank-' later in the string. We might also note that the most

salient word in the quotation from Emmet is 'epitaph'; its [p] and [f] echo the onomatopoeic fart, deflating the heroic gesture as it is made. This link is all the stronger because Joyce has implanted it in the reader's mind in the chapter's prelude, where it occurs in the initially uninterpretable 'My eppripfftaph' (11.6 1). The reader might also be induced to make a connection with another sign system, that of musical dynamics, where 'ppffff' would signal 'very soft' and 'very loud indeed.' (When Molly breaks wind in 'Penelope,' and also does her best to be quiet about it, she addresses the words 'piano' and 'pianissimo' to herself at the critical moment [18.907, 908].)

The onomatopoeic effect also relies on an *avoidance* of certain morphological associations where these would be irrelevant or distracting: this is one reason – we shall look at others in a moment – why the spelling *cran* with a *c*, though it would indicate exactly the same pronunciation as *kran* with a *k*, would seem less appropriate, as it would produce associations with cranberries or craniums or Stephen's erstwhile companion Cranly. And what if the tram went 'bramble' or 'gran, gran, gran . . .'?

(3) The passage relies on our knowledge not only of the conventions of graphology, phonology, and morphology, however, but also of those of the rhetorical device of onomatopoeia itself. To take one example, the convention that a repeated letter automatically represents a lengthened sound is not to be found among the rules of the English language; the spelling of *gaffer*, for instance, does not imply that the medial consonant is pronounced at greater length than that of *loafer*. The rules cannot handle a succession of *more* than two repeated letters at all. But we have no difficulty with Joyce's triple *Fff*, which we interpret as an indication of marked duration, and such breaches of the graphological rules function, in fact, as strong indicators that we are in the presence of an onomatopoeic device.

The conventions of onomatopoeia relate not just to spelling, however, but also to the associations evoked by sounds and letters. Within the tradition of English poetry, the onomatopoeic associations of /s/ and /ʃ/ are more appealing than those of /f/, though there is nothing intrinsically beautiful about the former or ugly about the latter. [. . .]

More generally, to respond to onomatopoeia of any kind it is necessary to have learned how to do so, because it means overriding the normal procedures of language comprehension whereby the sound functions, in Saussure's vocabulary, entirely as a differential entity and not as a positive term. [. . .] In sum, onomatopoeia requires *interpretation* as much as any other system of signs does; it is a convention among conventions. [. . .]

(4) Although we have been discussing onomatopoeia as if it were a purely aural device, it is evident that the effect of these sequences is partly visual. [. . .] A mere glance at the passage, in fact, signals to the eye the presence of sequences of letters which go beyond the normal configurations of written English, and the visual patterns contribute to the mimetic impressions received by the reader – the short, visually contrasted segments of 'Fff! Oo. Rrpr'; the identical repetitions of 'kran kran kran'; the undifferentiated extension of 'Kraaaaaa,' with a run of letters all the same height; and the more varied continuities (and presumably sonorities) of 'Pprrpffrrppffff,' where the graphic shapes not only differ from one another but protrude above and below the line. (The reader familiar with musical scores might even respond

subliminally to this up-and-down movement as a representation of pitch changes.) The unpronounceable examples mentioned earlier rely even more on apprehension by means of the eye: they remain resolutely visual, rendering any attempt to convert them into sound arbitrary and inadequate. One does not have to go to *Finnegans Wake* to find a text in which neither eye nor ear is sufficient on its own; indeed, one does not even have to go to Joyce or to 'experimental' writing.

(5) Turning now to the common notion that onomatopoeia constitutes an unusually precise representation of the physical qualities of the external world, we may ask how successful we would be in identifying the sounds referred to by these strings of letters outside the specific context of this passage from *Ulysses*. Joyce in fact poses this question at the beginning of the chapter, as if to underline the point in advance. Among the brief fragments that open 'Sirens' are the following, without any accompanying explanation:

> Fff! Oo! (11.58)
> Rrrpr. Kraa. Kraandl. (11.60)

These enigmatic scraps, like all the items in the list, convey very little in terms of the fictional setting and can be interpreted only retrospectively. Appearing where they do, they highlight the dependence of linguistic formations – onomatopoeic and otherwise – on their immediate context. Thus our 'hearing' of the tram in the final passage of 'Sirens' depends entirely on a clue not given in the prelude, the word 'tram' itself, without which we could make no sense of the onomatopoeic sequence. And the fart has already been carefully prepared for earlier in the chapter, without, it is true, anything so gross as the word 'fart' crossing Bloom's mind or the text's surface. (Molly, in a similar predicament at the end of the book, is not so squeamish.) Several intimations of flatulence have appeared at intervals on the preceding pages:

> Rrr. (11.1155)
> Rrrrrrrsss. (11.1162)
> . . . bloom felt wind wound round inside.
> Gassy thing that cider: binding too. Wait. (11.1178)
> . . . then all of a soft sudden wee little wee little pipy wind.
> Pwee! A wee little wind piped eeee. In Bloom's little wee. (11.1201)
> Rrrrrr.
> I feel I want . . . (11.1216)
> Wish I could. Wait. (11.1224)
> I must really. Fff. Now if I did that at a banquet. (11. 1247)
> Must be the cider or perhaps the burgund. (11. 1268)

The final release is therefore the culmination of a little private drama, a kind of interior dialogue, and we are left in no doubt as to the sound represented by the letters on the page before us. (Though some readers of refined sensibilities may have taken the problem to be the less embarrassing one of an urge to belch: the text seems to offer this possibility in its references to the gassiness of the cider and to the Persian custom of burping at banquets, and in the apparent, if deceptive, hint in 'Must be the bur.' Such an uncertainty as to oral and anal alternatives would be entirely in keeping with the rest of the episode [. . .].) The same letters can in fact perform very different onomatopoeic tasks: in *Ulysses* a sequence of *e*s stands not only for a release of wind, as in 'A wee little wind piped eeee,' but for a stick trailing along a path ('Steeeeeeeeeeeephen!' [1.629]), a creaking door ('ee: cree' [7.50] and 'ee' [11.965]), a turning doorhandle (['Theeee!' [15. 2694]), and a distant trainwhistle ('Frseeeeeeeefronnnng' [18.595], 'Frseeeeeeeeeeeeeeeeeeeefrong' [18.874], 'sweeeee . . . eeeee' [18.908]). In the last example the context does not allow us to distinguish that trainwhistle from Molly's own anal release.

(6) For onomatopoeia to work at all, however, it is not enough to know from the context what sound is supposed to be represented; it is also necessary to have some prior familiarity with that sound. [. . .] Bloom produces a sound with which we are all familiar, but we are less likely to know what a 1904 Dublin tram sounded like and so are less likely to be impressed by the imitative appropriateness of Joyce's phonetic formulae. To take a more extreme example, readers who do not know the sound of a badly adjusted gaslight (among whom I number myself) will not be able to find out what it is from the letters given to represent the noise in the 'Circe' episode: 'Pooah! Pfuiiiiiii!' (15.2280). (We might suspect, from the much more helpful lexical description '*the gasjet wails whistling*,' that there is a Circean extravagance about this utterance as about so many utterances in that chapter, but even if the representation were as accurate as letters could make it, we would still be little the wiser.) Onomatopoeia is not a means of gaining knowledge about the world; after all, we can praise a literary text for the precision of its descriptions only if we are already fully acquainted with what the text purports to be describing.

(7) Even when these two conditions, an unambiguous situating context and prior familiarity with the sound, are met, the imitative effects of onomatopoeia – even of this very direct type – remain extremely imprecise. What, for instance, are we to make of 'Oo'? Is this a voiced (or thought) exclamation of Bloom's? An accompanying burp? A noisy passage in the anal performance? (As every actor knows, the letter 'O' can represent a wide variety of speech sounds.) Are the 'rrr' sequences here and earlier to be taken as stomach rumbles, or as premonitory activity in the bowels? And what aspects of the tram's sound are represented? The other noises made by trams in the novel provide no help: earlier they are to be heard 'honking' (5.131) and 'clanging ringing' (7. 10), and in 'Circe' a sandstrewer bears down on Bloom, 'its trolley *hissing* on the wire,' while the motorman '*bangs* his footgong' and the brake '*cracks* violently' (15.186, 187, 190). One reader, at least, does not even hear a tram at the end of 'Sirens,' but something more euphonious: David Hayman, in a plot summary of *Ulysses*, refers to Bloom's 'carefully releasing a final fizzle of fart to the sound of band-music.' (Hayman 1981: 142; cf. 112–14, where Hayman takes Bloom's thoughts about a drummer in a military band as evidence that there is a real band on the Liffey quay). Most readers would no doubt regard this as a highly idiosyncratic interpretation, but it does testify to the lack of a wholly obvious sonic referent.

Only a few nonvocal sounds, in fact, can be imitated with any degree of closeness by the speech organs, and the significance (and pleasure) to be drawn from Bloom's fart lies partly in its exceptional character: it is unusually amenable to vocal imitation in being a sound produced by an orifice of the human body. This fact enables the sequence 'fff' to be appropriate in both the ways open to onomatopoeic imitation, in its articulatory processes and in its acoustic properties – it is both produced like and sounds like a fart. (Even then, we take little pleasure in accuracy of imitation for its own sake: a more precise rendition of a fart than 'Pprrpffrrppffff' would be 'Fffffffffffff.') Few of the sounds that we hear, and that writers attempt to convey, are as well qualified as this one is for imitative representation. We might even say that the only fully successful onomatopoeia occurs when the human voice is imitated, which is what written language, in a sense, does all the time – except, that is, when it is attempting nonlexical onomatopoeia.

(8) A further complication is most obvious in the case of nonlexical onomatopoeia, though it remains a possibility in all onomatopoeic devices. The reader who responds to these strings of letters as attempts at direct representation of familiar sounds is likely to go beyond the normal phonological rules of English in essaying an imitation (in the imagination if not in actual utterance) more accurate than language normally permits. Doing so amounts to treating the sequences as instructions to the reader: [*sound of fart*], [*sound of passing tram*]. If we look at it in this way, mimetic precision in the string of letters is completely unnecessary, and the reader is in fact likely to do a better job of imitating or imagining the sound required if he or she is unhindered by the writer's attempt to make it compatible with the normal phonological properties of the English language. Difficulty in pronunciation according to the normal rules of English may also encourage the reader's inventiveness: strictly speaking, for example, it is impossible to give a plosive any degree of duration, but the doubling of *p* in the final onomatopoeic effusion of 'Sirens' may suggest a continuant very close to the sound represented. And most readers probably take the unpronounceability of 'Mrkrgnao!' as an invitation to imitate a cat's cry in a way less stylised than the conventional 'Miaow!'. In 'Circe' Joyce plays with the curious relationship between stage directions describing utterances and the utterances themselves, as in the gasjet's wailing whistle, and we might ask whether in 'Lestrygonians' Davy Byrne's yawn 'Iiiiichaaaaaaach!' (8.970), which Hugh Kenner praises for its 'deftness of rhythmic imitation' (Kenner 1980: 85), would even be recognised without a prior announcement of what is coming. (When Byrne is assigned a similar string of letters in 'Circe' – 'Iiiiiiiiaaaaaaach!' (15. 1697) – interpretation is again aided by the stage direction [*'yawning'*].) At the same time, the extraordinary sequence of letters clearly gives the reader more scope for a bravura performance and in so doing provides greater pleasure than would a mere 'Davy Byrne yawned loudly.'

It can be demonstrated, then, that any sense of appropriateness which an example of nonlexical onomatopoeia may produce is not primarily the result of an unusually close resemblance between the sounds of language and the sounds of the external world. This being the case, it is easier to understand how the experience can be accompanied by a heightened consciousness of the sounds of language themselves. Indeed, the inevitable incongruity of such devices frequently intrigues and amuses the reader, even while the letters successfully perform their referential duties. Jakobson's double emphasis seems justified, therefore, at least as far as nonlexical

onomatopoeia is concerned: the series of linguistic sounds *and* their referents receive simultaneous, if separate, enhancement. But this pleasurable double foregrounding is achieved by something other than the art of imitation.

ISSUES TO CONSIDER

An important point of theory to emerge from Attridge's study is his contention that the use even of nonlexical onomatopoeia, that most mimetic of stylistic devices, is not of itself sufficient to represent directly the object or activity it echoes. This is because recognition depends on a series of other in-text indicators, and even when two important conditions – an unambiguous situating context and prior familiarity with the sound – are met, the imitative potential remains imprecise. Attridge's point articulates a broad principle about stylistic analysis which was rehearsed in B4; namely, that linguistic structures do not embody textually aspects of the 'real world' but instead serve as gateways to the understanding and interpretation of those texts *vis-à-vis* their relationship to the real world.

Some suggestions follow.

Activity 

- ❑ Although his focus is principally on the style of a single literary text, much of what Attridge says has general validity and his observations can therefore be translated to other textual practices – this is always the test of an insightful and far-reaching stylistic analysis. Developing this, reference was made in A4 to the importance of sound symbolism in the 'advertising jingle', and this is a type of discourse that lends it itself well to the study of both lexical and nonlexical onomatopoeia. For example, a long-running British advertisement for a popular stomach and headache remedy displays the dropping of two effervescent tablets into a glass of water. In both its billboard and televisual versions, this activity is accompanied by the written logo 'Plink, plink, fizz'. Can you (i) identify the types of onomatopoeic devices at work in this jingle and (ii) think of other ads where similar stylistic techniques are used?
- ❑ Following from the previous suggestion, here is another advertising text (for a local bakery) which displays an interesting sound texture:

  This is the bread
  To greet any guest
  Because it's the bread
  That mother knows best.

  Drawing on any of the relevant material offered across this thread, try to provide an account of sound patterning, including metrical structure, in this advertising jingle.
- ❑ English words which begin with 'sl' are often thought to be onomatopoeic because they frequently connote an unpleasant action or thing. Can you list five 'sl' words that have an unpleasant feel to them? Now, can you think of any words which begin with 'sl' but which do *not* have such connotations? If you succeed

at the latter task, what does this say about the supposed unpleasantness of 'sl' words in English? Do the historical origins of the words (that is, whether they are Anglo-Saxon or Latinate in derivation, for example) have any bearing on their supposed onomatopoeic qualities?

D5

STYLE VARIATION IN NARRATIVE

This reading, by Mick Short, examines the use of graphological deviation as an indicator of viewpoint in Irvine Welsh's novel, *Marabou Stork Nightmares*. After providing an interpretative summary of its plot line (see unit A5), Short explores the narrative structure of Welsh's novel which, unusually, comprises three interwoven 'levels' of narration, all produced by the same narrator. Although graphological deviation is normally seen as the preserve of stylistic experimentation in poetry, Short's analysis, which is orientated principally towards the opening of the novel, demonstrates how prose fiction can draw on this level of language for stylistic effect. Short also develops in a theoretically more rigorous way some of the terms, such as *viewpoint*, *focaliser* and *reflector*, which have been used across this strand.

The work of Irvine Welsh featured in unit C2 where a passage from *Trainspotting* formed the principal focus of attention. This Scottish writer is renowned, indeed infamous, for his grimly realistic portrayals of criminal counter-cultures and of the social consequences of violence and drug addition. With its sociolinguistic code the lower status urban vernacular of Edinburgh, and its frequent mixing of levels and structures of language, Welsh's work is challenging, often disturbing and at times unsuitable, as it were, for the stylistically faint-hearted. Nevertheless, and as Short's analysis demonstrates, the writing of this novelist pays many useful dividends in stylistic terms.

Graphological deviation, style variation and point of view in *Marabou Stork Nightmares* by Irvine Welsh

Mick Short

Mick Short (reprinted from *Journal of Literary Studies/Tydskrif vir Literatuurwetenskap* 15, 3/4, 1999, p. 305–23).

Introduction

In this article I want to provide an account of Irvine Welsh's *Marabou Stork Nightmares* (1995), based mainly on a representative stylistic analysis of the opening of the novel. I have chosen to concentrate on this rather bizarre and disturbing novel because, in spite of its horrific qualities, I think it has considerable intrinsic artistic merit (something which I hope my analysis will begin to show). [. . .]

[B]elow I will give an interpretative summary of the novel, to which I will then link a stylistic commentary of its opening. But for those who have not already read the novel, it will be helpful to experience how the novel begins [see Figure D5.1] without such explanation (I have numbered the sentences for ease of reference).

(1) It.was.me.and.Jamieson.

(2) Just us.

(3) On this journey, this crazy high-speed journey through this strange land in this strange vehicle.

(4) Just me and Sandy Jamieson.

(5) But they were trying to disturb me, trying to wake me; the way they always did. (6) They willnae let this sleeping dog lie. (7) They always interfere. (8) When the cunts start this shite it makes things get aw distorted and I have to try to go deeper.

(9) DEEPER. (10) Things get dis up - - - - (12) - We're just going to take
coming your temperature,
start Roy. (13) Have you got the
I bedpan, Nurse Norton?
(14) Number Twos now Roy,
(11) I lose control when they interfere - - - and time for Number Twos.
(15) —Yes, he's looking brighter this morning, isn't he, Nurse Devine? (16) You're brighter this morning, Roy lovey.

(17) Aye right ye are, take your fuckin hand oot me fuckin erse.

(18) DEEPER

(19) DEEPER - (20) Sandy Jamieson is my best friend down here. (21) A former professional sportsman and an experienced hunter of man-eating beasts. (22) I enlisted Jamieson's aid in a quest I have been engaged in for as long as I can remember. (23) However, as my memory is practically non-existent, this could have been a few days ago or since the beginning of time itself. (24) For some reason, I am driven to eradicate the scavenger-predator bird known as the Marabou Stork. (25) I wish to drive this evil and ugly creature from the African continent. (26) In particular, I have this persistent vision of one large blighter, a hideous and revolting specimen, which I know somehow must perish by my own hand.

Figure D5.1 Extract from *Marabou Stork Nightmares*: Irvine Welsh (1995: 3–4)

An interpretative summary of Marabou Stork Nightmares

Irvine Welsh is probably best-known for *Trainspotting*, a novel about the drugs culture in Britain which was also made into a highly successful film. In *Marabou Stork Nightmares*, drug-taking is a minor theme, but the subject-matter of the novel is also extremely distasteful. [. . .] The I-narrator is a young Edinburgh Scot who is lying in hospital in a coma, caused, as we discover towards the end of the novel (on p. 255 of a novel which ends on p. 264), by a failed suicide attempt. He had tried to kill himself – while watching a video of his favourite football team (the Edinburgh side, Hibernian FC, or 'Hibs') – using the pain-killer, paracetamol, and a plastic bag over the head, as recommended in a book he had read called *Final Exit: The Practicalities of Self-Deliverance and Assisted Suicide for the Dying.*

If the passage above was your first experience of *Marabou Stork Nightmares*, you may have found it initially difficult. This is because the events of the story are presented out of chronological sequence, and in an apparently piecemeal and disorganised fashion by an unconscious narrator who is in a vegetative state. At the outset of the novel he is fantasising about himself and an imaginary friend, Sandy Jamieson, who are supposedly in South Africa on an extraordinary 'quest' to kill the Marabou Stork. To make matters even more difficult for the reader, there are three distinct 'levels' of narration in the novel, through which the I-narrator, Roy Strang, is continually shifting/being shifted by external intervention. The deepest level is the South African fantasy narration concerning his hunt for the Marabou Stork, and the highest is one where the narrator is aware of what is going on around him in the Edinburgh hospital as he drifts towards consciousness (something which is never fully achieved, but which he gets closer to as the novel proceeds). The middle level is a rather jumbled, and sometimes contradictory, account of Roy Strang's life leading up to his attempted suicide, his resulting vegetative state (which he has been in for two years) and his eventual death at the end of the novel.

It could be argued that the novel has three distinct narrations, where the same narrator tells three stories at the same time, but I prefer to call them three *levels* of narration because (a) they all have the same narrator and the same 'default' narratee (the reader), (b) as the novel proceeds, the narrative levels 'interact' and reflect one another more and more and (c) there is textual evidence (see below) to suggest that we are meant to see the three narrations as a series of connected levels. The top level and the middle level are, in any case, part of the same general fictional world (what Ryan 1991 would call the 'text-actual world'), the top level coinciding with what appears to be the narrator's coding time ('what is happening to the I-narrator in his fictional now') and the middle level being what happened to the I-narrator/what the I-narrator did in his fictional past. The deepest level of narration is distinct from the other two in that it is a fantasy (what Ryan 1991: 119 calls a 'fantasy-universe'). But the connections and correspondences between it and the two levels of the text-actual world are so many that they begin to interpenetrate, and become 'explanations of one another', as we will see below.

The movements from one level of narration to another, sometimes forced by external stimuli and sometimes by connections made within the mind of the narrator, are clearly meant to be representative of a mind drifting towards, and away from, consciousness. Our major tasks as readers, then, are (a) to work out when we are in which narrative level, and why, (b) to construct a characterisation and narrative structure for the text which explains how Roy Strang came to be in a coma and (c) to make sense of the connections which become apparent among the different levels of narration, many of which do not become clear until the last few pages of the novel.

For example, on p. 255, when the suicide attempt is being described, the footballer on the video, who is gesticulating at the referee, is called Jimmy Sandison, allowing us to see that Sandy Jamieson, Roy's friend in the Marabou Stork fantasy, is an imaginative metathetic creation derived from the footballer's name, something we have been prepared for by the fact that on occasion the I-narrator 'mis-refers' to Sandy as 'Jimmy' (e.g. p. 169). In Ryan's terms, then, Roy Strang's fantasy universe is clearly prompted by the text-actual world in which he lives. [. . .]

When Roy is ten, the family emigrates to South Africa [. . .] [b]ut the dream of a new life for the family in South Africa is not realised. John Strang is jailed for attacking a taxi-driver when drunk, and the rest of the family returns to Edinburgh a year and a half after they had emigrated. For Roy, who [. . .] has his father's love for nature, and for wild animals in particular, the South African period was a very mixed experience. His uncle, a paedophile, secretly abuses him, forcing him into both oral and anal sex, but at the same time showers him with presents, including wonderful trips to safari parks to see the animals.

As a young man, Roy has a good job working for an insurance company as an IT specialist, but in his spare time he satisfies his now ingrained thirst for violence as a member of a 'casuals' football gang who fight other such gangs. It is this activity which results in his eventual downfall. He and his pals gang-rape a young woman called Kirsty, also forcing her to have anal and oral sex with them. These activities are reminiscent of what Roy's uncle forced him to do in South Africa, and, in his fantasy universe, (a) of what he 'sees' his girlfriend doing with his fantasy friend, Sandy Jamieson, near the beginning of the novel (p. 5) and (b) the various distasteful activities of a businessman in the fantasy called Lochart Dawson, a figure who resembles Roy's uncle Gordon in a number of ways. Ironically, it later transpires that, unbeknown to Roy, Kirsty was romantically attracted to him at the time he raped her.

The gang is arrested, but at their trial they are all acquitted through the adversarial skills of an experienced lawyer who, at the same time is clearly very unsympathetic to the young men. Roy's initial account of the rape depicts him as an unwilling participant, something which later appears not to be true, but which helps to suggest his growing sense of guilt. [. . .]

In the last few pages of the novel, Kirsty secretly visits Roy in hospital. Her experience of the rape and the humiliation of the trial make her want to take systematic revenge on those who raped her. She has already killed one of the gang, and now she proceeds to kill Roy by stabbing him with a pair of scissors, after first removing his eyelids, and then cutting of his genitalia and stuffing them into his mouth. This process parallels both her own rape and the other events referred to above, in the text-actual world and Roy's fantasy universe, which I have already said are reminiscent of that rape.

And what of the Marabou Stork? As the novel proceeds, the leader of the Marabou Storks which Roy is hunting in his fantasy universe accrues more and more connections with Roy himself in his remembered text-actual world. In that world, he sees Marabou Storks for the first time, with his father, when his uncle Gordon, who has already systematically abused Roy sexually, takes the family to the Kruger National Park. Roy sees the Storks destroy and eat some pink flamingos, and that night he has his 'first Marabou Stork nightmare' (p. 74). As a young boy, then, he is a victim, the equivalent of the flamingos, and uncle Gordon is the oppressor, the equivalent of the Marabou Stork. But when Roy describes Kirsty immediately after the rape (p. 190), he does so in terms which resembles the damaged flamingos, and by extension he has also changed status from flamingo to Marabou Stork. After the rape he has more nightmares in which he clearly associates Kirsty with the flamingos, and himself and his friends with the Storks (pp. 221, 233). Roy's pursuit of his personal Marabou Stork in his fantasy universe thus appears to be a subconscious attempt to come to terms with, and defeat, his own evil. But he never destroys the Stork, never really catches up with it. And indeed, at the moment of his death, when his fantasy universe and the text-actual world finally coincide on the last page of the novel (p. 264), he clearly sees himself as the Marabou Stork: 'Captain Beaky, they used to call me at school . . . I spread my large black wings . . .' This coincidence of narrative levels means that he dies at the same time in both his fantasy universe and the text-actual world. This is indicated by the fact that people and objects from the fantasy universe and the text-actual world are now represented as if they are in the same textual world. He is both stabbed by Kirsty in the Edinburgh hospital and shot by his erstwhile fantasy friend in 'South Africa', and his nurse can do nothing to help:

> I can move my lidless eyes, I can see my cock dangling from my mouth and I can see the scissors sticking out from my neck. . . . Patricia runs to get help but she's too late because Jamieson's facing me and he's pointing the gun and I hear it going off and it's all just one big
>
> **Z.**

The novel thus ends with a final marked graphological device using a letter which is conventionally associated with sleep, and hence, by extension, death. However, the normal comfortable associations for sleep are minimised here as a consequence of the fact that in the previous twenty-three pages (i.e. from p. 241 onwards) graphologically marked forms of this letter have systematically been associated with the 'Z' of the posters in the Zero Tolerance campaign against rape and sexual oppression. In real life, this campaign has had a considerable impact in Edinburgh in recent years and, in the fictional world of the novel, Roy's exposure to the posters is partly responsible for his increasing feelings of guilt. Whether, as the blurb on the back cover of the paperback suggests, these feelings of guilt and Kirsty's final treatment of him amount to a final 'redemption' is, however, not so clear. [. . .]

A stylistic commentary on the opening passage in relation to the rest of the novel

It will be apparent from the discussion above that *Marabou Stork Nightmares* has an extremely distasteful subject matter, which could deter some from reading it. But it is also an extremely interesting novel. In particular, it is sophisticated narratologically, and this complex narratological structuring has well-worked-out interpretative consequences. This narratological innovation is, in turn, signalled/controlled through considerable linguistic invention, which we can now explore through a detailed examination of the novel's opening.

The novel opens with what in the 20th century has become a fairly standard *in medias res* device, presenting what must be new information to the reader as if it were given information, to draw the reader into seeing events from the narrator's viewpoint and with his ideological assumptions. However, the technique is taken to quite an extreme here. In the first four sentences we are not told who the narrating 'I' is, who Sandy Jamieson is, where the characters are, or what exactly they are doing. And in spite of the repeated use of the quasi-deictic natural spoken narrative use of 'this' in sentence (3), we do not know what journey they are on, or why it is crazy, which land they are in, or why it is strange, and what vehicle they are in, and why that vehicle is strange. These matters become a bit more clear in sentences (20)–(26), but Africa is not narrowed to South Africa until p. 13 of the novel, when it can be deduced from a small child offering sexual services 'for rand.' We are thus made to struggle hard for coherence. The issue of the identity of the vehicle mentioned in (3) is even more problematic. It is referred to as a jeep on p. 2, and this assumption holds for a while, but by p. 8 it has apparently become some sort of aircraft, probably a helicopter. It is this sort of changing and contradictory characterisation which leads the reader to assume that we are being presented with some sort of fantasy universe.

In addition to the oddities of the given-new structure, the first few sentences of the text are characterised by syntactic and graphological oddity. Sentences (2)–(4) are minor sentences grammatically and are also separated from one another by line-spaces. Sentence (1) is grammatically complete, and has the standard narrative past tense, which leads us to assume this tense as a background default for the next three minor sentences. But sentence (1) is also very deviant orthographically, full stops separating the words instead of spaces. Indeed, this oddity caused a problem for me when I numbered the sentences for ease of presentation. Should what I have labelled as sentence (1) really be represented as five separate sentences? I decided not to do this because the first five words form a grammatically normal English sentence and only the sentence-initial word and the final word, a proper name, begin with upper case letters.

These features need explanation, although it would be impossible for a reader to find a satisfactory one from the first few sentences alone. In content terms, they are, of course, sentences describing the narrator's fantasy universe which I outlined above, and once we have deduced that the narrator must be in a coma, we can relate the minor sentence construction, the stops among the words in the first sentence and the line spaces among the other sentences as indicative of a mind having some difficulty in getting going at the beginning of the narration: they thus represent mental disjunctions, which, like the deviant given-new information structure, can be put down to a mind struggling to cope.

GRAPHOLOGICAL DEVIATION AND STYLE VARIATION

In spite of the minor sentence syntax, the first four sentences would appear to be reasonably characterised as Standard English. However, there is a switch in sentences (6)–(8), within the first orthographically normal paragraph, to the representation of a non-standard Scots dialect. Later on in the novel, when we know where the narrator comes from, we will be able to characterise this dialect as working class Edinburgh Scots. The orthographic indicators of a Scots dialect are 'willnae' for 'won't', 'shite' for 'shit' and 'aw' for 'all' [see C2 – P.S.]. This indication of a pronunciation change also corresponds with the introduction of a rude scatological vocabulary ('shite', 'cunts').

This marked style shift also needs explanation, of course. What appears to happen is that the real Roy Strang, as yet un-named, begins to appear in these sentences, where, note, the tense has also changed from past to present. When Roy 'speaks' in his fantasy narration, however, he uses a Standard English which is at the same time marked as belonging to a kind of upper class between-the-wars RAF Biggles-speak, which is parodic of what might be called the 'English of Empire'. The only clear indicators of this style in the passage quoted in 1 above are the narrator's reference to his friend by last name only, and the word 'blighter' in sentence (26). But in the following page of text the word 'blighter' appears again, along with 'Wizard!' (meaning 'great!'), 'Yuk!', 'yukky' and 'a cunning but somewhat morally deficient native fellow'. This pattern of 'Biggles-speak' for the fantasy universe narration and Edinburgh Scots for the text-actual world narrations is used consistently throughout the novel and helps to contrast brutal reality with a wish-world (see Ryan 1991: 117–18) which the narrator appears to be struggling towards but does not properly achieve mentally, let alone physically.

So far I have studiously avoided discussion of sentence (5), which begins the paragraph I have been discussing. Its tense is consistent with that of the first four sentences, and there are no orthographic indications of Edinburgh Scots. But it is orthographically connected to the Edinburgh Scots narration, and the unanchored, given-information use of 'they' also coheres better with the 'they' of sentences (6)–(7) and 'the cunts' of (8) than with sentences (1)–(4). Indeed, in the fantasy universe narration, sentences (1)–(2) appear to rule out the possibility of reference to individuals other than the narrator and Jamieson. Sentence (5) thus appears to be a transition sentence which moves the reader from one level of narration to the next. It also indicates something which is true throughout the novel, namely that it is not possible to associate particular tenses exactly with particular levels of narration. Although the text-actual world in the narrator's 'coding-time fictional present' is usually accorded the present tense, and the fantasy universe narration and the narration of the text-actual world in the narrator's past are mainly in the past tense, there are 'janus-faced' sentences like (5) from time to time, and there are also some other textually strategic tense shifts within the default tense for a particular narrative level.

GRAPHOLOGICAL DEVIATION AND VISUALLY SYMBOLIC EFFECTS

The narrator's response to what he sees as interference by the as yet non-specific outsiders is to 'try to go deeper'. This phraseology is then used as the trigger for the first of a series of 'graphology-symbolic' representations which can be found throughout the novel, and which provide textual evidence for the notion, which I introduced above, that the different narrations are best seen as levels of the same narration. As I said, the narrator represents the unfolding of his fantasy universe as the deepest level of narration, and that of his presently experienced coding time as the highest. In the opening to the novel which I am concentrating on, there is no clear representative of the middle level, the narrator's past in the text-actual world (although, interestingly, the narratorially ambivalent sentence (5) could be seen as relating to this middle level as well as to the other two). A clear characterisation of this middle level in relation to the other two can be seen on pp. 48–9, for example.

The first 'graphology-symbolic' movement between the narratorial levels of the novel (sentences (9)–(19) of the passage) is complex, as a result of the fact that it contains an upward movement embedded inside a downward one. Elsewhere, in more simple cases, when the narrator moves down a level, this is usually represented symbolically by the word 'DEEPER' in capitals repeated on three successive lines. A series of dashes of varying length occur after the final 'DEEPER', apparently representing the size of the mental pause between the effort to go deeper and the resumption of the lower (in this case fantasy universe) narration. Sometimes, as here, the instances of 'DEEPER' are directly under one another. On other occasions they are 'raked' rightwards down across the page as in:

DEEPER

DEEPER

DEEPER

Although the normal representation involves a three-fold repetition of the word, larger or smaller repetitive sequences sometimes occur, appearing to indicate the amount of effort needed to move between levels. For example, the narrator needs a sequence of nine raked repetitions of 'DEEPER' on p. 40 to stop thinking about the attractive Nurse Devine (a play on 'divine') and get back to his fantasy.

Not surprisingly, when the narrator moves upwards between narrative levels, the words go up the page, sometimes vertically, as in the passage we are discussing, and sometimes raked from left to right. In the passage under discussion the reader needs to go down five lines from the uncompleted word 'dis' to 'I lose control . . .' in order to read up and then down again through the block of nurse-talk on the right-hand side of the page. Note also here the effect of sentence (10) ending in the middle of a word as Roy struggles unsuccessfully to stay in his fantasy universe. In context it would appear that the uncompleted word is 'disturbed' or 'disrupted', and so 'dis' is itself graphology-symbolic (note the lack of a final hyphen – as in 'din-', which would normally be used in writing to indicate an interrupted item).

A further graphology-symbolic effect that can be seen in (9)–(19) relates to font and type-size. Sentences (12)–(16) are in a different and considerably smaller type face than those surrounding them. These sentences, with their stereotypical euphemisms and friendly vocatives, clearly represent a conversation between two nurses, Nurse Norton and Nurse Devine who also 'interact' with Roy as they care for him. This conversation is important for us in beginning to make sense of the movements among narrative levels in the novel, and we also glean the name of the narrator from their conversation. The change in type size is thus an appropriate foregrounding device for the reader. But it also appears that the particular size (smaller than the surrounding type) can be seen as representative of Roy's viewpoint relation to what they say. They interrupt his fantasy universe thoughts, causing him to rise up through the narrative levels, but at the same time they appear to be less important or less vivid for him than what he 'hears' inside his head. This symbolic use of type size and related features like capitalisation is a feature to be found throughout the novel. For example, on p. 15, when his parents are leaving after a visit, their farewells ('CHEERIO SON! CHEERIO ROY!') are in capitalised small print to represent an increase in volume and pitch variation compared to the rest of their speech (cf. also the exclamation marks). But the fact that even the capitalised words are still in the smaller type size indicates their lack of interest from Roy's perspective.

In the novel's opening passage, Roy 'responds' to what the nurses say with his most dialectally marked sentence in the passage ((17) 'Aye right ye are, take your fuckin hand oot me fuckin erse.'). Six of the twelve words are non-standard in some way, and three of them are also taboo words. When Roy uses 'fucking' in his fantasy universe it is spelled normally, but here the spelling indicating a dialect pronunciation omits the final 'g' and does not even signal its omission by the conventional apostrophe. But in spite of the anger of Roy's response, there is no indication that the nurses hear him. There is no indication that those in the hospital hear him anywhere else in the novel either, so we must assume that (17), and sentences like it, must be Direct Thought, not Direct Speech (see Short 1996: Ch. 10).

Elsewhere in the novel, graphological foregrounding devices like capitalisation, italicisation, unusual spellings and so on are also often used within this Direct Thought mode to indicate simultaneously Roy's dialect and the strength of his attitude:

> – Awright son!
> AW FUCK! *THIR* HERE.
>
> (p. 10)

In this section, although my analysis has not been exhaustive by any means, I hope to have shown that graphological deviation and patterning and style variation are important factors in how viewpoint shifts, and in particular how movements among the levels of narration are controlled in the opening to *Marabou Stork Nightmares.* Indeed, the use of graphological deviation to signal viewpoint occurs in a number of his works, and so can be seen as part of Irvine's overall style. Moreover, the features seen in the opening passage of *Marabou Stork Nightmares* are representative of, and also explained by, what happens in the rest of the novel. Perhaps one final point to note is that sentence (23) ('However, as my memory is practically non-existent, this could have been a few days ago or since the beginning of time itself.') is one of a number of clear indications in the novel, both in its direct statement and the accompanying hyperbole, that the narrator is unreliable. This correlates with the extraordinary movements we have seen in the rest of the passage, and with the fact that the narrator does not always face reality direct in the rest of the novel. For example, as I have already pointed out, he first characterises his role in the rape of Kirsty as less bad than it really is, and nowhere in the novel does he appear to be able to confront his own evil directly, having to resort instead to the symbolic quest to kill the Marabou Stork in his fantasy universe.

[. . .]

Marabou Stork Nightmares is an extraordinary novel. Its extremely distasteful subject-matter and the attitudes of the characters portrayed will be enough to dissuade many from reading it at all. But I hope to have shown that it also has considerable artistic interest in general narratological terms, in its linguistic detail and the inter-relations between this linguistic detail and the larger-scale narratological structuring. [. . .]

ISSUES TO CONSIDER

It is important to reiterate that the scope of Mick Short's article is wide-ranging and that it makes many general points of interest for narrative stylistics. In this respect it ties in directly with the issues covered both in this strand and in strand 7 on point of view.

Some suggestions follow.

- On the basis of Short's analysis, to what extent can you align the various narrative techniques he uncovers in Welsh with the six-part model of narrative proposed in A5? Are all the features he uncovers readily positioned in the model or are further categories or expansions to the model warranted?
- Graphological effects are more commonly associated with poetry than with prose fiction, although Laurence Sterne's *Tristram Shandy*, published in the 1760s, is the first novel in English to make extensive use of symbolic graphological representation. If you have read the novel, to what extent are the techniques of analysis developed by Short applicable to Sterne's narrative? What other works of prose fiction do you know of that employ graphological deviation and to what sort of stylistic effect?
- 'Orientational metaphors' are used to express emotional states through physical direction, as in GOOD IS UP, BAD IS DOWN and so on (see further thread 11). To what extent can the graphologically symbolic patterns in Welsh be considered orientational metaphors? In terms of the narrator's orientation, which narrative level – the higher, middle or lower – is the positive preference? For example, does 'up' necessarily equate with 'good' in the discourse world of *Marabou Stork Nightmares*?

TRANSITIVITY AT WORK: A FEMINIST-STYLISTIC APPLICATION

D6

This reading is a famous feminist-stylistic application of the model of transitivity where Deirdre Burton uses the framework to explore relationships of power in a passage from Sylvia Plath's semi-autobiographical novel *The Bell Jar*. Burton argues provocatively for a political dimension in textual interpretation and suggests that links between literary analysis and political standpoint can be articulated clearly through systematic and principled methods of analysis – precisely the sorts of methods that are offered by stylistics. Before you read Burton's article, you should refamiliarise yourself with the basic model of transitivity as outlined in A6.

One further note of contextualisation is necessary on the reading that follows. When Burton wrote her paper, the transitivity framework was to some extent in its infancy and in the intervening years the model has undergone various revisions and refinements, a natural progression which has been reflected in subsequent work in stylistics. One important revision was the addition of 'behavioural processes', a category which, as noted in A6, sits at interface between material and mental processes. Although this type of process does not feature in the version of the model used by Burton, its absence is compensated for to some degree by an expanded interpretation of material processes. This expanded category draws a primary distinction between *event* processes, where the Actor is inanimate (as in 'The lake shimmered'), and *action* processes, which are performed by an animate Actor. Action processes may themselves be further subdivided into *intention* processes, where the Actor performs the process of doing voluntarily and *supervention* processes, where the process of doing just happens. Thus, while a process like 'Mary kissed Clare' is clearly material-action-intention, a process like the 'The boy coughed loudly' is (arguably) accidental and would therefore be coded as material-action-supervention. Figure D6.1 is a network which explains the way material processes are subdivided in Burton's study. Of course, the problem with a classification that relies on judgments about 'intention' is that in the absence of full contextualisation we can never really know whether or not a particular action was done accidentally or deliberately. For this reason, these subdivisions for material processes dropped out of later versions of the transitivity model, just as the category of behavioural processes came progressively more to the fore.

Although I have not attempted to alter to the newer framework any of the original classifications in Burton's study, it is important to bear in mind that her study draws on just one version of a theoretical model that has proved popular in stylistics. Indeed, her study is a good exemplum of the 'three Rs' at work because it is *rigorous*, its methods are *retrievable* and its analysis can be *replicated* using different versions of the same analytic model.

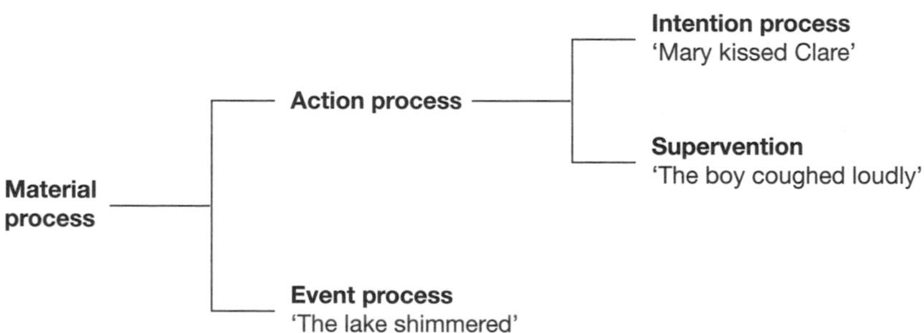

Figure D6.1 Subdivision of material processes in Burton's study

Through glass darkly: through dark glasses. On stylistics and political commitment – via a study of a passage from Sylvia Plath's *The Bell Jar*

Deirdre Burton (reprinted from Ronald Carter (ed) *Language and Literature: An Introductory Reader in Stylistics* London: George Allen and Unwin, 1982, p.195–214)

Deirdre Burton

[. . .] The piece of prose fiction I am going to consider in some detail is a short passage from Sylvia Plath's autobiographical novel *The Bell Jar*. It is a passage which details her experience of electric-shock treatment as a 'remedy' for severe depression. Readers may care to look ahead at this point, to where the text is given, in order to contextualise general points made here. Essentially, I will be analysing aspects of clause construction and, in a preliminary reading of the passage, readers may find it useful to pay specific attention to the simple question 'who does what to whom?'.

Here, then, I want to consider two issues as preliminaries to that analysis. First, I want to map out a model of some relevant features of clause construction in general, against which any text can be charted, and our Plath text will be charted. Secondly, I want to discuss why this type of analysis is particularly relevant to the issues raised in the introduction, and similarly why this specific text was chosen for analysis.

The model of processes and participants in the structure of clauses that I shall draw here is adapted from ideas in the work of Halliday (1970, 1973, 1978). Let me quickly try to explain why processes and participants are a strong place to begin analysis [. . .]. If the analyst is interested in 'making strange' the power relationships that obtain in the socially constructed world – be it the 'real' world of public and private social relationships or the spoken and written texts that we create, hear, read, and that ultimately construct us in that 'real' world – then, crucially, it is the realisation of *processes* and *participants* (both the actors and the acted upon) in those processes that should concern us. Ultimately, I want to suggest, with Sapir (1956), Whorf (1956) and Volosinov (1973 [1930]), that the 'world' is linguistically constructed. But rather than a crude Whorfian view, which might lead us to believe that we are trapped and constrained by that linguistic construction, I want to suggest a far more optimistic line of thought. Simply, once it is clear to people that there are alternative ways of expressing 'reality', then people can make decisions about how to express 'reality'; both for others and themselves. By this means, we can both deconstruct and reconstruct our realities to an enabling degree.

And this brings me to an explanation of why the Plath text seemed peculiarly appropriate to a feminist-linguistic polemic.

Where the topic of 'women and literature' is concerned, there are three immediate areas of thought and study that are being researched:

(1) Images of women in literature written by males – particularly in relation to details of social history. This is, of course, work that draws upon, and contributes to, a 'new' feminist version of that history. (See Rowbotham, 1973a, 1973b.)
(2) Images of women in literature written by feminist women. This may well involve finding them in the first place. (See Showalter 1977; Rich 1977)

(3) Images of women in literature by women who were not/are not feminists – either by 'free' choice, or because they were unaware that that choice was available to them.

Sylvia Plath's work and life can clearly be seen in relation to the third point here. Reading her prose, poems and letters, and reading about her, in the context of the raised consciousness and women's support groups of the 1970s and 1980s, is a moving, and disturbing, experience. It is so easy for us to locate her contradictions, dilemmas and pressures as they are expressed by her texts. It is so easy to see her writing herself *into* a concept of helpless victim, and eventually, perhaps, into suicide itself. Her texts abound in disenabling metaphors, disenabling lexis, and – I wish to demonstrate here – disenabling syntactic structures.

[. . .] I want to assert the importance of perceiving those sorts of forces, pervasive in the language around us, and would maintain that both individuals and social institutions require analytical access to knowledge about the intricacies of the relationship between linguistic structures and reality, such that, with that knowledge, reality might be reconstructed in less damaging ways – and again, I would emphasise, with regard to both individuals and social institutions.

I do not, by any means, wish to suggest that only women 'are' victims, or construct themselves as such. If this were a text written by a man (and there are, of course, similar texts), then it would be open to similar sympathetic analysis and discussion. However, that seems to me to be a job for somebody else to do, given that life is short and we must follow our immediate priorities. My general message is: stylistic analysis is *not* just a question of discussing 'effects' in language and text, but a powerful method for understanding the ways in which all sorts of 'realities' are constructed through language. For feminists who believe that 'the personal is political' there is a burning issue which has to be investigated immediately, and in various triangulated ways. We want to understand the relationships between severe and crippling depression that many women experience and the contradictory and disenabling images of self available for women in models of literature, the media, education, folk notions of the family, motherhood, daughterhood, work, and so on. [. . .] Any reader with any other radical political commitment should see what follows as a model to appropriate and to be made relevant to his or her own convictions. [. . .]

On reading the passage, readers repeatedly formulate the following sorts of responses:

(1) the persona seems quite helpless;
(2) the persona seems 'at a distance', 'outside herself', 'watching herself', 'detached to being with – and then just a victim';
(3) the medical staff seem more interested in getting the job done than caring.

In order to understand something of what is happening in the language of this passage, that gives rise to such responses, the following instructions enable us to get a firmer grasp of the persona's 'reality' as constructed in the clause-by-clause make-up of the text as a whole:

(1) isolate the processes *per se*, and find which participant (who or what) is 'doing' each process;
(2) find what sorts of process they are, and which participant is engaged in which type of process;
(3) find who or what is affected by each of these processes.

First, then, here is the text with sentences numbered for ease of reference, and processes isolated and underlined.

THE TEXT

(1) The wall-eyed nurse *came* back. (2) She *unclasped* my watch and *dropped* it in her pocket. (3) Then she *started tweaking* the hairpins from my hair.

(4) Doctor Gordon *was unlocking* the closet. (5) He *dragged out* a table on wheels with a machine on it and *rolled* it behind the head of the bed. (6) The nurse *started swabbing* my temples with a smelly grease.

(7) As she *leaned over to reach* the side of my head nearest the wall, her fat breast *muffled* my face like a cloud or a pillow. (8) A vague, medicinal stench *emanated* from her flesh.

(9) 'Don't worry,' the nurse *grinned* down at me. (10) 'Their first time everybody's scared to death.'

(11) I *tried to smile*, but my skin *had gone stiff*, like parchment.

(12) Doctor Gordon *was fitting* two metal plates on either side of my head (13) He *buckled* them into place with a strap that dented my forehead, and *gave me a wire to bite.*

(14) I *shut* my eyes.

(15) There *was* a brief silence, like an indrawn breath.

(16) Then something *bent down* and *took hold* of me and *shook* me like the end of the world. (17) Whee-ee-ee-ee-ee, it *shrilled*, through an air crackling with blue light, and with each flash a great jolt *drubbed* me till I *thought* my bones *would break* and the sap *fly out* of me like a split plant.

(18) I *wondered* what terrible thing it *was* that I *had done.*

(Plath 1986 [1963]: 151–2)

Given this simple skeleton analysis, we can abstract out the Actors in each process, and spell out the lexical realisation of each of the processes associated with them:

Sentence No.	Actor	Process
1	nurse	came back
2a	nurse	unclasped
b	nurse	dropped
3	nurse	started tweaking
4	doctor	was unlocking
5a	doctor	dragged out
b	doctor	rolled
6	nurse	started swabbing

7a	nurse	leaned over to reach
b	nurse's body part	muffled
8	nurse's body contingency	emanated
9a	n.a.	n.a.
b	nurse	grinned
10	n.a.	n.a.
11a	persona	tried to smile
b	persona's body part	had gone stiff
12	doctor	was fitting
13a	doctor	buckled
b	doctor's equipment	dented
c	doctor	gave . . . to bite
14	persona	shut
15	–	was
16a	something (electricity)	bent down and took hold
b	something (electricity)	shook
17a	something (electricity)	shrilled
b	electricity part	drubbed
c	persona	thought
d	persona body part	would break
e	persona body part	fly out
18a	persona	wondered
b	–	was
c	persona	had done

The analysis is simple, but the resultant table above gives access to a clear, general picture of who is doing what and when in the persona's description of the 'world' around her. The first half of the text gives the Nurse and Doctor performing all actions (16–10). We have a brief mention of the persona as Actor (11), and then the Doctor and his equipment dominate the action (12, 13). We have another brief mention of a negative persona as Actor (14), the electricity as Actor in a very positive sense (16–17) and finally the persona as Actor – in a hypothetical sense at least. We shall be able to say more about the types of process below. A simple counting of Actors and their actions shows us very little:

nurse (including body parts) as Actor: 8
doctor (including his equipment) as Actor: 7
electricity as Actor: 4
persona (including body parts) as Actor: 7

This is interesting in view of the often expressed pre-analytic response, 'the persona doesn't *do* anything'. Clearly, we can see what readers 'mean' when they say that, but we have to pursue the analysis further, and rephrase the response to capture the 'reality' of the text. What this analysis does lay bare is the *succession* of Actors in the scene. The Nurse, for example, drops out after sentence 9, although she has

certainly played the major part in the action till then (eight clauses out of eleven), and has been the focus of the persona's (and therefore our) attention. The Doctor, his equipment and the persona interact together, then he drops out and is superseded by a succession of clauses where the 'something' takes over very forcefully. Finally the persona is left acting alone.

Charting through the *types* of processes involved allows us much more room for discussion:

1	nurse came back = material-action-intention
2a	nurse unclasped = material-action-intention
b	nurse dropped = material-action-intention
3	nurse started tweaking = material-action-intention
4	doctor was unlocking = material-action-intention
5a	doctor dragged out = material-action-intention
b	doctor rolled = material-action-intention
6	nurse started swabbing = material-action-intention
7a	nurse leaned over to reach = material-action-intention
b	nurse's body part muffled = material-action-supervention
8	nurse's body contingency emanated = material-event
9a	n.a.
b	nurse grinned = material-action-intention
10	n.a.
11a	persona tried to smile = material-action-intention
b	persona's body part had gone stiff = material-event
12	doctor was fitting = material-action-intention
13a	doctor buckled = material-action-intention
b	doctor's equipment dented = material-action-supervention
c	doctor gave . . . to bite = material-action-intention
14	persona shut = material-action-intention
15	- was = relational
16a	something took hold = material-action-intention
b	something shook = material-action-intention
17a	something shrilled = material-action-intention
b	something drubbed = material-action-intention
c	persona thought = mental-cognition
d	persona's body part would break = material-action-supervention
e	persona's body part fly out = material-action-supervention
18a	persona wondered = mental-cognition
b	- was = relational
c	persona had done = material-action-intention

Here, the overwhelming fact revealed by the analysis is the definite preponderance of the selection of the option material-action-intention; twenty clauses out of thirty make this choice. A closer consideration brings out the following interesting features of the text. First, all the Nurse's actions are material-action-intention processes;

though where the Nurse's body is the Actor we have supervention or event processes, so that the effect is of her deliberately carrying out determinate actions, in the persona's environment, while her body produces contingent, 'accidental', yet none the less substantial effects on her thought-world also. Similarly all of the Doctor's actions are material-action-intention processes, but, like the Nurse's body, his equipment produces effects on the environment tangentially, as it were. The electricity is also only represented in terms of material-action-intention processes. Thus, all three of these major Actor-participants are seen as overwhelmingly 'in control' of whatever events take place. They are presented and given as being in charge of the construction of the reality that the persona perceives and expresses.

But what of the patient herself? Her attempt at what is (technically) a material-action-intention process (11a) fails. Her related body-part action is similarly only an 'accidental' event, that is, beyond her control (11b). At sentence 14, she succeeds in a material-action-intention process but, whereas all the other actors are doing constructive, concrete tasks by that option, her contribution is to shut her eyes – to remove herself from the scene. At 17c and 18, she has the only mental-internalised-cognition processes in the passage – a fact which makes it absolutely clear that the piece is very much – and only – from her point of view. At 17d and e we are given two possible (but hypothetical) supervention processes for her body parts – so, again, material actions that are not part of the actual reality, but only subordinated possible outcomes of others' actions. And, finally (18c), her 'successful' material-action-intention process is located away in the past, in mysterious circumstances.

This further analysis, then, gives us a little more scope in the way of accounting for our understanding of the persona's conception of her world. The next analysis, which isolates who or what is affected by each process takes us a little further:

1 nurse affects ø by intention process
2a nurse affects persona's possession by intention process
b nurse affects persona's possession by intention process
3 nurse affects persona's possession by intention process
4 doctor affects equipment by intention process
5a doctor affects equipment by intention process
b doctor affects equipment by intention process
6 nurse affects persona's body part by intention process
7a nurse affects persona's body part by intention process
b nurse's body part affects persona's body part by intention process
8 nurse's body contingency affects ø by event process
9a n.a.
b nurse affects persona by intention process
10 n.a.
11a persona affects ø by intention process
b persona's body part affects ø by event process
12 doctor affects equipment by intention process
13a doctor affects equipment by intention process
b doctor affects persona and equipment by intention process

14 persona affects persona's body part by intention process
15 ø affects the environment by relational process
16a something affects persona by intention process
b something affects persona by intention process
17a something affects ø by intention process
b something affects persona by intention process
c persona affects persona's body part by cognition process
d persona's body part affects ø by supervention process
e persona's body part affects ø by supervention process
18a persona affects ø by cognition process
b ø affects ø by relation process
c persona affects ø by intention process (hypothetical)

Reading this skeleton gives us a firmer grasp of the abstract reality of the persona's world. Massively, it is the Nurse who affects both the persona's possessions and body parts (2a, 2b, 3, 6, 7, 8) and, in one instance, the whole of her (9b). The Doctor, on the other hand, uses his intention processes to affect equipment (4, 5a, 5b, 12, 13a, 13c) and, in one localised area, via the persona's body part (13a) and the equipment (13b), the persona herself (13c). At this point he disappears from her world view. The electricity, not surprisingly, continually affects the whole persona (16a, b, 17a, b).

And the patient herself? At 11a she affects nothing – despite her intentions. At 11b her body part affects nothing. At 14 she successfully affects her own body – but remember that this is her escapism clause. At 17c she again 'successfully' carries out a cognition process on her own body – but remember that the resultant effect is only hypothetical. At 17d and e, 18a and c, the remaining clauses which have the persona as Actor, the persona and her body parts still affect nothing at all.

This third analysis, then, gives us a much neater and more delicate way of addressing ourselves to readers' responses. Obviously we could discuss much more in this text, and I do not mean to suggest that this is a 'full analysis'. Nevertheless, by pursuing these important sets of related features in this way, we have begun to refine our understanding of the 'reality' presented by this text. [. . .]

To sum up let me offer the following programme of eight points, which I see the teacher of stylistics as pursuing. It assumes students with an interest in literature in general, but little or no linguistic knowledge. Points 1–4 are, I take it, uncontentious; points 5–8 are offered as a programme for radical stylistics.

(1) Stylistics can be part of a programme to enable students to handle competently a coherent and comprehensive descriptive grammar, which can then be used in either literature-oriented studies, or linguistics-oriented studies.
(2) It is always at least a 'way in' to a text.
(3) It can shift discussion to awareness of effects that are intuitively felt to be in a text in the process of reading it, and a contingent 'making strange' of those effects and feelings simultaneously. It is towards 'knowing how' as well as 'knowing that' (Ryle 1949).

(4) It can spell out a shared vocabulary for describing the language of any text – whether those effects are straightforward or ambiguous.
(5) Crucially, stylistics can point the way to understanding the ways in which the language of a given text constructs its own (fictional) reality.
(6) It should then point the way towards understanding the ways in which language constructs the 'reality' of everyday life – and an awareness that always *must* do so. So that, in a sense, everyday 'reality' can usefully be seen as a series of 'fictional' constructs – as texts open to analysis and interpretation in just the same way as texts marked out for literary study are.
(7) This would lead to an awareness of the importance of perceiving the constituent parts of the fictions we live *in* and *by*, if only to map them against alternative constructions of reality.
(8) Finally, this would lead to an understanding that the fictions (both large and small) that we live in and by can be rewritten. Both individually and collectively. As reform or revolution, whichever is more appropriate.

As for my title? See it as notes for a poem, on Sylvia Plath, Women, Feminism, Radical Stylistics, academic work in general. Optimistic notes.

ISSUES TO CONSIDER

As with a number of the scholars whose work constitutes Section D, Burton raises many areas for further stylistic investigation in the course of her article. However, you might wish to consider additionally the following issues:

- ❑ Burton uses a version of the transitivity model that has been partly reworked in subsequent linguistic research. A useful exercise is to comb through the Plath text using the version of the analytic model presented in A6 and B6, concentrating in particular on Plath's use of *behavioural processes* (as they relate to the persona's actions) and on her use of *meronymic agency* (as it relates to her depiction of the nurse).
- ❑ Rewrite the paragraph from *The Bell Jar* from the point of view of either the Nurse or the Doctor, staying as close as possible to the words of the original text. What overall changes to the transitivity profile are brought about by your rewrites? What sorts of processes now dominate? Look again at these rewrites once you have completed unit 7, on point of view. To what extent do your rewrites involve a realignment in the visual perspective of each of the characters in the scene?
- ❑ Since Burton's study, certain critical theorists have suggested that feminism has given way to a so-called 'post-feminist' era. Using the transitivity model, you could evaluate this claim by looking at other texts by and/or about women. Are there any novels or short stories that you have read which portray women through what Burton calls 'disenabling' patterns of language, whether metaphorical, lexical or grammatical in design? Is Burton's feminist-stylistic polemic as viable today as it was on its publication in 1982?

POINT OF VIEW

D7

Activity ✪

Because of its length and the breadth of its coverage, Mick Short's reading in D5 'doubles up' as a useful follow-up reading for this section. As well as addressing the 'Issues to consider' section posted there, it is also worth following up the second of the three exercises suggested for Deirdre Burton's reading in the previous unit. For example, do your rewrites of *The Bell Jar* passage make use of any of the modal frameworks suggested in C7? And to what extent is it possible to make a connection between patterns of transitivity and patterns of modality in narrative fiction?

Activity ✪

With reference to this thread on point of view, three types of point of view modalities were proposed. In terms of your own reading experience, do you think three categories are enough? Can you think of a genre of writing which is marked by a modal profile that is different from the three types proposed here?

Activity ✪

Finally, what about the modality of 'second person' narratives, as embodied in Italo Calvino's postmodern novel *If on a Winter's Night a Traveller* (1981) or Ray Bradbury's science fiction short story 'The Night' (1948)? What is there about fiction written in the second person that is different from both first and third person narratives? And how can we go about accommodating such fiction in a model of narrative style?

SPEECH AND THOUGHT PRESENTATION

D8

Key to activities in unit A8

Here are the suggested solutions to the practice examples posted in unit A8:

a 'I know this trick of yours!' (FDS)
I know this trick of yours! (FDS – freest form)
She said that she knew that trick of his. (IS)
She knew that trick of his! (FIS)
She spoke of his trickery. (NRS)

b 'Can you get here next week?' (FDS)
Can you get here next week? (FDS – freest form)
He asked if she could get there the following week. (IS)
Could she get there the following week? (FIS)
He enquired about her plans for the next week (NRS)

c 'Why isn't John here?' (FDT)
Why isn't John here? (FDT – freest form).
She asked herself why John wasn't there. (IT)
Why wasn't John there? (FIT)
She pondered John's absence. (NRT)

Note: the reporting clause here is 'she asked *herself*' (and not 'she asked') suggesting not externalised speech as such but an internalised process more characteristic of thought presentation.

d 'We must leave tonight.' (FDS)
We must leave tonight. (FDS – freest form)
She said that they had to leave that night. (IS)
They had to leave that night. (FIS)
She stressed the urgency of their time of departure. (NRS)

Note: the NRS form feels cumbersome – which tends to underscore the point made in A8 about those situations when it is sometimes easier to use an explicit mode of speech presentation.

e 'Help yourselves.' (FDS)
Help yourselves. (FDS)
He urged them to help themselves. (IS)
He encouraged them to tuck in. (NRS)

Note: This is one of those situations when no FIS form is possible. The grammatical block is activated here by the verb 'help' which is in its *imperative* form. Imperatives have no Subject elements (see A3) and cannot be backshifted to the past tense. Although the IS form gets around the problem by making the verb infinitive ('to help'), the FIS form needs to use a backshifted past. The result, 'Helped themselves', just doesn't make sense.

D9 LITERATURE AS DISCOURSE: THE LITERARY SPEECH SITUATION

This reading is taken from Mary Louise Pratt's grounding-breaking book, *Toward a Speech Act Theory of Literary Discourse*, which was published in the 1970s. Pratt's emphasis throughout her monograph is generally on the nature of literature as discourse and more specifically on the speech act status of various types of literary 'utterance'. Her perspective is one which views literary communication as dynamic action, and following the tenets of speech act theory, as action which is brought about by utterances in real contexts of use. Pratt develops and illustrates this strongly interactive conceptualisation of literary discourse using a range of models in pragmatics and conversation analysis and, of course, in speech act theory and natural language philosophy of the sort embodied in the work of Austin (1962), Searle (1969) and Grice (1975). As the reading reveals, she also makes use of Labov's model of narrative narrative which featured across strand 5 of this book. The particular excerpt reproduced here outlines the 'literary speech situation', exploring principally the communicative dynamic between the literary 'speaker' and, what Pratt terms, the literary *Audience.*

The literary speech situation

Mary Louise Pratt (reprinted from chapter four of Pratt, M. L. (1977) *Toward a Speech Act Theory of Literary Discourse* Bloomington: Indiana University Press, pp. 100–19.

Mary Louise Pratt

[. . .] The fact that storytellings, unlike other conversational contributions, require the consent of the nonspeaking participants and that the request for this consent is explicitly built into the formal structure of natural narratives suggests, I believe, a rather important generalisation about what it means to be an audience. Natural narratives formally acknowledge that in voluntarily committing ourselves to play the role of audience, we are accepting an exceptional or unusual imposition. This claim, I believe, holds for voluntary audience roles in general and is crucial to our understanding of the appropriateness conditions bearing on many kinds of speech situations, including literary ones. I am claiming that in speech situations in which no one person is clearly in authority, the unmarked case [. . .] is that all participants have equal access to the floor and that among peers, an unequal distribution of such access is marked and brings with it a redistribution of obligations and expectations among the participants. This is a broad generalisation, and it merits a good deal more analysis than I am able to give it here. It is clear, though, that equal-access-to-the-floor rules play an important role in many situations other than conversation. Such rules are considered crucial in decision-making gatherings of almost any kind, so that in many societies, including our own, the turntaking rules for such gatherings are explicitly set down (in the 'rules of order') and a presiding officer is appointed solely to enforce them. There are clear, pragmatic motives behind such procedures. Battles for the floor can easily paralyse conversation when disagreements arise. Hence, it is not surprising that speech situations that are specifically tailored to presenting and settling disagreements should possess some other less time-consuming mechanism – the chairman and his rule book – for guaranteeing the equitable allocation of turns. Understandably, speech situations that presuppose disagreement, notably debates of any kind, make particular use of strict equal access rules and time allotments. Notice that in such institutionalised speech situations, wherever there are rules prohibiting interruptions of a current speaker, there are also rules guaranteeing potential next-speakers a chance for a turn. In societies with egalitarian values the right to a turn, that is, freedom of speech, in part defines one's equality to one's fellow citizens.

What happens, then, when we give up our access rights to a fellow speaker, when we agree of our own free will to become an Audience? (I am using the capitalised 'Audience' in this discussion to mean voluntary audience, as opposed to audiences who, by virtue of inferior status in the situation, have no floor rights to give up, e.g., employees addressed by their boss). For one thing, our expectations of the speaker increase, and his obligations to us likewise increase. He had better make sure, in other words, that his contribution is 'worth it' to us. Boring lectures and bad jokes annoy us more than boring turns in conversation, because we expect more of lectures and jokes, and we expect more because we cannot without rudeness stop the speaker, correct him, have our own say, change the subject, or walk out before he has finished. At most we can indicate our displeasure by some nonverbal means like facial expression or body posture. Audiences in this sense are indeed captive, and speakers addressing Audiences are obliged to make the captivity worthwhile. [. . .]

It is important to note that a speaker's having an authority over his subject matter which his Audience lacks does not erase his indebtedness when the Audience is a voluntary one. The storyteller knows something his Audience does not, yet he is indebted to them for consenting to listen. A lecturer or after-dinner speaker may be invited to talk because he is an 'expert'; nevertheless, in our society at least, he is obliged by convention to treat his Audience as equals and thus to assume a debt to them precisely because they have chosen to attend. Such a speaker will very likely address his Audience as 'my fellow X's'. The voluntary aspect of the Audience role, in other words, serves to establish a peer relation between speaker and Audience whether or not one existed before, because the context assumes such a relation. Students attending compulsory lectures need not and should not be thanked by the professor for their attention; students voluntarily attending the same professor's public lectures do merit his thanks like anyone else in the Audience. This presupposed peer relation which obtains in fact or by convention between speakers and voluntary Audiences explains why we frequently accuse boring or unsatisfactory speakers of conceit or contempt for their Audiences. They are felt to have treated us as inferiors and thus to have claimed illegitimate authority over us. Failure to maintain this peer relation by talking 'up' or 'down' to one's Audience is the public speaker's worst sin. By the same token, attending a speech by a famous personage confers status on the Audience since for the time they are peers of the personage. 'Getting' an obscure allusion in a literary work has the same effect.

I have said that in compensation for the asymmetrical distribution of turn-taking rights that prevails in speaker/Audience situations, the Audience is entitled to expect more of the speaker than they would if they were playing a participant Role. 'More' is a very unsatisfying way of characterising nonparticipant as opposed to participant expectations; however, there does seem to be one area of speaker/Audience relations in which this increase in expectations is explicitly acknowledged. As a rule, in giving up floor rights, Audiences gain the right to pass judgment on the speaker's contribution. Conventionally, a space is allotted at the end of a performance in which the Audience is offered the floor for the purpose of addressing its judgment to the performer(s), and the performance is not over until this has occurred. A repertory of noises and gestures is available for indicating Audience judgments, including handclapping, knee-slapping, egg-throwing, foot-stomping, cheers, whistles, laughter, boos, hisses, and standing up. At public events, applause intensity is considered a very meaningful indication of Audience judgment. [. . .] In the case of artistic performances and books, printed reviews are an important and obvious exercise of the Audience's right to judge. In addition, I have already mentioned the kind of approving commentary which follows a successful natural narrative and the dreaded 'so what?' response to an unsuccessful one. Some such commentary invariably follows a natural narrative in conversation. Notice, however, that when no evaluative commentary occurs, a judgment is nevertheless understood to have been expressed, and a very damning one at that. The fact that silence itself counts as a judgment in speaker/Audience situations provides important support for the claim that the act of judging is presupposed to be an integral part of the speaker/Audience exchange. These evaluative rituals can be seen as a way of giving the erstwhile nonparticipants a 'turn'; the fact that this turn is specifically set aside for judging indicates the degree to which the speaker addressing an Audience puts himself in jeopardy. A performer who satisfies is said in English to have 'acquitted himself.' Notice too that this judging goes on whether or not the performer is present to hear it, as anyone knows who has listened in on the buzz of evaluative commentary with which departing Audiences fill the corridors of theatres and lecture halls. We seldom applaud films anymore, there being no live addressees to receive the applause, but we do invariably talk about them on the way home.

It may be that the act of expressing judgment, preferably in the performer's presence, is the Audience's way of reclaiming the peer status which it has voluntarily placed in jeopardy, or of counterbalancing the asymmetry of the speaker/Audience relation. By more or less formally building the judicial act into the performance itself, we create a different, delayed kind of symmetry to replace turntaking. This identification of nonparticipation with judging extends beyond formal, institutionalised manifestations such as applause. [. . .] Voluntary nonparticipation in conversation is labelled non- or anti-social. Perhaps because of the particularly silent and solitary nonparticipation the literary speech situation imposes, judging is felt to be a central part of the reader's role in literature. Indeed, it is only rather recently that we have begun to perceive literary studies as concerned with anything other than evaluation.

[. . .]

To sum up the argument as it applies to verbal behavior, I am proposing that we recognise the speaker/Audience relation as one of the possible role structures that may obtain between the participants in a speech situation. This role structure is marked with respect to the unmarked situation among peers, in which all participants have equal access to the floor. Participants who become an Audience temporarily waive their access rights. The speaker who wishes to address an Audience must request and receive permission to do so; his request counts as an imposition on his interlocutors and thereby places him under obligation to them. For the Audience, ratifying the speaker's request for unique floor access counts as a favour done and entitles the Audience, first, to expect the speaker will repay them via the special quality of what he says during his special floor time and, second, to pass judgment on his success when his turn is over. The speaker's indebtedness and the Audience's right to judge persist even when the speaker has actually been invited to take the floor and when the other participants are present for the sole purpose of being an Audience. I have argued that this role structure can account for certain formal features of natural narratives and of the conventions surrounding public performances and that it accurately represents the attitudes of the participants in those situations. Just as the appropriateness conditions for conversation have to include a specification of the turn-taking system, so the appropriateness conditions for natural narratives, public speeches, and many other speech act types will have to specify the marked redistribution of rights, obligations, and expectations that suspension of turn-taking brings with it.

The analysis holds for literary speech situations, too, and must do so if it is to hold at all. Our role in the literary speech situation has the main formal characteristic I have been using to define an Audience: we knowingly and willingly enter a speech situation in which another speaker has unique access to the floor. The formal similarities I noted earlier between natural narrative and literary narrative are readily explained if we posit a similar disposition of speaker and Audience with respect to the message in both types. Titles, subtitles, chapter headings, and summaries, for example, perform the 'request for the floor' role of Labov's abstracts and similarly correspond in function to the public speaking conventions just discussed. Readers of literary works usually feel that the writer is under obligation to make their attention worthwhile, and that they have the right to judge what he has done. Hence, even though we are not imprisoned by a book the way we are by a lecture hall or an oral anecdote, we do not put down a bad book with indifference or neutrality but rather with annoyance, frustration, disappointment, and anger at the author. We throw it across the room. Nor are most writers unaware of their indebtedness to the Audience. The 'dear reader' remarks common to eighteenth- and nineteenth-century novels, like the 'my fellow X's' address of the orator, are readily interpreted as acknowledgments of the peer relation which holds between author and reader, of the sense of obligation the author feels as a result of that relation, and of his awareness of being in jeopardy. From the beginnings of literature to the present, iconoclastic works of literature have often come to us accompanied by prefaces, built-in self-defenses very much akin to the moderator's credentials list. If their role were purely discursive or commentative rather than defensive, prefaces would be as well or better placed at the end of the book. But they aren't. And even writers who profess not to 'give a damn what the public thinks' are usually careful if not eager to apprise us of this fact. Certainly, not caring what the Audience thinks is not the same as not wanting to be read and applauded. In short, the author's 'authority' in a literary work, like the authority of the speechmaking 'expert,' does not suffice to put him in the clear with the reader.

Even these rudimentary similarities between literature and other speaker/Audience situations are enough to tell us that speaker and Audience are present in the literary speech situation, that their existence is presupposed by literary works, that they have commitments to one another as they do everywhere else, and that those commitments are presupposed by both the creator and the receivers of the work. Far from being autonomous, self-contained, selfmotivating, context-free objects which exist independently from the 'pragmatic' concerns of 'everyday' discourse, literary works take place in a context, and like any other utterance they cannot be described apart from that context. Whether or not literary critics wish to acknowledge this fact – and they sometimes have not – a theory of literary discourse must do so. More importantly, like so many of the characteristics believed to constitute literariness, the basic speaker/Audience situation which prevails in a literary work is not fundamentally or uniquely literary. It is not the result of a use of the language different from all other uses. Far from suspending, transforming, or opposing the laws of nonliterary discourse, literature, in this aspect at least, obeys them. At least some of the expectations with which readers approach literary works cannot be attributed directly to the fact that the utterances are literary works or works of fiction but rather to more general appropriateness conditions governing speaker/Audience relations in the most familiar and commonplace speech contexts (to say nothing of activities not primarily verbal). To put it the other way round, the nonparticipant Audience role, which has been considered a key

to literary response, is a familiar component of many other speech situations as well. The role is not part of the rhetoric of fiction but of the rhetoric of Audience-ship which is itself defined in relation to the rhetoric of conversation.

ISSUES TO CONSIDER

Activity

In the context of Pratt's reading, it is worth revisiting Short's schema which was introduced in unit A9 of this thread. Although designed to explain the embedding of interactive levels in drama, the schema has much relevance to what Pratt says about literary communication generally. To this extent, can you locate on the schema the interactive position of her concept of Audience? Can you also design similar interactive schemata, indicating embedded interaction where appropriate, to account for the particularised literary speech situations of any novels or poems you have read. (Alternatively, you can use the passages provided in section C for this activity, especially those in C1, C2, C4 and C8). As a more specific follow-up activity, Julian Barnes' short novel *Love etc* (2000) makes for an intriguing study of the literary speech situation. Without giving too much away, Barnes' novel is relayed entirely through the unmediated utterances of its three main characters who appear to speak directly to the reader. This unusual interactive situation can be explored using the models of dialogue and discourse introduced across this thread.

More suggestions follow:

- Pratt suggests that because the literary speech situation imposes 'silent and solitary nonparticipation', judging is felt to be a central part of the reader's role in literature. How accurate a reflection is this of your own reading experience?
- In what contemporary discourse contexts do we agree to become an Audience in the sense outlined by Pratt? Following from this, to what extent has modern interactive media affected the concept of the Audience? Does being an Audience still require the concession of the floor to the speaker? Or has the communicative dynamic of interactive film and television made the relationship between speaker and Audience more problematic or tenuous?

COGNITIVE STYLISTICS: THE POETRY OF EMILY DICKINSON

D10

In this reading, Margaret Freeman offers a cognitive stylistic analysis of certain grammatical patterns in the poetry of Emily Dickinson. In that it commonly breaches everyday grammatical rules, Dickinson's use of language can be challenging and it often makes heavy interpretative demands on the reader. Of many structures that might productively inform a cognitive stylistic analysis of her work, it is Dickinson's special use of the '*-self* anaphor' which is the focus of Freeman's study. An *anaphor* is an item of language which refers back to some antecedent in a text. More specifically, the term -self *anaphor* describes grammatical items like reflexive pronouns ('herself', 'oneself') which have no fixed meaning of their own and which therefore require a local textual referent for their interpretation. For example, in the sequence 'Mary hurt herself', the meaning of the reflexive *-self* anaphor 'herself' can only be retrieved by locating it anaphorically in the earlier reference to 'Mary'. Freeman also draws on the concept of *deixis* (see A2) in her analysis and argues, with respect to Emily Dickinson, that this poet's *-self* anaphors are grounded in mental spaces, and, furthermore, that their use signals a projection from one mental space into another.

Grounded spaces in the poetry of Emily Dickinson

Margaret Freeman

Margaret Freeman (a redaction by the original author of a 1997 article entitled 'Grounded spaces: deictic *-self* anaphors in the poetry of Emily Dickinson' *Language and Literature*, 6, 1, 7–28).

When the first edition of a selection of Emily Dickinson's poems appeared in 1890, literary reviewers, especially in England, criticised her poems for being unmetrical and ungrammatical (Buckingham 1989). Critics today are much more tolerant of such poetic 'violations'. Tolerance or intolerance, however, do nothing to illuminate poetic practice. Critics assume that such practices are *ad hoc* and random or arise from 'poetic licence', the belief that the principles underlying the language of poetry are different *in kind* from conventional usage. I accept neither of these positions. Instead, I believe that grammatical usage results from both a social construct and a personal idiolect. Furthermore, I adopt the approach of recent cognitive linguistic theory that the grammar of a language cannot be determined simply on the linguistic level alone, but must take into account the cognizing processes of the embodied mind (Lakoff and Johnson 1998). Poetic language *is* different from conventional language, but they both share the same principles of conceptual integration (Fauconnier and Turner 2002). When the grammar of a poet diverges from conventional usage, the reason for the divergence lies in the way the poet experiences and conceives the world. What is needed is a theory that will account for the conceptual models underlying the choices a poet makes. Consider, for example, the seemingly anomalous use of the *-self* anaphor form 'Himself himself' (in **boldface**) in line 6 of the following Dickinson poem:

[1] A Spider sewed at Night
Without a Light
Upon an Arc of White

If Ruff it was of Dame
Or Shroud of Gnome
Himself himself inform.

Of Immortality
His Strategy
Was Physiognomy.
(F1163/J1138; ms., lines 1–6)[1]

Under any standard grammar of English, this use of the *-self* anaphor is considered ungrammatical. In spite of much recent linguistic work on anaphor, the grammatical rules that purport to govern the use of the pronoun forms in English that carry the *-self* suffix do not entirely explain why *-self* anaphors appear when and where they do in actual or 'natural' language use. As recent work in cognitive linguistics has shown, the failure of both traditional and transformational (what Taylor (1989) calls 'autonomous') grammar to fully account for this usage arises from commitment to a traditional, objectivist view that grammar generates meaning and that meaning can be characterised by the tools of formal logic. More insidiously, this commitment in itself banishes the mind's imaginative, analogical processes to the realm of fantasy and 'untruth', the so-called realm of the poets. According to both traditional grammar and the government binding conditions of transformational theory, Dickinson's use of *-self* anaphors seems haphazard and inconsistent. (See, for example, Reinhart and Reuland's (1993: 713) discussion, where they explicitly exclude forms like 'Himself criticised himself'.) However, analysed in the light of 'mental space' or, as it is now known, conceptual integration theory (Fauconnier 1994; Fauconnier and Turner 2002), Dickinson's *-self* anaphors are perfectly regular. Although Dickinson's grammar is not *prototypical*, it is nevertheless *grammatical*, and the principles of that grammar can be discovered and described. In autonomous grammar, deixis is also poorly understood; in English, *-self* anaphor forms, despite received theory to the contrary, can indeed be deictic in their usage. If Dickinson's poetry is considered ungrammatical in its use of *-self* anaphors, it is so because of the limitations of the grammar, not the limitations of her language. Under this view, poetic licence is not freedom *from* the constraints of grammar but freedom *to* construct grammars that conceptualise the poet's world view. Understanding a poet's grammar can help us understand the poet's world view and, through it, our own. [. . .]

We exist in a world constrained by time and space. As Merleau-Ponty (1962) notes, we live always in the existential present, at a particular physical location. Thus at any instant of time we are 'grounded' in what we can call our 'reality space', and the point of view or perspective we take on our experiences of the world around us is conditioned by the particular facets of the domain structuring that space, a domain that includes our social-cultural knowledge and experiences, our memories, and so

1 References to Dickinson's poetry include the poem numbers from the Franklin (F) and Johnson (J) editions, followed by the 'Fascicle' or 'Set' number in which the poem appears, or 'ms.' if not in either (See Franklin 1981, 1998, and Johnson 1963). Line breaks follow the manuscripts, not the printed editions. Variants in the manuscript are placed in square brackets or at the end (depending on how they appear in the manuscripts), and I have retained Dickinson's spelling throughout.

on (our *Idealised Cultural Cognitive Model* or ICCM). As humans, however, we are able to transcend the limits of that reality space by conceiving of other 'mental spaces'. These mental spaces can change time (past or future) and space (other locations) as well as creating other kinds of dimensions such as hypothetical or counterfactual spaces. Fauconnier (1994) has shown how we dynamically construct these mental spaces in the way we think and reason, and Fauconnier and Turner (2002) have developed the theory further to show how we are able to create new thoughts from these spaces in additional 'blended' spaces.

Under this theory, grammatical forms are not simply a matter of syntax or logical relations but arise from the interaction and integration of the ways in which we conceive our experiences. An example can be seen in the famous sentence quoted in McCawley (1981), 'I dreamed that I was Brigitte Bardot and that I kissed me'. In any traditional view of grammar, the structure *Noun Phrase – Verb – Noun Phrase* would produce a reflexive pronoun in the second noun phrase, as in 'Harry cut himself'. However, in the dream sentence, the *-self* anaphor rule is blocked by the cross-space identity connectors that in the dream space link 'I' to Bardot and 'me' to the speaker. In Dickinson's poetry, as we shall see, the identification of counterparts in connected mental spaces forms a complex web of projected *-self* anaphors and deictic movement between spaces. [. . .]

Dickinson's *-self* anaphors are triggered in mental spaces as projections of *subjects/agents* of their originating spaces, according to the following rule:

> *When a subject/agent in one space projects an additional mental space, its pronoun counterpart in the projected space will take the corresponding* -self *anaphor form.*

In example (2), the second pronoun reference occurs within a hypothetical mental space that is projected from the speaker's reality space through the space-builder 'wonder' (pronouns marked in **boldface,** space-builders by <u>underline</u>):

[2] **We** <u>wonder</u> it was not
Ourselves
Arrested it – before –.
(F446/J448; Fascicle 21, lines 8–10)

Mental space theory accounts for the distribution of anaphors. In example (3), the *-self* anaphor included in the subject noun phrase 'Myself and It' is projected from the originating space, subject 'I', as we would expect. 'It', however, refers to 'the Day' which occurs within the space projected by 'But when' and therefore does not appear as a *-self* anaphor:

[3] **I** rose, and all was plain –
<u>But when</u> the Day declined
Myself and It, in Majesty
Were equally – adorned –
(F613/J356; Fascicle 29, lines 10–13)

The following poem is more complex:

[4] **We** can but follow to the
Sun –
As oft as **He** go down
He leave **Ourselves** a
Sphere behind –
(F845/J920; Set 4b, lines 1–5)

The subject/agent 'we' in the originating space triggers its counterpart 'Ourselves' in the mental space as predicted. Since the two references to 'He' both appear within the same mental space, the *-self* anaphor form does not occur. However, 'He' refers to the 'Sun', which *does* occur in the original, speaker's 'reality' space, but as it is not the subject/agent of the originating space, it does not trigger a *-self* anaphor.

The subject/agent constraint does not preclude double mental spaces with two subjects (*italics* indicate second coreferential subjects):

[5] <u>To think</u> just how the fire will
burn –
Just how *long-cheated eyes* will turn –
To wonder what **myself** will say,
And what *itself*, will say to me –
(F199/J207; Fascicle 10, lines 11–15)

Here the speaker is projecting a fantasy of arriving home late. 'I' is the underlying subject of the space-builder 'to think', triggering a mental space in which 'long-cheated eyes' is a subject. The second space-builder, 'to wonder', can be read as doubly triggered, from the initial 'I' of the speaker, but also from the 'long-cheated eyes', so that two subjects occur with *-self* anaphors in the resulting mental space.

When mental spaces are multiply embedded, the subject in one space will project its own *-self* anaphor into the mental space projected from it:

[6] <u>If</u> *God* could make a visit –
Or ever took a Nap –
So not to see us – <u>but they</u>
<u>say</u>
Himself – a Telescope

Perennial beholds us –
Myself would run away
From Him – and Holy Ghost – and All –
(F437/J413; Fascicle 15, lines 10–17)

Here, the conditional space is projected by the speaker, thus triggering the first person *-self* anaphor in its space (line 16). However, within the conditional space, in which

'God' is a subject, a contrastive space is created with the words 'but they / say', and the subject 'God' projects onto the third person *-self* anaphor in its own embedded mental space.

The appearance of 'itself' in example (7) indicates that *-self* anaphors are projected not from the syntactic but from the conceptual subject of the parent space:

[7] **All these** – <u>remind</u> us of the
place
That Men call 'Paradise' -
Itself be fairer -
(F544/J575; Fascicle 28, lines 18–25)

The space-builder 'remind' creates a hypothetical space in which 'all these' is equated with 'the place' called 'Paradise'. 'All these' refers to the signs that have been described in the previous stanzas that stand for heaven. The projection from space to space allows noun phrases like 'All these', 'the place', 'Paradise', and 'Itself' to be linked. The *-self* anaphor 'itself' thus can be licensed by one form (all these) and agree grammatically with another (the place, Paradise). [. . .]

There are exceptions to the grammatical rule as formulated. Other poems indicate that the form of an anaphoric reference will shift as the perspective shifts between the mental spaces that are projected, and pronominal references *cross over* into other spaces:

[8] **I** almost strove to clasp
his Hand,
Such Luxury – it grew -
That <u>as</u> **Myself** – could pity
Him -
[<u>Perhaps</u> he – pitied **me** – /He – <u>too</u> – could pity **me** -]
(F570/J532; Fascicle 25, lines 19–24)

The speaker fantasises a mental space in which there might be someone else besides herself 'Of Heavenly Love – forgot -'. She considers reaching out to 'clasp his Hand', and in that mental space of projected fantasy refers to herself as 'Myself'. The 'Perhaps' (or 'too') also serves as a space-builder, but this time, the first person *-self* anaphor does not occur. Whereas she, as 'Myself', can pity him in that mental space she has fantasised, he might pity her, not in that same fantasised space (which would trigger 'myself' in line 24), but in her own reality space, where the *-self* anaphor is not triggered. The crossing of mental spaces is what causes the effectiveness and power of the ending. If 'myself' is substituted in that final line, the result would be to stay in the same mental space of fantasy; there would be no crossing of spaces into the speaker's reality space, and the power of the ending would be lost.

On one occasion, Dickinson herself had second thoughts about what form to use. In the poem, 'I took my power in my hand', in which the speaker compares herself with David, two variants, 'me' and 'I' are suggested for the second *-self* anaphor:

[9] I aimed my Pebble – <u>but</u>
Myself
Was all the One that fell -
Was it Goliah – was too
large -
<u>Or</u> + was **myself** – too small?
+ just **myself** – Only **me** – **I** -
(F660/J540; F 30, lines 7–12)

The first use of 'Myself' in this stanza is predicted by the projection of the subject 'I' into the contrasted mental space set up by 'but'. The second 'myself' is interesting. It occurs in a mental space set up by 'Or'. If the originating space is the sentence immediately preceding, then 'Goliah' is the subject of that space, and 'myself' should not be triggered, as the variants indicate. However, if both spaces are multiply projected from the first sentence of the stanza, 'I aimed my Pebble -', then 'myself' would be triggered, as indicated in the original and first variant offered. It is, of course, impossible to know what Dickinson was thinking in her suggested variants, but this example raises interesting questions about structuring domains and speaker point of view and perspective. As multiple mental spaces are generated, the grounding perspective or point of view can shift from one space to another. [. . .]

Examples (8) and (9) seem to indicate that the *-self* anaphor deictically grounds the self in the mental space into which it is projected. The following discussion shows that this is in fact the case.

It would appear that whenever there is anaphoric reference in a mental space to the subject/topic of the originating space, the *-self* anaphor should occur. However, in example (10a), where a mental space is created through the space-builder 'wondered', the anaphor is 'me', not 'myself':

[10a] **I** <u>wondered</u> which would
miss **me**, least,
And when Thanksgiving, came,
If Father'd multiply the plates -
To make an even Sum -
And <u>would</u> it blur the
Christmas glee
My Stocking hang too high
For any Santa Claus to reach
The Altitude of **me** -
(F344/J445; Fascicle 16: stanzas 4–5)

The poem, which begins ''Twas just this time, last / year, I died', is a narrative, being told from the perspective of the grave. Through the space-builders, 'know', 'thought', 'wondered', the speaker in the grave projects the events of real life that are going on without her. Had Dickinson used the *-self* anaphor in these stanzas, she would have been deictically projecting the speaker into that mental space of life, thus 'grounding' the speaker in the objective scene (Langacker 1987, 1991). However, the very point of the stanzas is that the speaker is physically absent from the mentally projected scene of real life, as she imagines the people in that space missing her presence. In these stanzas, then, when she refers to herself, the speaker crosses over from the mental space of life to her reality space of death and therefore the anaphoric reference does not take the *-self* form.

The last stanza contrasts the mental spaces of the entire poem, between life and death:

[11b] But this sort, grieved **myself**,
And so, I thought the other
way,
How just this time, some
perfect year -
Themself, should come to **me** -
(stanza 6)

Now the *-self* anaphor occurs, as thinking about life creates a mental space in which the speaker projects her grief. The poem ends in yet another projected space, 'some perfect year', and in this 'other way' space, the *-self* form is attributed to they who are agents in that other space in life and who will come to the speaker's reality space in death: 'Themself, should come to me -'.

When crossovers occur with shifts in focus, perspective, and point of view, *-self* anaphors may thus not appear. In the poem that begins 'Those fair – fictitious People -', for example, three lines with parallel linguistic forms appear to be inconsistent in pronoun use:

Remembering ourselves (line 14)
Anticipating us (line 20)
Esteeming us (line 24).

The poem creates mental spaces for both the dead and the living, and the *-self* anaphor occurs only when the subject self in the mental space of the living is projected into the mental space of the dead. The speaker, looking at representations of the dead, and wondering where they are, trusts they are 'in places perfecter' (stanzas 1–3). The next stanza projects into the space of the dead from the speaker's reality space through the space-building phrase 'trust', triggering the *-self* anaphor in the projected mental space as the dead become the subject of that space. Starting with the next line, the *perspective* also shifts from the reality space of the speaker to that of the dead through the space building comparative terms 'yet' and 'where', contrasting the state of the dead in their space to that of the living in the originating (speaker's reality) space:

[11a] Remembering **ourselves**, we trust -
Yet Blesseder – than we -

Through Knowing – where we
only [hope/guess]
[Receiving/beholding] – where we – pray -
(F369/J499; Fascicle 18, stanza 4)

Although the dead 'know' in their domain where we can 'only hope' in ours, they also experience, as we do, 'Expectation', and, as the poem shifts into the mental space of the dead as the *originating* space, the subject of that space is 'the dead' not 'we', so the pronoun in the now projected space of the living takes the regular, not the -*self* anaphor form:

[11b] Of Expectation – also -
Anticipating **us**
With transport, that would
be a pain
Except for Holiness -
(stanza 5)

Now it is the speaker's space that is 'away' in 'Exile', and the final stanza ends in the domain of the dead:

[11c] Esteeming **us** – as Exile -
Themself – Admitted Home -
Through [gentle/curious -/*easy* -] Miracle of
Death -
The way **ourself** – must come -
(stanza 6)

Though the anaphor 'ourself' appears to be in the speaker's reality space, in fact it is being projected from the perspective of the mental space of the dead with the deictic words 'must come', as is 'themself', with the word 'admitted'. It is, however, still governed by the 'parent' space of life now. By projecting the self from life into the world of the dead, whether as the speaker's reality space as in 'Themself, should come to me -', or the projected mental space as in 'The way ourself, must come -', Dickinson makes the world of the dead an integral part of our own.

Dickinson's 'Spider' poem quoted in example (1) is one of those cases of ungrammaticality people characteristically point to, and it is true that under any autonomous theory of language, Dickinson's poetry is considered ungrammatical. However, the explanatory power of cognitive grammar lies in its ability to account for what people actually say, rather than creating arbitrary boundaries between what grammar can and cannot generate. The seemingly anomalous use of the double -*self* anaphor in 'Himself himself inform' of example (1) can be explained by mental space theory. In the poem, the subject 'Spider' is projected onto the -*self* anaphor subject of the conditional space set up by the 'if' space-builder. The reflexive object is then preposed before the verb (a typical Dickinson move) to get the line 'Himself himself inform'.

Given conceptual integration theory, Dickinson's *-self* anaphors are perfectly regular. Her use of the *-self* anaphor in projected mental spaces has the effect of making the self deictically present – grounding the self – in that space; not any self but the self as subject/agent in the originating space.

But what are the consequences of Dickinson's manipulation of the *-self* forms in this as in other poems? The spider builds his web at night. Only he can give shape to or 'in-form' the nature of his projection of himself into his web as he builds it. The grounding of the self in the space of the web is both strategic and physical: whether it be the accoutrements of living – the 'ruff of dame' – or the accoutrements of the dead – 'the shroud of gnome' – the spider is building his immortality. But it has to occur through a *physical* projection of 'himself' into his work – the web, his physiognomy. If the spider's web is to have any meaning, then the spider must project itself as a deictic presence in the world. We need to project the self into the world to change the world, to give it meaning, to create the web. This poem is not only a poem about poetry, it is a poem about how poetry works in the world.

By projecting *-self* anaphors from the subject/agent in one mental space into its counterpart in another, Dickinson creates for us a world of possibilities, a world in which things can happen and be made to happen through the agencies of the self. Under a cognitive grammar account, we not only understand the principles underlying Dickinson's grammar, we understand the way she uses the *-self* anaphor to create a presence of self in the world – of the dead and of the living.

ISSUES TO CONSIDER

Freeman's reading intersects in interesting ways with other work on deixis and the poetic voice, notable among which is Green's study of deixis and the poetic persona (Green 1992). Green concentrates on lyric poetry, and his analysis includes a very useful typology of stylistic features (125–6) for this particular literary genre. It is also worth following up Freeman's other work on Emily Dickinson where she approaches this poet's complex writing from yet further cognitive-stylistic perspectives. See, for example, M. Freeman (1995), (2000) and (2002).

More suggestions follow:

- Consider the sort of approach developed by Freeman here in relation to other poetry which is often considered grammatically 'deviant'. To what extent does her approach work with writers other than Dickinson? You can cross-refer to texts reproduced in other units of the book, such as those by e e cummings (B2), Edwin Morgan (D3) or even Gerard Manley Hopkins (B4 and D12).
- A major feature of Freeman's cognitive stylistics is her emphasis on deixis. To what extent is the 'poetic voice' delineated by deictic markers in other genres of poetry? For example, does deixis feature significantly in 'autobiographical poetry' of the sort written by Sylvia Plath, Allen Ginsberg or George Herbert? Alternatively, does deixis feature in 'dramatic monologue poetry' such as that found in the work of Robert Browning and John Donne, in the sonnets of Shakespeare and even in rap lyrics?

D11

COGNITIVE STYLISTICS AND THE THEORY OF METAPHOR

Peter Stockwell's article explores, challenges and ultimately rejects a important and widely accepted theory of metaphor comprehension. This theory, known as the *Invariance Hypothesis*, postulates that our understanding of a metaphor works in one direction only. Whereas our conceptualisation of the *target* domain of the metaphor (see unit A11) is affected and altered by the use of the metaphor, our conceptualisation of its source domain (that is, the concept we draw upon to develop the metaphor), remains unaffected. Thus, in the metaphor WAR IS CLEANING, which was discussed in A11, the thing we are trying to describe (our conception of war) is configured into a new way of thinking, although in the process we do not revise our mental schema of the source domain (our conception of cleaning).

More specifically, Stockwell draws on the concept of the Idealised Cognitive Model (see unit A10) in order to explore the Invariance Hypothesis as it relates to the processing of metaphor. According to Stockwell, the Invariance Hypothesis places a constraint on the ways in which ICMs are used to understand new experiences in a metaphorical mapping, allowing only the receiver's knowledge about the target domain of the metaphor to be altered. Using some examples from literature to support his case, he demonstrates that *both* domains are altered in a metaphorical mapping, an observation which suggests that the basic assumption of asymmetry in metaphorical mapping is ill-founded. Stockwell therefore rejects the Invariance Hypothesis as it relates to the reading of literature and in its place suggests an alternative source for a solution to the problems which the Invariance Hypothesis was invented to solve.

The inflexibility of invariance

Peter Stockwell (reprinted from *Language and Literature*, 1999, 8, 2, 125–42).

Peter Stockwell

[. . .] In general, cognitive linguistics has attempted to demonstrate how all representations of reality are based on metaphorical habits, conventionalised into domains of knowledge labelled *Idealised Cognitive Models* (or ICMs) (Lakoff 1987; [see also unit A10–P.S.]). These are presented as dynamic, radial structures that are altered by experience. They are *dynamic* in the sense that the categories of knowledge they represent can alter during on-going discourse in the world. They are *radial* in the sense that the arrangement of items in the structure displays prototype effects, such that there are central and peripheral examples of the category. Put most simply for illustration, 'apples' and 'oranges' are good, central examples of the 'fruit' category, whereas 'mangoes' and 'tomatoes' are not so central. Categories are thus seen not as absolutes but as culturally-determined and potentially fluid continua of knowledge. A 'potato' isn't simply 'not-a-fruit'; rather it is just a very bad example of a 'fruit'.

[. . .] underlying metaphorical mappings of ICMs are so ingrained in our usage that we barely perceive their metaphorical force at all: in the context of a popular romantic novel, 'She surrendered to his advances' is a realisation of the LOVE IS WAR metaphorical mapping of ICMs. The dozens of other realisations of this metaphor,

and associated isomorphisms such as ARGUMENT IS WAR, POLITICS IS WAR, SPORT IS WAR and so on, all point to the habituated and accustomed nature of much of the evidence from everyday language on which cognitive linguistics rests.

[. . .] The simplest version [of the Invariance Hypothesis] is as follows:

> *The Invariance Hypothesis: Metaphorical mappings preserve the cognitive typology (this is, the image-schema structure) of the source domain.*
>
> (Lakoff 1990: 54)

The need for a restriction on the information which is mapped between ICMs is apparent when counter-intuitive anomalies are thrown up. Turner [. . .] gives the LIFE IS A JOURNEY metaphor as an example, where JOURNEY is the source domain and LIFE is the target. Life is structured and understood in terms of a journey, in the expressions, 'He's getting nowhere in life, She's on the right track, and, He arrived at a new stage in life' (from Turner 1990: 248). In this example, the Invariance Hypothesis constrains us from saying, 'First I was getting somewhere in life and then I got off to a good start' (Turner 1990: 249), since the physical order of passing points on the path in a journey cannot be violated by the metaphorical mapping. It is the Invariance Hypothesis that explains here the anomalous meaning which 'disturbs us badly' (Turner 1990: 249).

[. . .] The central point is the *unidirectionality* of the isomorphism. Our idea of LIFE is structured by our familiar idea of a JOURNEY, but we do not conversely revise our idea of JOURNEYS on the basis of metaphors in which they are equated with LIFE. The cognitive typology of the source domain, JOURNEY, remains inviolable in this mapping. Turner (1990: 253–4) goes on to demonstrate that, when in life we might make a decision (understood as taking a fork in the path on the journey), then we cannot un-make that decision, though we could, on a journey, certainly retrace our steps and take the other fork. If the Invariance Hypothesis were not applied here, then the LIFE IS A JOURNEY metaphor would also allow us forks in paths that irrevocably disappear once we have chosen one way to go!

[. . .] As mentioned above, there is an assumption associated with the Invariance Hypothesis that there is a unidirectionality in the mapping of items and structure in conceptual metaphor. It would seem on first glance that this is the case with the TIME IS SPACE metaphor discussed by Lakoff (1990: 57). The fact that SPACE is the base (source) ICM in this example seems obvious, since

> we have detectors for motion and detectors for objects/locations. We do not have detectors for time (whatever that could mean). Thus, it makes good biological sense that time should be understood in terms of things and motion.
>
> (Lakoff 1990: 57)

TIME is thus the target ICM. We understand it in terms of our familiar idea of three-dimensional space. Indeed, H.G. Wells' (1895) time traveller explains 'time' to his dinner guests in precisely these terms, as an extension into 'four-dimensional' space at right angles to our familiar world, just before he literalises the metaphor by sweeping off into the future.

Lakoff (1990: 57) goes on to point out contradictory vectors in the TIME IS SPACE conceptual metaphor: 'The time has passed' and 'He passed the time'. For each, he argues that these simply illustrate that there are different correspondences of the metaphor. But this means that a single conceptual metaphor can be manifested and realised by a variety of utterances which reframe the detail in the mapping of ICMs slightly in the process. This conclusion would mean that cognitive linguistic methodology can produce more 'openness' in possible interpretation than it has been accused of [. . .].

More importantly, I would argue that examples such as 'The time has passed' or 'He passed the time', compared with 'Liverpool is three days' sailing from here', show a reversal of the conceptual metaphor: TIME IS SPACE and SPACE IS TIME. Each concept is understood in terms of our conventional understanding, by now well established, of the other. There is a consistency here in the mathematical logic that the two sides of an equational expression can be reversed without any change in meaning or value. The Invariance Hypothesis seeks to restrict such a reversal, acting (to apply another ICM mapping) like a conceptual non-return valve.

In any case, it is not true to say that we don't have detectors for time: we have watches, clocks and a calendar (where progress through space represents time). These are indexes of time rather than detectors, strictly, but our tools have always and increasingly become extensions of our biology in ways that must affect our language, if the root of metaphor is the everyday and habitualised that Lakoff and Johnson (1980) claim it is. Rather than being unidirectional, it would seem that conceptual metaphor, even in the TIME IS SPACE example, might be *interanimating*. [. . .]

Let me give a couple of examples to illustrate this. The first is a phrase from a Paul Simon song, 'Diamonds on the Soles of His Shoes', in which a poor boy is walking down the street, 'empty as a pocket'. Here the ICMs of the boy's EMPTY LIFE and the general notion of POCKETS are mapped together. However, what results from this phrase is two ideas: the boy's life is like a pocket (a small insignificant container personal to him), but the type of pocket that is evoked by this mapping with the poor boy is an empty one. *Both* domains of the mapping have been altered (or specified) in the mapping.

The second example is of a different sort, and demonstrates what I have elsewhere (Stockwell 1996: 13) called 'flashpoint reference'. This is when a noun phrase invokes a referent but the utterance (usually through the predicate or a negation particle) immediately revokes or cancels the referent from active memory (see Stockwell (1994, 1996) for a fuller account of this). This happens in T.S. Eliot's poem *The Waste Land*:

Sweet Thames, run softly, till I end my song.
The river bears no empty bottles, sandwich papers,
Silk handkerchiefs, cardboard boxes, cigarette ends
Or other testimony of summer nights. The nymphs are
departed.
And their friends, the loitering heirs of City directors;
Departed, have left no addresses.

(Eliot 1963: 70)

Here, the 16th century Elizabethan River Thames is invoked, firstly by the quotation of the coda to each stanza of Spenser's *Prothalamion* (1596), and then by the description of the river in its pre-industrial pre-urbanised state, clean and unpolluted by social rubbish. Of course, in describing the non-existence of the litter, the poem simultaneously invokes the image of the modern, dirty, degraded river as well, even in the act of denying it all. The two image-schemas of Elizabethan river and 20th century river are mapped together dialectically to suggest a comment on the degradation of the modern world; and the movement from the high art of the Elizabethan Renaissance to the rather tawdry and sleazy mundane concerns of modern times is further suggested. The mapping itself, in other words, can be *thematised*, in this literary context, and this action involves moving *beyond* the simple mapped restructuring of image-schemas.

When discussing 'image metaphors', Lakoff (1990: 66) cites several poetic examples as 'one-shot metaphors', in which both image-schemas are conventional, but the mapping is novel or striking [. . .]. Lakoff cites the surrealist writer André Breton's line: 'My wife . . . whose waist is an hourglass', to argue that such 'part-whole' mappings can be explained using the Invariance Hypothesis. He suggests it provides an answer to the question of which parts of the source domain are mapped to the target (and which parts of image-schematic structure are left behind). In this example, the curvy shape of the hourglass is mapped onto the poet's wife's body, but presumably the flowing sand inside, the glass coldness and perhaps the notion of time running out (literalised and dramatised in the hourglass) are not mapped. It is from such literary examples that Lakoff and Turner generalise the Invariance Hypothesis.

Let's look at the Breton example in detail. The line is most commonly found in English in the translation by Edouard Roditi of Breton's poem 'Freedom of Love'. [. . .] It begins:

> My wife with the hair of a wood fire
> With the thoughts of heat lightning
> With the waist of an hourglass
> With the waist of an otter in the teeth of a tiger
> My wife with the lips of a cockade and of a bunch of stars of the last
>   magnitude
> With the teeth of tracks of white mice on the white earth
> With the tongue of rubbed amber and glass
> My wife with the tongue of a stabbed host
> With the tongue of a doll that opens and closes its eyes
> With the tongue of an unbelievable stone [. . .]
>
> (Breton/Roditi in Germain 1978: 69)

This is a poem generated by surrealism. A multi-media art movement flourishing in Europe in the 1920s and '30s, surrealism had as one of its main objectives the destruction of rationalist and bourgeois thought by unusual juxtaposition. This collage technique manifested itself in verbal art mainly in the form of highly striking and deviant metaphor, of which the Breton passage above provides several good examples. [. . .]

Verbal art in surrealism is founded on isomorphism, but it is a very different conception from that posed within cognitive linguistics through the Invariance Hypothesis. Here is a perception of language that is transcendental and uses metaphor to go beyond everyday meaning, in order to reframe fundamentally our view of the world and ourselves. In other terms, here is a perception of language that is dialectical and uses metaphor to go beyond the familiar understandings of ICMs, in order to recast all our ICMs and retroactively alter our perceptions of base *and* target in our conceptual experience. This is metaphor as interanimation, in which the process of 'metaphoring' encourages us to see the familiar world in a new light as a synthesis of base and target mapping.

Let me demonstrate this by returning to the opening of Breton's poem quoted above. Each line contains a single metaphorical mapping, except the fifth which maps the wife's lips with two bases (a 'cockade' and 'stars'). Her 'waist' is mapped with two ICMs, and lines 7–10 map her 'tongue' with four different things. Applying the Invariance Hypothesis to a reading of this would predict only incoherence, as Turner points out (Turner 1990: 248) [. . .]. On first inspection the Breton passage is not exactly like this: in the line, 'My wife with the lips of a cockade and of a bunch of stars of the last magnitude', two distinct sources are mapped onto one target; and in the last four lines of the quoted passage, four distinct sources ('rubbed amber and glass', 'a stabbed host', 'a doll' and 'an unbelievable stone') are mapped onto one target ('tongue'). However, if the whole poem is read as a general conceptual mapping in which the poet's wife is the target ICM, then there are possibly 75 distinct components of very diverse ICMs, and there are 11 source ICMs even just in the passage from the beginning of the poem I quoted above. All of these map, sometimes severally, onto particular components of the 'wife'. If the passage is to be read as surrealism, then simple incoherence does not seem an adequate account of this poem.

This paper began by noting that ICMs are radial structures that display prototype effects. They are built up by accumulated experience and are constantly being revised and altered to a greater or lesser degree. Those ICMs that are revised the least constitute the individual's relatively stable view of the world and the things in it. Those that are revised the most encompass new experiences, unfamiliar things, items of debate or uncertainty, or perhaps areas of which the person does not have a strong opinion and has been swayed by the arguments in various incoming bits of language.

The aspect of cognitive linguistics that is essential here is the notion of prototype effects: categories are not absolutes but are fluid continua of knowledge. Together with the notion of radiality, this means that ICMs have central, secondary and peripheral elements in their structures. The central problem which the Invariance Hypothesis was invented to solve is a consequence of the question of how to decide which elements are mapped and which are left behind. This question can be answered directly, without any need for Invariance.

The key idea here is *salience*. This involves a judgment of match between the incoming text and the individual's expectations and propensities. In other words, it is a readerly notion as well as a text-based one. Let me outline the process of encountering a metaphorical structure-mapping, as follows, by recalling again the example from Breton that Lakoff (1990) suggested: 'My wife . . . with the waist of an hourglass'. In the discussion above, I suggested that the curvy shape of the hourglass was mapped, but presumably not the flowing sand inside, nor the glass coldness and perhaps not the notion of time running out. But why not? And why 'presumably'? Certainly this seems intuitively right. So how do we decide that the line is not about the poet's wife's similarity to these other things?

It seems that the notion of the *shape* of the hourglass is the most salient feature. Maybe this has become conventionalised (and thus comes to mind most readily) in the phrase 'hourglass figure'. It is plausible to suggest that the centrally prototypical feature of the 'hourglass' ICM is its distinctive shape. In any case, what seems to happen is that once this feature has been mapped onto the target ('wife'), then that is satisfactory enough to carry on with the reading of the poem. This was enough for me on my first reading. The flowing sand inside is a relatively secondary feature, and one that I only began to consider when I re-read the line in the article by Lakoff. But I can see no salience in this feature for my reading of the poem, so I don't think it is mapped to my image-schema of the 'wife'. [. . .]

Unfamiliar ICMs are only unfamiliar once, and after several practices of the mapping the pattern becomes conventionalised. It then becomes difficult to see which is source and which target [. . .]. [I]t is plausible to suppose that we become accustomed to approaching novel metaphors using the same interpretative strategies: that is, we look for the most salient features – on the basis of their prototypical ordering – that will produce a satisfactory reading for the context in hand. I have tried to demonstrate how changing contexts and reading purposes can account for different interpretations, within this model.

The key ideas outlined in this paper include the notion that image-schematic structure-mappings are *interanimating* rather than unidirectional, and this allows meaning and interpretation to be *dialectical* and *exponential* to the surface realisation of the proposition. The notion that ICMs are *radial* and display *prototype effects* allows an account of which features are mapped and which left behind, subject to *salience.* This notion, related to the pragmatic description of relevance, centres on the purpose of reading a particular text, joined to a recognition that genres encourage readers to interpret in particular ways. And finally, it is a key idea that ICM-construction is not treated as a completed process prior to the reading experience, but that reading itself serves to refine and revise the features, structures and domains of knowledge. [. . .]

My main interest is in cognitive poetics, which I believe is able to provide a coherent, valid and workable theory of literature (as argued clearly by M. Freeman [see Reading D10–P.S.]). The Invariance Hypothesis curtails the perception of metaphor as creative. It limits our understanding, condemning us to see things only in the way that we have always seen them. It would prevent us from seeing how we could possibly genuinely perceive anything new or challenging. It cannot explain the capacity of language for reference to a new sense beyond source and target, that is embodied in surrealist poetry, science fiction, and all imaginative works of art. Such limitations are counter to the larger, more fundamental claims of cognitive linguistics concerning the linguistic basis and embodiment of culture and perception. Here, I have sought to preserve the general value of cognitive linguistics, while escaping the inflexibility of invariance.

ISSUES TO CONSIDER

Stockwell's paper illustrates well how stylistics can be used to rethink ideas about language and linguistics. Indeed, it addresses a question posed at the very start of this book, in A1, which asks 'What can stylistics tell us about language?'. Specifically, Stockwell orientates his analysis of examples from literature towards the Invariance Hypothesis as conceived in cognitive linguistics, which then allows him to challenge the theory and suggest an alternative solution. In the light of Stockwell's solution, it is worth revisiting the passage from Jeanette Winterson provided in unit C11. A key question to ask of the passage is whether it is only one side of the metaphorical expression, our understanding of misery, which is altered in the mapping, or is our perception of the numerous source domains altered also? In other words, are Winterson's metaphors *interanimating* in the sense proposed by Stockwell?

More suggestions follow:

- Take an anthology of poetry and write down every metaphor you can find across any five pages of print. Consider what mappings between source and target domain are involved, which elements are mapped and whether the literary expression really does affect your impression of the source domain as well as the target domain.
- Using the selection of metaphors provided in C11 as a starting point, develop a comparative analysis of the sorts of metaphors you typically find in specific discourse contexts. What sorts of metaphors, for example, do you commonly find in advertising? Or in tourist information, popular science, cook books and so on?

STYLE AND VERBAL HUMOUR

D12

This reading is taken from Walter Nash's book *The Language of Humour* and it explores some of the stylistic techniques that are used in the development of comic styles of writing. Nash is particularly interested in *allusion* and in the role it plays in the compositional make-up of humorous discourses like parody. The topics broached in this reading make numerous implicit intersections with material in other units of this book; this includes intertextuality (see A5), the comic function of allusion and intertextuality (C1 and C2), grammar and style (B3) and sound symbolism (strand four). In all, Nash's reading is an excellent illustration of 'applied stylistics' in that it shows how the stylistic method can serve to identify and explicate various techniques of creative writing.

Allusion and parody

Walter Nash

Walter Nash (reprinted from chapter five of Nash, W. (1985) *The Language of Humour* Harlow: Longman, pp.74–102.

Allusion in the very broadest sense is never absent from our discourse; always there is some fact of shared experience, some circumstance implicit in the common culture, to which participants in a conversation may confidently allude. For families, friends, neighbours, colleagues, there is a generic knowledge of the affairs of the day – of politics, of social questions, of sports and entertainments, of current notions and phraseology. Such knowledge informs a good deal of what we say to each other, making its point even when its presence is veiled.

What we commonly understand by 'allusion', however, is something more explicit and overt, something for which the word 'citation' might be a more accurate name. These citations often have a function that goes beyond the mere decoration of a conversational exchange. They are a kind of test, proving the credentials of the initiated, baffling the outsider. In effect, they are a device of power, enabling the speaker to control a situation and authoritatively turn it to his own advantage. [. . .]

In an allusion, however, the cited text need not be from a poem: or any other recognised piece of literature. Virtually any well known form of words – from the language of politics, of advertising, or journalism, of law and social administration – will serve the requirements of wit. A music critic, reviewing a performance of Bruch's violin concerto, notes the unusually slow tempi adopted by the soloist, Shlomo Mintz; and jocosely adds his supposition that this violinist is 'one of the too-good-to-hurry Mintz'. British readers can laugh at this, because they will almost certainly recognise the allusion to an advertising jingle no longer in use but popular in its day:

> Murraymints, Murraymints,
> Too-good-to-hurry mints.

The allusion is impudently funny, and at the same time makes a criticism that might have been more woundingly phrased; the reviewer does not use expressions like 'cloying', or 'self-indulgent', but something of the kind may be implied in his quip. Once again, we can regard the allusion as a controlling element in discourse; here, its effect is both to direct and to deflect the severity of criticism.

[. . .] allusion can be an important, indeed cardinal, device in the structure of comic texts. Furthermore, wherever allusions occur some excursion into parody is possible; the parodic line often begins with the allusive point [. . .]

Robert Graves sees an image of parody in the folk myth of the witch who invisibly stalks her victim, following close on his heels and imitating his gait so aptly that she at last possesses it, and can make him stumble at will. This striking comparison suggests that parody appraises – learns the way of walking – in order to ridicule and discomfit. But not all parody is hostile; many acts of literary caricature and burlesque show affectionate familiarity with the things they imitate, and are a form of positive criticism, of stylistic analysis, and ultimately of tribute. If there are malign witches, there are also benevolent warlocks, who learn the steps in order to show just how well the 'victim' dances. Parody of a personal style often aims to do just that. It is the shortest and most concrete way of commenting on typical features of syntax, lexicon, phonology, prosody, and all the apparatus of learned dissertation.

The point is illustrated by the following attempt, on my part, to parody the distinctive poetic idiom of Gerard Manley Hopkins:

G. M. Hopkins takes lunch in the restaurant car

Ah, waiter, are there any any, where are, tell me, come,
  Napkins, lovely all-of-a-starch-staring
Linen, preferably, or pauper-seeming paper, waiter? Wearing
  My gaygear goodsuit, ah, my dear, dim was it? dumb?
Well, this train's tripping and track-truckling as I sipped
  Soup, did, ah God, the hot of it! – yes, slipped, flipped
Into my lap, slapping, of this clear consomme, some
  Spoonflung flashes, splashes for bosom's bearing.

Bring me a – coo – lummy here dab, here dry with a kerch-
  ief, tea-towel, toilet-roll, oh-dear-then-a-doyly, but merely
A move (with a mercy, man) make! Oh what a slanting that
  sheerly,
  What with the canting curve of the, what with the lilt of the
  lurch,
Hurled leaping lapward, all in a skirl, the dear drenching.
  There was a splash to abash one quaintly, ah, there was a
  quenching!
Since when, on seat's edge sodden I pensive perch,
  Picking at lunch unlovely, unappetising nearly.

The intention of this light-hearted exercise is certainly not to stage a satirical attack on a sage and serious poet. The parody aims affectionately at the comprehension of certain stylistic mannerisms, and it is the parodist who is at risk here, should the purport of his mimetic tricks go unrecognised. To say what these 'tricks' are, and how they reflect the devices habitually used by the poet, is to embark on a primary course in Hopkinsian poetics. Here are the familiar prosodic and phonetic idiosyncrasies, the 'sprung rhythm' with its jostling clusters of strong accents, the linking alliterations and assonances, the internal rhyming, the 'rove over' rhyme (*with a kerch/ief, tea towel* etc). Here also are the characteristic syntactic patterns: the interrupted constructions, the parentheses, the ellipses, the bold departures from normal word order, the phrasal modifiers, the liking for certain phrase types (eg the 'of-genitive', *the X of Y*, and the 's-genitive' with participial noun, *the Y's Xing*). The vocabulary, too, clearly purports to represent Hopkins' lexical preoccupations – the abundant compounds and phrasal adjectives, the deviant semantics (as in 'the *lilt* of the lurch', 'all in a *skirl*'), the liking for words suggesting rapid and violent action or motion (*hurl* is a favourite).

The validity of these brief analytical notes can be tested against the poet's work. Anyone interested enough to make the test might possibly mark in passing some apparently direct verbal borrowings from Hopkins' poems, or perhaps some general resemblances of phraseology between the parody and the original corpus. Although these correspondences were not consciously sought when the parody was made, memory has indeed been at its sneaking craft, as a few examples may show:

Hopkins:	'How to keep – is there any any, is there none such, nowhere known some, bow or brooch . . .' ('The Leaden Echo and The Golden Echo')
Parody:	'Ah, waiter, are there any, any, where are, tell me, come, Napkins . . .'
Hopkins:	'. . . to-fro tender trambeams truckle at the eye' ('The Candle Indoors')
Parody:	'This train's tripping and track-truckling . . .'
Hopkins:	'But how shall I . . . make me a room there: Reach me a . . . Fancy, come faster-' ('The Wreck of the Deutschland')
Parody:	'Bring me a – coo – lummy – here dab, here dry . . .'
Hopkins:	'The girth of it and the wharf of it . . .' ('The Wreck of the Deutschland')
Parody:	'. . . the hot of it'
Hopkins:	'. . . and blue-beak embers, ah my dear, Fall . . .' ('The Windhover')
Parody:	'My gaygear goodsuit, ah, my dear, dim was it . . . ?'

Such echoes, however, are ultimately of minor interest and are perhaps irrelevant to the question of whether or not the parody is effective. A test of good parody is not how closely it imitates or reproduces certain turns of phrase, but how well it *generates* a style convincingly like that of the parodied author, producing the sort of phrases and sentences he might have produced. Borrowing the terminology of language acquisition, we might say that the parodist displays a competence, learns to 'speak Hopkins' and to produce Hopkinsian utterances which he has never heard before.

Something, therefore, is *added* to an effective and interesting parody; it is not solely or even primarily an exercise in specific allusion to certain textual loci, but an attempt at a *creative allusiveness* that generates the designated style. To this, add one further element: the intrusion of the parodist's own idiom, or at all events of a patently alien accent (*dim was it? dumb*?; *coo – lummy –*) confessing to the irreverent act, reminding the reader, should he need reminding, that this is not the style itself, not a blatant forgery, not an attempt to pass off as genuine a gobbet of pastiche, but something that remains from first to last a piece of jocose mimicry. The apparent ineptitudes of the clown are at one and the same time the setting for his burlesque act and his admission that it *is* a burlesque and nothing more. [. . .]

There arises the question of how we recognise a parody or a parodic intention; for here, as in other forms of humour, laughter depends on some framework of expectancy. Most commonly, as in our Hopkins parody, a title makes the directive signal, even suggesting the structure of the parodic joke. The reader is given some form of stylistic proposition; a poet's name is mentioned, and a content (eg: *lunch in the restaurant car*) is indicated. Thus he is led to presuppose a model of this type:

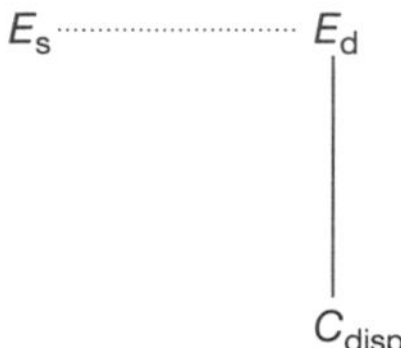

This represents two 'planes', of *expression* and *content.* E_s is the source-expression (eg Hopkins' style as observed in his poems), from which the parodic expression E_d is *derived.* The content of the parody is totally unHopkinsian; his usual subject-matter has been *displaced,* so to speak, by an untypical theme. Hence, E_d = 'derived expression', and C_{disp} = 'displacing content'.

The presuppositions encouraged by the title are confirmed, or at any rate tested, by the ensuing text; as we have seen, the E_d may pick up identifiable scraps from the E_s or, more broadly, may generate a phraseology suggestive of the E_s. If the parody is successful, the model-proposing title is strictly speaking unnecessary; nevertheless, it has a part to play, in orientating the reader. Were there no title, or were the title less explicit (eg: *Eminent Victorian in Hot Water*), he would have to make his own guess at the intended style. There would be an implied query – 'Guess who?' – which would turn the exercise from a humorous demonstration into a riddle or charade. The title, then, is part of a conditioning process that lets the reader in on the joke.

Yet in the absence of a title, even when the reader is not sure just what is being parodied, it may still be possible to recognise parodic intention. The parodist takes care as a rule to create notable discrepancies: discrepancies of 'fit' between expression and content, and discrepancies of style on the plane of expression itself. In the Hopkins parody, the mismatch of expression and content is boldly obvious, and must be so even to a reader with no knowledge of Hopkins. 'Cry like this over spilt soup?' he asks himself. 'This has to be a joke.' Similarly, he must have his doubts about the seriousness of a rhetoric that veers abruptly from the pseudo-poetic (eg: *bosom's bearing*) to the banally colloquial (*coo – lummy –*). Perception of stylistic discrepancy confirms his assumptions about the wayward content; what he has before him is either a piece of absurdly ill-judged writing, or an essay in buffoonery, *probably* of a parodic nature. [. . .]

The domain of parody is, to be sure, a large and varied one – so much so, that we inevitably come across texts that are not centrally parodic, in terms of a clearly definable model, but which wear a parodic *aura,* and are full of echoes of half-remembered writings. They might be called *pseudoparodies.* Here is an example of pseudoparody, produced during a tutorial on composition and creative writing, as an illustration of some rhetorical techniques:

> Milkmen everywhere. Milkmen up the Avenue; milkmen down the Grove. Milkmen on the High St, where it winds between banks of shops stacked with plastic footwear and cutprice washing machines; milkmen in the alleys that meander past the dirty backyards of dormant pubs. Milkmen rattling their bottles in areas and basements; milkmen wheedling incorrect sums from harassed housewives; milkmen with dejected horses; milkmen with electric floats, stuck at the traffic lights where the main road forks left past the grim grey majesty of the multi-storey car park.

The composition of this was haunted by the troubled sense of writing to a hidden model. Readers of the passage may have the impression of having met something like it elsewhere, and in their mental rummagings for a source may possibly remember the first page of Dickens' *Bleak House* [see unit B3 – P.S.]. [. . .]

Clearly, the 'milkman' exercise is an example of parodic recollection. It is not closely or pointedly imitative of the Dickens passage. If it were a deliberate and conscious parody, it would imitate the original's subtle variations of clause and sentence length, and its picture of a suburban High Street would offer some sort of iconographic parallel to the programme of the Dickensian Thames, which is followed from the meadows above London, through the city, and out to the estuary marshes. There is no conscious modelling of one passage on the other; but there is a hazy recollection of rhetorical procedures. We see, for instance, how the pseudoparody has picked up some linguistic features of its Dickensian original, eg the rarity of finite verbs, and the frequency of participle clauses and adverbial constructions. [. . .] These echoes suggest that a powerfully or idiosyncratically written passage, like the splendid opening of *Bleak House*, can lodge in a reader's mind a stylistic record for later reference. [. . .]

Elements of parody are so important in the style of comedy that the creation of a parodic texture may sometimes appear to be the exclusive principle of any comic work [. . .] One might certainly argue that one of the *axes* of comic writing – the 'style-axis', if we like to call it that – is a progression of allusions, parodic hints, pseudoparodies.

ISSUES TO CONSIDER

It is interesting to observe how prominent is the principle of ironic echo (see A12) in Nash's parodies – indeed, Nash himself elaborates in some detail the stylistic impetus for his pastiches of both Hopkins and Dickens. Worth mentioning in passing is that both of these pastiches embody a particular kind of parodic humour known as *high burlesque*. This technique works by presenting trivial subject matter in an ornate or high-flown style of presentation, while *low burlesque* (a technique much favoured incidentally by the Monty Python team) works by presenting serious subject matter in a trivial or informal way. In general, Nash's reading emphasises the interdependence of creative writing and stylistic analysis: in a sense, you cannot write a parody without first of all undertaking some kind of stylistic analysis, no matter how intuitive or informal that analysis may be.

Some suggestions follow:

Activity 

- David Lodge's novel *Thinks* (2002) makes for an interesting study in style, not least because of the multiplicity of styles its author employs. Many of these styles are direct parodies of other writers' work. Worth following up in view of the material covered both in C2 and D5 of this book, is a parody which involves a treatise on the subject of bats written in the style of Irvine Welsh.
- The following excerpt is from a parody by Woody Allen. Set in the Europe of the 1920s, a fictional persona imagines a series of encounters with the distinguished literati of that period. This sequence covers his meeting with Ernest Hemingway:

  > . . . we came upon Hemingway. Bronzed and bearded now, he was already beginning to develop that flat prose style about the eyes and mouth . . . We had great fun in Spain that year and we travelled and wrote and Hemingway took me tuna fishing and I caught four cans and we laughed . . .
  >
  > (Allen 1975: 91–3)

  Hemingway's prose style has come under scrutiny in this book, in B3 and in C8. What stylistic resemblance can you detect between the Hemingway material presented in those units and the Woody Allen parody? What are the key features of Hemingway's style that Allen is echoing? Working from the relevant distinction drawn in A12, are there any aspects of the Allen text that you feel make it shade into *satire*?

FURTHER READING

WHAT IS STYLISTICS?

- Lecercle's attack on stylistics, entitled 'The current state of stylistics', was published as Lecercle (1993). Wales (1993a) is a riposte to Lecercle which appeared in a subsequent issue of the same journal.
- Representative samples of feminist stylistics, cognitive stylistics and discourse stylistics are, respectively, Mills (1995), Semino and Culpeper (2002) and Carter and Simpson (1989). An overview of the aims and scope of 'pedagogical stylistics' is Clark and Zyngier (2003). An accessible general introduction to the discipline is Verdonk (2002) – a book which incidentally also has *stylistics* in its title – while Wales's dictionary of stylistics (2001) offers compact definitions of the key terms and topics in the field. Finally, Barry (2002) contains a chapter on stylistics written from the perspective of critical theory. A useful exercise would be to compare the angle taken on stylistics in Barry's description with that taken in this book.

GRAMMAR AND STYLE

- A useful introduction to grammar and vocabulary, which offers a much fuller treatment than can be accommodated within a single unit like this, is Jackson's textbook in the RELI series (Jackson 2001).

RHYTHM AND METRE

- Attridge (1982) is an important book on the rhythms of verse, while Leech (1969) remains an authoritative account of this and other features of the language of poetry. Scholarly articles by Cureton (1994) and Fabb (2002) offer more advanced treatments of metre.
- Brazil's paper on the intonation patterns of reading aloud makes some illuminating observations on how people can read a piece of poetry in different ways (Brazil 1992). His study shows how metrical emphasis in verse is open to a variety of interpretations.

NARRATIVE STYLISTICS

- The definitive stylistic introduction to narrative is Toolan (2001). A version of the six part model proposed here is used by Simpson and Montgomery (1995) in an extended stylistic analysis of Bernard MacLaverty's novel *Cal* (and see further C6). Leech and Short (1981) offer a comprehensive introduction to the stylistic techniques of prose fiction while Simpson (1997a) contains a chapter outlining a workshop programme in narrative stylistics.

STYLE AS CHOICE

- The full, authoritative account of transitivity is Halliday (1994: 106–75). Detailed summaries of the model may also be found in Eggins (1994: 220–70) and Thompson (1996: 76–116).

STYLE AND POINT OF VIEW

- Fuller treatments of point of view in fiction can be found in books by Fowler (1996) and Simpson (1993), while useful scholarly articles on the topic include Sasaki (1994) and Chapman (2002).
- The terms *homodiegetic* and *heterodiegetic* come from Genette's study of narrative discourse (Genette 1980), although a useful introductory summary can be found in Rimmon-Kenan (1983).

REPRESENTING SPEECH AND THOUGHT

- Full and authoritative accounts of speech and thought presentation can be found in Leech and Short (1981) and Short (1996). The categories proposed in this unit are based largely on those accounts.

DIALOGUE AND DISCOURSE

- A more comprehensive survey of the areas covered in this unit can be found in Simpson (1997a: 129–78), while Simpson and Hall (2002) offers an overview of more recent developments in the field of discourse stylistics. A useful collection of papers on the stylistic analysis of dialogue (including film dialogue) is Culpeper *et al* (1998), while Herman (1996) is a monograph-length study of dramatic discourse from a stylistic perspective.
- The authoritative study of politeness phenomena, of which stylisticians have made extensive use over the years, is Brown and Levinson (1987). Other key work in pragmatics is Austin's seminal work on speech acts and illocutionary force (Austin 1962) and Grice's development of a model of conversational implicature (Grice 1975).

COGNITIVE STYLISTICS

- Two key publications in this area are related textbooks by Stockwell (2002) and Gavins and Steen (2003). The former is a general introduction to the field, covering its history, development and methods, and the latter a collection of readings offering practical advice and exercises for cognitive stylistic exploration. A collection of more advanced papers is Semino and Culpeper (2002).
- The idea of an Idealised Cognitive Model was first developed by Lakoff (1987; and see also readings D10 and D11). Other influential studies in cognitive linguistics and Artificial Intelligence, which have shaped the development of cognitive poetics, are Gibbs (1994); Lakoff and Johnson (1998); Fauconnier (1994); Fauconnier and Turner (2002) and Schank and Abelson (1977; and see further B10).

METAPHOR AND METONYMY

- Good introductions to metaphor include Kövecses (2002) and Goatly (1997), and chapter 8 of Stockwell (2002) is also very useful. Two of the more 'classic' books on metaphor are Brooke-Rose (1958) and Ortony (1979) while seminal publications in cognitive linguistics which focus on metaphor are Lakoff and Johnson (1980), Lakoff (1987) and Lakoff and Turner (1989). The stylistician Gerard Steen has written extensively on metaphor over the years, of which a representative sample of his work includes: Steen (1994, 1999a, 2002a and 2002b). Also relevant is a co-edited collection of papers, Gibbs and Steen (1999).

STYLISTICS AND VERBAL HUMOUR

- Accessible introductory books on the language of humour include Chiaro (1992), Ross (1998) and Crystal (1998).
- Both Redfern (2000) and Culler (1998) are book-length treatments of puns, the latter with a specifically literary orientation. Leech (1969: 209–14) contains a useful section on punning in poetry. Simpson (2003) is a comprehensive study of the discourse of satire which contains a short overview of different forms of verbal humour. It also includes an account of the complex relationship between parody and satire.

DEVELOPMENTS IN STYLISTICS

- The stylistician Willie van Peer has written extensively on foregrounding theory, two representative samples of which are a book (van Peer 1986) and a later article (van Peer 1993).
- Cook (1994) contains an excellent overview of both the Russian Formalist and Prague School movements, while Durant and Fabb (1990: 32–4) includes a useful chronological map showing how these movements developed in the context of related developments in critical theory.

- Wales's study of Philip Larkin's poem 'Church Going' makes for an interesting synthesis of the techniques of rhetoric with the methods of stylistics (Wales 1993b).

LEVELS OF LANGUAGE AT WORK: AN EXAMPLE FROM POETRY

- Traugott and Pratt (1980) is a generally informative book in stylistics which also contains a short analysis of the same cummings poem. Their analysis draws on a very different model of language to the one adopted here, so the two studies should make for an interesting point of comparison. The fact that it is possible for different scholars to approach the same text with different models of analysis illustrates well the point made in A1 on the importance of stylistic method being *replicable*.
- Widdowson's influential and highly readable book on stylistics includes a revealing analysis of Robert Frost's poem 'Dust of Snow', with semantic patterning at the fore of the analysis (Widdowson 1975: 38ff).
- Other stylistic work focussed specifically on e e cummings includes Simpson (1997a: 44ff) and van Peer (1987).

SENTENCE STYLES: DEVELOPMENT AND ILLUSTRATION

- Leech and Short (1981) contains a number of detailed analyses of prose fiction which pay particular attention to patterns of grammar. A number of the papers collected in both Carter (1982) and Verdonk (1993a) also offer accessible explorations of style and grammar.

INTERPRETING PATTERNS OF SOUND

- Attridge (1988) has a chapter which explores in depth many of the issues raised in this unit, while Nash (1986) is an article which looks at the problems involved in teaching sound symbolism in a stylistic context. Montgomery *et al* (1992: 86–9) contains a useful short section on the problems associated with interpreting sound patterns in poetry.

DEVELOPMENTS IN STRUCTURAL NARRATOLOGY

- Toolan has applied Propp's categories to a passage from Joyce's short story 'Eveline' (2001: 17–22), and this analysis, along with his general development of this model of narrative structure, is accessible and informative. See also Durant and Fabb (1990:182–6) for a useful explication of Propp's model.

STYLE AND TRANSITIVITY

- Simpson (1993: 86–118) contains an application of an admittedly older version of the model of transitivity, along with a more detailed review of the Fish-Halliday debate than has been attempted here. Toolan (1998: 75–104) provides a useful outline of the transitivity model and offers for analysis an intriguing passage from J. M. Coetzee's novel *Life & Times of Michael K.*
- Halliday's and Fish's papers have been usefully gathered together in two collections of articles in stylistics, D. Freeman (1981) and Weber (1996). A more recent study of Golding's *The Inheritors*, offering an extensive exploration of transitivity, is Hoover (1999). Hoover's book takes Halliday's work in many new directions and it is also a further illustration of the principal of 'replicability' in stylistic method (A1). Both Shen (1988) and Toolan (1990) are two of the many good ripostes to Fish that have been written by stylisticians over the years.

APPROACHES TO POINT OF VIEW

- The four-way account of point of view is from Uspensky (1973) with summaries and adaptations in Fowler (1996).

TECHNIQUES OF SPEECH AND THOUGHT PRESENTATION

- Again, full surveys of speech and thought presentation can be found in Leech and Short (1981) and Short (1996). Fludernik (1993) is a more advanced monograph-length study which includes substantial treatment of speech and thought presentation. Article length publications include a debate on the topic played out between Simpson (1997b) and Short *et al* (1997).

DIALOGUE IN DRAMA

- Simpson (1998) develops in more detail the idea of incongruity as a feature of the absurd in drama. This essay also connects incongruity to theories of humour (see also unit A12). Tan (1998) offers advice on how to write a stylistic analysis of drama dialogue. In no way a definitive guide to the writing of essays in stylistics, Tan's paper nonetheless contains a number of useful suggestions about how to organise a response to a passage of play dialogue. Another version of Burton's structural model of discourse, with a more pedagogical-stylistic emphasis, can be found in Burton (1982b).

DEVELOPMENTS IN COGNITIVE STYLISTICS

- In addition to the references posted throughout this unit, useful theoretical context for cognitive stylistics is provided by Steen and Gavins (2003), Stockwell (2000) and (2003), and by the editors' foreword in Semino and Culpeper (2002).
- Another important cognitive-stylistic model, which complements usefully those outlined here, is provided in Semino's study of 'world creation' in poetry and other texts (Semino 1997). Jeffries (2001) and Semino (2001) form two sides of a provocative and entertaining debate about the usefulness for stylistic analysis of schema theory and related concepts in cognitive linguistics.

STYLES OF METAPHOR

- A special issue of the journal *Language and Literature* (2002, 11, 1), edited by Gerard Steen, is devoted to metaphor identification, and readers will find in that issue many useful suggestions about how to identify and track metaphors in literature. M. Freeman (2002) explores the 'body' of a poetic text, making a number of connections between the visual form of a poem and its cognitive import. This paper is therefore a good follow-up to the sorts of issues raised in this unit about the connection between metaphor and graphological experimentation. McRae's (1998) study of the language of poetry, which is a generally valuable stylistic survey of poetic technique, contains a short exercise based around the McGough poem and other visually striking poems.

IS THERE A 'LITERARY LANGUAGE'?

- The 'literary language' issue has been addressed in various stylistics publication, but the treatments in Fowler (1996) and Carter and Nash (1990) are especially useful. Tambling (1988) approaches the issue from a range of perspectives in his useful book on the subject. Finally, the problems involved in modelling a stylistic description of *literature* are addressed in van Peer (1991) and Steen (1999b).

STYLE, REGISTER AND DIALECT

- Hess (1996) is an insightful exploration of code-switching in literature. Two articles on the representation of dialect in literature are Toolan (1992) and (2000), while Cooper (1994) is a study of dialect in the novels of Thomas Hardy. A special issue of the journal *Language and Literature* (2001, 10, 2) is devoted to dialect analysis, specifically to the representation of African-American varieties of English in the work of Mark Twain and Harriet Beecher Stowe. Antilanguages in literature are the principal focus of attention in both Tsen (1997) and in a chapter of Fowler (1981).

- Corbett (1997) offers an excellent general overview of the language of Scottish literature while Mick Short's essay in Reading D5 explores another of Irvine Welsh's novels, *Marabou Stork Nightmares.*

GRAMMAR AND GENRE: A SHORT STUDY IN IMAGISM

- There are numerous literary-critical treatments of Imagism and of the life and work of Ezra Pound, although it should be noted that rarely does this work engage in any rigour with stylistic issues associated with Imagist poetry. On the other hand, Crisp (1996) is a scholarly article in stylistics which is devoted to the significance of the 'image metaphor' in the work of Pound and other poets. Although quite advanced theoretically, Crisp's article, which includes a commentary on 'In a station of the Metro' makes for rewarding reading.

STYLES IN A SINGLE POEM: AN EXPLORATION

- Brearton and Simpson (2001) is an article on the poetry of Michael Longley which balances literary critical methods and the methods of stylistics. Brearton (forthcoming) is book-length study of the same poet's work.
- Verdonk (1993b) offers an analysis of a range of levels of language in a Seamus Heaney's poem 'Punishment', paying particular attention to patterns of *deixis* (see A2).

A SOCIOLINGUISTIC MODEL OF NARRATIVE

- Burton (1980) is an important stylistic exploration of drama dialogue which contains a full chapter on Ionesco's *The Bald Prima Donna.* Both Simpson (1997a: 101–27) and Toolan (2001: 143–77) contain detailed accounts of the Labov model, along with a number of suggested stylistic applications.

TRANSITIVITY, CHARACTERISATION AND LITERARY GENRE

- Nash (1990) is an engaging general account of the language of popular fiction, which examines narrative techniques beyond those covered in this unit.
- Mills (1995: 143–9) looks at transitivity from a feminist perspective, while Wareing, in two articles in which the transitivity model features, examines popular fiction written for women (Wareing 1990; 1994).

EXPLORING POINT OF VIEW IN NARRATIVE FICTION

- This unit is based on a (dangerously) simplified version of a framework set out in Simpson (1993), and readers are urged to consult the fuller model for further detail and illustration. Other books which cover point of view are Rimmon-Kenan's textbook (1983) and Genette's influential study (1980). Interesting articles on point of view include Sasaki (1994) and Chapman (2002).

EXPLORING DIALOGUE

- Herman's extensive study of drama discourse includes a discussion of the way principles of social interaction can be brought to bear in the interpretation of play dialogue. (Herman 1996: 6 and *passim*). Birch (1991) is a generally interesting study of drama which balances critical theory with some insights from stylistics. Simpson (2000) includes a study, with an emphasis on discourse structure, of patterns of comic dialogue in the popular Irish sitcom *Father Ted.*

COGNITIVE STYLISTICS AT WORK

- Gavins and Steen's (2003) collection contains applications to text, by different stylisticians, of a variety of models in cognitive stylistics. Most closely reflecting the interests of this unit are individual papers in the collection by Gavins, who explores a Donald Barthelme novel using text world theory and by Emmott, who examines 'twists in the tale' in fiction from a cognitive-discourse perspective.
- Wales (1992) is a book-length treatment of the style of James Joyce (and on this topic, see again reading D4 by Derek Attridge).

EXPLORING METAPHORS IN DIFFERENT KINDS OF TEXTS

- With reference to the exploration of metaphor in text, each of the chapters in Kövecses (2002) book on the subject is accompanied by helpful practical activities, while useful exercises are distributed throughout Goatly's book on metaphor (Goatly 1997). Articles on metaphor with a text-based or practical orientation include Crisp (2003) and Heywood *et al* (2002).

REFERENCES

Attardo, S. (2001) *Humorous Texts: A Semantic and Pragmatic Analysis* Berlin: Mouton de Gruyter.

Attridge, D. (1982) *The Rhythms of English Poetry* Harlow: Longman.

Attridge, D. (1988) *Peculiar Language: Literature as Difference from the Renaissance to James Joyce* London: Methuen.

Austin, J. L. (1962) *How to do Things with Words* London: Clarendon Press.

Bakhtin, M. M. (1986) *Speech Genres and other Late Essays* Austin: University of Texas Press.

Ball, M. J. and Rahilly, J. (1999) *Phonetics: The Science of Speech* London: Edward Arnold.

Barnett, L. (1964) *The Treasure of Our Tongue* New York: Academic Press.

Barry, P. (2002) *Beginning Theory: An Introduction to Literary and Cultural Theory* 2nd edition. Manchester: University of Manchester Press.

Bex, A., Burke, M. and Stockwell, P. (eds) (2000) *Contextualized Stylistics* Amsterdam/ Atlanta, GA: Rodopi.

Birch, D. (1991) *The Language of Drama* Basingstoke: Macmillan.

Blamires, H. (1988) [1966] *The New Bloomsday Book* London: Routledge.

Bolinger, D. (1965) *Forms of English: Accent, Morpheme, Order* [Abe, I. and Kanekiyo, T. (eds)] Cambridge: Harvard University Press.

Brazil. D. (1992) 'Listening to people reading', In Coulthard, M. (ed.) *Advances in Spoken Discourse Analysis* London: Routledge, 209–41.

Brearton, F. (forthcoming) *Reading Michael Longley* Newcastle upon Tyne: Bloodaxe.

Brearton, F. and Simpson, P. (2001) '"Deciphering otter prints": language, form and memory in the poetry of Michael Longley', *The Honest Ulsterman: Special Feature on Michael Longley*, 110, 17–31.

Breton, A. (1969) *Manifestoes of Surrealism* [translated by R. Seaver and H. R. Lane] Ann Arbor, MI: University of Michigan Press.

Brooke-Rose, C. (1958) *A Grammar of Metaphor* London: Secker and Warburg.

Brown, P. and Levinson, S. (1987) *Politeness* Cambridge: Cambridge University Press.

Buckingham, W. J. (ed) (1989) *Emily Dickinson's Reception in the 1890s: A Documentary History* Pittsburgh: University of Pittsburgh Press.

Burton, D. (1980) *Dialogue and Discourse: A Sociolinguistic Approach to Modern Drama Dialogue and Naturally Occurring Conversation* London: Routledge and Kegan Paul.

Burton, D. (1982a) 'Through glass darkly: through dark glasses', In Carter, R. and Burton, D. (eds) (1982) *Literary Text and Language Study* London: Edward Arnold, 195–214.

Burton, D. (1982b) 'Conversation pieces', In Carter, R. and Burton, D. (eds) (1982) *Literary Text and Language Study* London: Edward Arnold, 86–115.

Carter, R. (ed) (1982) *Language and Literature: An Introductory Reader in Stylistics* London: George Allen and Unwin.

Carter, R. and Burton, D. (eds) (1982) *Literary Text and Language Study* London: Edward Arnold.

Carter, R. and Nash, W. (1990) *Seeing through Language: A Guide to Styles of English Writing* Oxford: Blackwell.

Carter, R. and Simpson, P. (eds) (1989) *Language, Discourse and Literature: An Introductory Reader in Discourse Stylistics* London: Unwin Hyman.

Chapman, S. (2002) '"From their point of view": voice and speech in George Moore's *Esther Waters*', *Language and Literature,* 11, 4, 307–23.

Chiaro, D. (1992) *The Language of Jokes: Analysing Verbal Play* London: Routledge.

Clark, U. and Zyngier, S. (2003) 'Towards a pedagogical stylistics', *Language and Literature* 12, 4, 339–51.

Cook, G. (1994) *Discourse and Literature* Oxford: Oxford University Press.

Cooper, A. (1994) '"Folk speech" and "book English": re-presentations of dialect in Hardy's novels', *Language and Literature* 3, 1, 21–42.

Corbett, J. (1997) *Language and Scottish Literature* Edinburgh: Edinburgh University Press.

Crisp, P. (1996) 'Imagism's metaphors – a test case', *Language and Literature* 5, 2, 79–92.

Crisp, P. (2003) 'Conceptual metaphor and its expressions', In Gavins, J. and Steen, G. (eds) (2003) *Cognitive Poetics in Practice* London: Routledge, 99–113.

Crystal, D. (1998) *Language Play* Harmondsworth: Penguin.

Culler, J. (ed) (1988) *On Puns: The Foundation of Letters* Oxford: Blackwell.

Culpeper, J. (2001) *Language and Characterisation: People in Plays and Other Texts* Harlow: Longman.

Culpeper, J., Short, M. and Verdonk, P. (eds) (1998) *Exploring the Language of Drama: From Text to Context* London: Routledge.

Cureton, R. (1994) 'Rhythm and verse study', *Language and Literature,* 3, 2, 105–24.

Durant, A. and Fabb, N. (1990) *Literary Studies in Action* London: Routledge.

Eggins, S. (1994) *An Introduction to Systemic-Functional Linguistics* London: Pinter.

Emmott, C. (1997) *Narrative Comprehension* Oxford: Clarendon Press.

Fabb, N. (2002) 'The metres of "Dover Beach"', *Language and Literature* 11, 2, 99–117.

Fauconnier, G. (1994) *Mental Spaces: Aspects of Meaning Construction in Natural Language* Cambridge: Cambridge University Press.

Fauconnier, G. and Turner, M. (2002) *The Way We Think: Conceptual Blending and the Mind's Hidden Complexities* New York: Basic Books.

Fish, S. (1981) 'What is stylistics and why are they saying such terrible things about it?', In Freeman, D. (ed.) (1981) *Essays in Modern Stylistics* London: Methuen, 53–78.

Fludernik, M. (1993) *The Fictions of Language and the Languages of Fiction* London: Routledge.

Foucault, M. (1986) 'What is an author?', In Adams, H. and Searle, L. (eds) *Critical Theory Since 1965* Gainesville: University Presses of Florida, 138–48.
Fowler, R. (1966) (ed) *Essays on Style and Language* London: Routledge and Kegan Paul.
Fowler, R. (1971) *The Languages of Literature* London: Routledge and Kegan Paul.
Fowler, R. (1981) *Literature as Social Discourse* London: Batsford.
Fowler, R. (1996) [1986] *Linguistic Criticism*, (2nd edition) Oxford: Oxford University Press.
Franklin, R. W. (ed.) (1981) *The Manuscript Books of Emily Dickinson*, 2 vols. Cambridge, MA, and London: The Belknap Press of Harvard University Press.
Franklin, R. W. (1998) *The Poems of Emily Dickinson* Cambridge, MA, and London: The Belknap Press of Harvard University Press.
Fraser, G. S. (1970) *Metre, Rhyme and Free Verse* London: Methuen.
Freeman, D. (ed.) (1981) *Essays in Modern Stylistics* London: Methuen.
Freeman, M. (1995) 'Metaphor making meaning: Emily Dickinson's conceptual universe', *Journal of Pragmatics*, 24, 643–66.
Freeman, M. (2000) 'Poetry and the scope of metaphor: Toward a cognitive theory of metaphor', In Barcelona, A. (ed.) *Metaphor and Metonymy at the Crossroads* Berlin: de Gruyter, 253–81.
Freeman, M. (2002) 'The body in the word: A cognitive approach to the shape of a poetic text', In Semino, E. and Culpeper, J. (eds) (2002) *Cognitive Stylistics* Amsterdam: John Benjamins, 23–47.
Garland, N. (1988) 'Political cartooning', In Durant, J. and Miller, J. (eds) *Laughing Matters: A Serious Look at Humour* Harlow: Longman Scientific and Technical, 75–89.
Gavins, J. (in press) 'Text-world approach to narrative', In *The Routledge Encyclopaedia of Narrative* New York: Routledge.
Gavins, J. and Steen, G. (eds) (2003) *Cognitive Poetics in Practice* London: Routledge.
Genette, G. (1980) *Narrative Discourse* New York: Cornell University Press.
Germain, E. B. (ed.) (1978) *Surrealist Poetry in English* Harmondsworth: Penguin.
Gibbs, R. W. jr. (1994) *The Poetics of Mind* Cambridge: Cambridge University Press.
Gibbs, R. W. jr. and Steen, G. (eds) (1999) *Metaphor in Cognitive Linguistics* Amsterdam: John Benjamins.
Goatly, A. (1997) *The Language of Metaphors* London: Routledge.
Graham, J. (1981) 'Flip, flap, flop: linguistics as semiotics', *Diacritics* 11, 1, 143–68.
Green, K. (1992) 'Deixis and the poetic persona', *Language and Literature*, 1, 2, 121–34.
Grice, H. P. (1975) 'Logic and Conversation', In Cole, P. and Morgan, J. (1975) *Syntax and Semantics III: Speech Acts*, New York: Academic Press, 41–58.
Halliday, M. A. K. (1970) 'Language structure and language function', In Lyons, J. (ed.) *New Horizons in Linguistics*, Harmondsworth: Penguin, 140–65.
Halliday, M. A. K. (1971) 'Linguistic function and literary style: an inquiry into the language of William Golding's *The Inheritors*', In Chatman, S. (ed.) *Literary Style: A Symposium* New York: Oxford University Press, 330–68. [Reprinted in Freeman, D. (ed.) (1981) *Essays in Modern Stylistics* London: Methuen 325–60]

Halliday, M. A. K. (1973) *Explorations in the Functions of Language* London: Edward Arnold.

Halliday, M. A. K. (1978) *Language as Social Semiotic* London: Edward Arnold.

Halliday, M. A. K. (1994) *An Introduction to Functional Grammar* 2nd edition. London: Edward Arnold.

Hayman, D. (1981) *Ulysses: The Mechanics of Meaning* 2nd edition. Madison: University of Wisconsin Press.

Herman, V. (1996) *Dramatic Discourse: Dialogue as Interaction in Plays* London: Routledge.

Hess, N. (1996) 'Code switching and style switching as markers of liminality in literature', *Language and Literature* 5, 1, 5–18.

Heywood, J., Semino, E. and Short, M. (2002) 'Linguistic metaphor identification in two extracts from novels', *Language and Literature* 11, 1, 35–54.

Hoover, D. L. (1999) *Language and Style in* The Inheritors Lanham, MD: University Press of America.

Hymes, D. (1972) 'On communicative competence', In Pride, J. B. and Holmes, J. (eds) *Sociolinguistics* Harmondsworth: Penguin, 269–93.

Jackson, H. (2001) *Grammar and Vocabulary* Routledge English Language Introductions. London: Routledge.

Jakobson, R. (1960) 'Closing statement: linguistics and poetics', In Sebeok, T. A. (ed) *Style in Language*, Cambridge: The MIT Press, 350–77.

Jeffries, L. (2001) 'Schema affirmation and White Asparagus: Cultural multilingualism among readers of texts', *Language and Literature*, 10, 4, 325–43.

Johnson, T. H. (ed) (1963) *The Poems of Emily Dickinson* 3 vols. Cambridge, MA: The Belknap Press of Harvard University Press.

Kennedy, C. (1982) 'Systemic grammar and its use in literary analysis', In Carter, R. (ed) (1982) *Language and Literature: An Introductory Reader in Stylistics* London: George Allen and Unwin, 82–99.

Kenner, H. (1980) *Ulysses* Unwin Critical Library. London: George Allen and Unwin.

Kövecses, Z. (2002) *Metaphor: A Practical Introduction* New York: Oxford University Press.

Labov, W. (1972) *Language in the Inner City* Philadelphia: University of Pennsylvania Press.

Lakoff, G. (1987) *Women, Fire, and Dangerous Things: What Categories Reveal about the Mind* Chicago and London: University of Chicago Press.

Lakoff, G. (1990) 'The Invariance Hypothesis: Is abstract reason based on image-schemas?', *Cognitive Linguistics* 1, 1, 39–74.

Lakoff, G. and Johnson, M. (1980) *Metaphors We Live By* Chicago, IL: University of Chicago Press.

Lakoff, G., and Johnson, M. (1998) *Philosophy in the Flesh* Chicago and London: University of Chicago Press.

Lakoff, G. and Turner, M. (1989) *More than Cool Reason: A Field Guide to Poetic Metaphor* Chicago, IL: University of Chicago Press.

Langacker, R. W. (1987) *Foundations of Cognitive Grammar* (Vol. 1, Theoretical prerequisites) Stanford: Stanford University Press.

Langacker, R. W. (1991) *Concept, Image, and Symbol: The Cognitive Basis of Grammar* Berlin and New York: Mouton de Gruyter.

Lecercle, J-J. (1993). 'The current state of stylistics', *The European English Messenger* 2, 1, 14–18.

Leech, G. N. (1969) *A Linguistic Guide to English Poetry* Harlow: Longman.

Leech, G. and Short, M. (1981) *Style in Fiction* Harlow: Longman.

Levin, S. R. (1962) *Linguistic Structures in Poetry* The Hague: Mouton.

McCawley, J. D. (1981) *Everything that Linguists have Always Wanted to Know about Logic (But were Ashamed to Ask)* Chicago, IL.: The University of Chicago Press.

McHale, B. (1987) *Postmodernist Fiction* New York: Methuen.

McRae, J. (1998) *The Language of Poetry* London: Routledge.

Merleau-Ponty, M. (1962) *Phenomenology of Perception* [trans. C. Smith.] London: Routledge and Kegan Paul.

Mills, S. (1995) *Feminist Stylistics* London: Routledge.

Montgomery, M., Durant, A., Fabb, N., Furniss, T. and Mills, S. (1992) *Ways of Reading: Advanced Reading Skills for Students of English Literature* London: Routledge.

Nash, W. (1985) *The Language of Humour* Harlow: Longman.

Nash, W. (1986) 'Sound and the pattern of poetic meaning', In D'Haen, T. (ed.) *Linguistics and the Study of Literature.* Dutch Quarterly Review, Studies in Literature 1. Amsterdam: Rodopi, 128–51.

Nash, W. (1990) *Language in Popular Fiction* London: Routledge.

Ortony, A. (ed) (1979) *Metaphor and Thought* Cambridge: Cambridge University Press.

Pope, R. (1995) *Textual Intervention* London: Routledge.

Pratt, M. L. (1977) *Toward a Speech Act Theory of Literary Discourse* Bloomington, Indiana: Indiana University Press.

Pratt, M. L. (1993) '"Yo soy la Malinche": Chicana writers and the poetics of ethnonationalism', In Verdonk, P. (ed) (1993a) *Twentieth Century Poetry: From Text to Context* London: Routledge, 171–87.

Propp, V. (1966) [1928] *The Morphology of the Folktale* Austin: University of Texas Press.

Redfern, W. (2000) *Puns: More Senses than One* 2nd edition. Harmondsworth: Penguin.

Reinhart, T. and Reuland, E. (1993) 'Reflexivity', *Linguistic Inquiry* 24, 4, 657–720.

Rich, A. (1977) *Of Woman Born: Motherhood as Experience and Institution* London: Virago.

Rimmon-Kenan, S. (1983) *Narrative Fiction: Contemporary Poetics* London: Methuen.

Ross, A. (1998) *The Language of Humour* London: Routledge.

Rowbotham, S. (1973a) *Woman's Consciousness: Man's World* Harmondsworth: Penguin.

Rowbotham, S. (1973b) *Hidden from History* London: Pluto Press.

Ryan, M-L. (1991) *Possible Worlds, Artificial Intelligence, and Narrative Theory,* Bloomington and Indianapolis: Indiana University Press.

Ryle, G. (1949) *The Concept of Mind* London: Hutchinson.

Sapir, E. (1956) *Culture, Language and Personality* Berkeley, California: University of California Press.

Sasaki, T. (1994) 'Towards a systematic description of narrative "point of view": an examination of Chatman's theory with an analysis of "The Blind Man" by D. H. Lawrence', *Language and Literature* 3, 2, 125–38.

Schank, R. C. and Abelson, R. P. (1977) *Scripts, Plans, Goals and Understanding* Hillsdale, NJ: Lawrence Erlbaum Associates.

Searle, J. R. (1969) *Speech Acts: An Essay in the Philosophy of Language* Cambridge: Cambridge: University Press.

Semino, E. (1997) *Language and World Creation in Poems and other Texts* Harlow: Longman.

Semino, E. (2001) 'On readings, literariness and schema theory: a reply to Jeffries', *Language and Literature,* 10, 4, 345–55.

Semino, E. and Culpeper, J. (eds) (2002) *Cognitive Stylistics* Amsterdam: John Benjamins.

Shen, D. (1988) 'Stylistics, objectivity and convention', *Poetics* 17, 3, 221–38.

Short, M. (1989) 'Discourse analysis and the analysis of drama', In Carter, R. and Simpson, P. (eds) (1989) *Language, Discourse and Literature: An Introductory Reader in Discourse Stylistics* London: Unwin Hyman, 138–68.

Short, M. (1996) *Exploring the Language of Poems, Plays and Prose* Harlow: Longman.

Short, M., Semino, E. and Wynne, M. (1997) 'A (free direct) reply to Paul Simpson's discourse', *Journal of Literary Semantics* 26, 3, 219–28.

Showalter, E. (1977) *A Literature of Their Own: British Women Novelists from Brontë to Lessing* Princeton, NJ: Princeton University Press.

Simpson, P. (1989) 'Politeness Phenomena in Ionesco's *The Lesson*', In Carter, R. and Simpson, P. (eds) (1989) *Language, Discourse and Literature: An Introductory Reader in Discourse Stylistics* London: Unwin Hyman, 170–93.

Simpson, P. (1992a) 'Teaching stylistics: analysing cohesion and narrative structure in a short story by Ernest Hemingway', *Language and Literature,* 1, 1, 47–67.

Simpson, P. (1992b) 'The pragmatics of nonsense: towards a stylistics of *Private Eye*'s "Colemanballs"', In Toolan, M. (ed.) *Language, Text and Context* London: Routledge, 281–305.

Simpson, P. (1993) *Language, Ideology and Point of View* London: Routledge.

Simpson, P. (1997a) *Language through Literature* London: Routledge.

Simpson, P. (1997b) 'A quadrant model for the study of speech and thought presentation' *Journal of Literary Semantics,* 26, 3, 211–18.

Simpson, P. (1998) 'Odd talk: studying discourses of incongruity', In Culpeper, J., Short, M. and Verdonk, P. (eds) (1998) *Exploring the Language of Drama: From Text to Context* London: Routledge, 34–53.

Simpson, P. (1999) 'Language, culture and identity: with (another) look at accents in pop and rock singing', *Multilingua,* 18, 4, 343–65.

Simpson, P. (2000) 'Satirical humour and cultural context: with a note on the curious case of Father Todd Unctuous', In Bex, A., Burke, M. and Stockwell, P. (eds) (2000) *Contextualized Stylistics* Amsterdam/Atlanta, GA: Rodopi, 243–66.

Simpson, P. (2003) *On the Discourse of Satire: Towards a Stylistic Model of Satirical Humour* Amsterdam: John Benjamins.

Simpson, P. and Hall, G. (2002) 'Discourse analysis and stylistics', *Annual Review of Applied Linguistics 22*, New York: Cambridge University Press, 136–49.
Simpson, P. and Montgomery, M. (1995) 'Language, literature and film: the stylistics of Bernard MacLaverty's *Cal*', In Verdonk, P. and Weber, J. J. (eds) *Twentieth Century Fiction: From Text to Context* London: Routledge, 138–64.
Steen, G. (1994) *Understanding Metaphor in Literature* Harlow: Longman.
Steen, G. (1999a). 'From linguistic to conceptual metaphor in five steps', In Gibbs, R. W. jr. and Steen, G. (eds) (1999) *Metaphor in Cognitive Linguistics* Amsterdam: John Benjamins, 57–78.
Steen, G. (1999b) 'Genres of discourse and the definition of literature', *Discourse Processes* 28, 2, 109–20.
Steen, G. (2002a) 'Metaphor in Bob Dylan's "Hurricane": Genre, language, and style', In Semino, E. and Culpeper, J. (eds) (2002) *Cognitive Stylistics* Amsterdam: John Benjamins, 183–210.
Steen, G. (2002b) 'Towards a procedure for metaphor identification', *Language and Literature: Special Issue on Metaphor Identification* 11, 1, 17–33.
Steen, G. and Gavins, J. (2003) 'Contextualising cognitive poetics', In Gavins, J. and Steen, G. (eds) (2003) *Cognitive Poetics in Practice* London: Routledge, 1–12.
Stockwell, P. (1994) 'How to create universes with words: Referentiality and science fictionality', *Journal of Literary Semantics* 23, 3, 159–87.
Stockwell, P. (1996) 'New wor(l)ds', *UCE Papers in Language and Literature – Special Issue: Science Fiction* 3, 1–18.
Stockwell, P. (2000) *The Poetics of Science Fiction* Harlow: Longman.
Stockwell, P. (2002) *Cognitive Poetics* London: Routledge.
Stockwell, P. (2003) 'Schema poetics and speculative cosmology', *Language and Literature*, 12, 3, 252–71.
Tambling, J. (1988) *What is Literary Language?* Bucks: Open University Press.
Tan, P. (1998) 'Advice on doing your stylistics essay on a dramatic text: an example from Alan Ayckbourn's *The Revengers' Comedies*', In Culpeper, J., Short, M. and Verdonk, P. (eds) (1998) *Exploring the Language of Drama: From Text to Context* London: Routledge, 161–71.
Taylor, J. R. (1989) *Linguistic Categorization: Prototypes in Linguistic Theory* Oxford: Clarendon Press.
Thompson, G. (1996) *Introducing Functional Grammar* London: Edward Arnold.
Thorne, J. P. (1965) 'Stylistics and generative grammars', *Journal of Linguistics*, 1, 49–59.
Toolan, M. (1990) *The Stylistics of Fiction: A Literary-linguistic Approach* London: Routledge.
Toolan, M. (1992) 'The significations of representing dialect in writing', *Language and Literature* 1, 1, 29–46.
Toolan, M. (1998) *Language in Literature* London: Edward Arnold.
Toolan, M. (2000) 'Quasi-transcriptional speech: A compensatory spokenness in Anglo-Irish literary fiction', In Bex, A., Burke, M. and Stockwell, P. (eds) (2000) *Contextualized Stylistics* Amsterdam/Atlanta, GA: Rodopi, 153–72.
Toolan, M. (2001) [1988] *Narrative: A Critical Linguistic Introduction* 2nd edition. London: Routledge.

Traugott, E. C. and Pratt, M. L. (1980) *Linguistics for Students of Literature* New York: Harcourt Brace Jovanovich.

Trudgill, P. (1983) 'Acts of conflicting identity: the sociolinguistics of British pop-song pronunciation', In P. Trudgill, *On Dialect* Oxford: Blackwell, 141–60.

Tsen, M. (1997) 'Symbolic discourse: mystical writing as anti-language', *Language and Literature* 6, 3, 181–95.

Turner, M. (1990) 'Aspects of the Invariance Hypothesis', *Cognitive Linguistics* 1, 2, 247–55.

Uspensky, B. (1973) *A Poetics of Composition* [trans. V. Zavarin and S. Wittig] Berkeley: University of California Press.

van Peer, W. (1986) *Stylistics and Psychology: Investigations of Foregrounding* London: Croom Helm.

van Peer, W. (1987) 'Top down and bottom-up: interpretative strategies in reading e e cummings', *New Literary History* 18, 3, 597–609.

van Peer, W. (1991) 'But what is literature? Towards a descriptive definition of literature', In Sell, R. (ed) *Literary Pragmatics* London: Routledge, 127–41.

van Peer, W. (1993) 'Typographic foregrounding', *Language and Literature,* 2, 1, 49–61.

Vendler, H. (1966) 'Review of *Essays on Style and Language* by Roger Fowler', *Essays in Criticism,* 16, 458–60.

Verdonk, P. (ed) (1993a) *Twentieth Century Poetry: From Text to Context* London: Routledge.

Verdonk, P. (1993b) 'Poetry and public life: A contextualised reading of Seamus Heaney's "Punishment"', In Verdonk 1993a, 112–33.

Verdonk, P. (2002) *Stylistics* Oxford: Oxford University Press.

Volosinov, V. M. (1973) [1930] *Marxism and the Philosophy of Language* [Trans. L. Matejka and I. R. Titunik] New York: Seminar Press.

Wales, K. (1992) *The Language of James Joyce* Basingstoke: Macmillan.

Wales, K. (1993a) 'On the stylistics of Jean-Jacques Lecercle', *The European English Messenger* 2, 2, 30–31.

Wales, K. (1993b) 'Teach yourself rhetoric: an analysis of Philip Larkin's "Church Going"', In Verdonk, P. (2002) *Stylistics* Oxford: Oxford University Press, 87–99.

Wales, K. (2001) [1990] *A Dictionary of Stylistics* 2nd edition. Harlow: Longman.

Wareing, S. (1990) 'Women in fiction: stylistic modes of reclamation', *Parlance* 2, 2, 72–85.

Wareing, S. (1994) '"And then he kissed her": the reclamation of female characters to submissive roles in contemporary fiction', In Wales, K. (ed.) *Feminist Linguistics in Literary Criticism* Woodbridge: Boydell and Brewer, 117–36.

Weber, J. J. (ed.) (1996) *The Stylistics Reader* London: Edward Arnold.

Wellek, R. and Warren, A. (1949) *Theory of Literature* New York: Harcourt Brace.

Werth, P. (1999) *Text Worlds: Representing Conceptual Space in Discourse,* London: Longman.

Whorf, B. L. (1956) *Language, Thought and Reality* [ed. J. B. Carroll] Cambridge, Mass.: MIT Press.

Widdowson, H. G. (1975) *Stylistics and the Teaching of Literature* Harlow: Longman.

PRIMARY SOURCES

This bibliography lists the primary sources for the texts used in the four sections of the book. Sources for shorter citations and illustrations of a line or two have not been included. Original dates of publication are given, where relevant, in square brackets.

Allen, Woody (1975) *Getting Even* London: Star Books.

Atwood, Margaret (1996) *Power Politics* Toronto: House of Anansi.

Banks, Iain (1993) *The Crow Road* London: Abacus.

Barnes, Julian (2000) *Love, etc* London: Picador.

Berkoff, Steven (1983) *Greek.* In *Decadence and Greek* London: Calder.

Conrad, Joseph (1995) [1912] *The Secret Sharer* Harmondsworth: Penguin.

cummings, e e (1954) [1939] 'love is more thicker', *Poems, 1923–1954* New York: Harcourt Brace Jovanovich Inc..

Dickens, Charles (1986) [1853] *Bleak House* Harmondsworth: Penguin.

Dickinson, Emily (1963) [various] *The Poems of Emily Dickinson* (ed. T. H. Johnson) Cambridge, MA: The Belknap Press of Harvard University Press.

Eliot, T.S. (1963) [various] *Collected Poems* London: Faber and Faber.

Fielding, Henry (1970) [1749] *Tom Jones* London: Pan Books Ltd.

Fitzgerald, F. Scott (1994) [1925] *The Great Gatsby* Harmondsworth: Penguin.

Hemingway, Ernest (1925) *In Our Time* New York: Charles Schribner's Sons.

Hemingway, Ernest (1960) [1952] *The Old Man and the Sea* London: Triad/Panther Books.

Ionesco, Eugene (1963) [1958] *The Bald Prima Donna* In *Plays Volume 1* [Translated by Donald Watson] Calder: London.

Ionesco, Eugene (1964) 'My critics and I', In *Notes and Counternotes* [Translated by Donald Watson] London: Calder.

James, Henry (2001) [1903] *The Ambassadors* Harmondsworth: Penguin.

Jerome, Jerome K. (1986) [1889] *Three Men in a Boat* London: Dent.

Joyce, James (1980) [1922] *Ulysses* Harmondsworth: Penguin.

Kafka, Franz (1985) [1925] *The Trial* Harmondsworth: Penguin.

Lodge, David (2002) *Thinks* Harmondsworth: Penguin.

Longley, Michael (1995) 'The Ghost Orchid', In *The Ghost Orchid* London: Jonathan Cape.

Longley, Michael (2000) 'The Comber', In *The Weather in Japan* London: Jonathan Cape.

Lowry, Malcolm (1984) [1947] *Under the Volcano* Harmondsworth: Penguin.

McEwan, Ian (1998) *Amsterdam* London: Vintage Books.

McGough, Roger (1971) '40-Love', In *After the Mersey Sound* Harmondsworth: Penguin.

MacLaverty, Bernard (1984) *Cal* Harmondsworth: Penguin.

Monty Python's Flying Circus (1971) BBC Television/Kettledrum Lownes Productions Ltd.

Morgan, Edwin (1966) 'Off Course', In *Poems of Thirty Years* Carcanet Press Ltd.

Morrison, Toni (1987) *Beloved* London: Vintage Books.

Nabokov, Vladimir (1986) [1955] *Lolita* Harmondsworth: Penguin.

Parker, Dorothy (1956) [1926] 'One Perfect Rose', From *The Portable Dorothy Parker* Penguin Books USA.

Pinter, Harold (1960) *The Dumb Waiter* London: Faber and Faber.

Plath, Sylvia (1986) [1963] *The Bell Jar* London: Faber and Faber.

Poe, Edgar Allan (1986) [1839] *The Fall of the House of Usher.* In *The Fall of the House of Usher and other Writings* (ed. D. Galloway) Harmondsworth: Penguin.

Pound, Ezra (1969) [1912] 'In a station of the metro', In *A Map of Modern English Verse* (ed. J. Press) Oxford: Oxford University Press.

Simpson, N. F. (1960) *One Way Pendulum* London: Faber and Faber.

Stoker, Bram (1998) [1897] *Dracula* Oxford: Oxford University Press.

Swift, Jonathan (1986) [1729] 'A Modest Proposal', In Abrams, M. H. (ed.) *The Norton Anthology of English Literature* New York: Norton, 2174–80.

Welsh, Irvine (1993) *Trainspotting* London: Minerva.

Welsh, Irvine (1995) *Marabou Stork Nightmares* London: Minerva.

Winterson, Jeanette (1993) *Written on the Body* London: Vintage Books.

Woolf, Virginia (1998) [1928] *Orlando* Oxford: Oxford University Press.

GLOSSARIAL INDEX

Where the page reference for a keyword is highlighted in **bold**, this indicates that a definition is provided or that the term is used in a context which makes its meaning clear. Other page references for keywords are to significant places in the book where the term or concept is also used. Page references for the literary authors cited in the book are also provided.